ECOLOGICAL PSYCHOLOGY

ECOLOGICAL PSYCHOLOGY

*Concepts and Methods for Studying the
Environment of Human Behavior*

ROGER G. BARKER

*Stanford University Press
Stanford, California   1968*

Stanford University Press
Stanford, California
© 1968 by the Board of Trustees of the
Leland Stanford Junior University
Printed in the United States of America
L.C. 68-21287

Preface

THE METHODS, theories, and data that are reported in this book issue from 20 years of research at the Midwest Psychological Field Station. My debt to my associates of these years is very great, for the ideas presented, as well as the data, are rooted in the work of many people. I regret that the sources of particular ideas are lost in the tangled skein of joint and separate efforts, so that I can make only general acknowledgment of indebtedness and appreciation to my many associates in research. But I wish to record special obligations to Herbert F. Wright, my long-time colleague, to Paul V. Gump, my more recent colleague, and to Phil Schoggen, my former student and later colleague, for their gifts of time, ideas, and encouragement. The contribution of my wife, Louise Shedd Barker, to these pages is beyond estimation.

A research program that continues for 20 years requires technical assistance of the highest order in keeping records and analyzing data. This has fortunately been provided by Isla Herbert, Dorothy Streator, and Marjorie Reed. During the course of these years computers have entered research science, and to Dan D. M. Ragle I am indebted for programming the old and new data.

The Midwest Psychological Field Station was established in Oskaloosa, Kansas, in 1947 by the author and Herbert F. Wright as a facility of the Department of Psychology, University of Kansas. An auxiliary station for comparative studies has functioned in Leyburn (code name Yoredale), Yorkshire, England, for a number of periods since 1954. The Field Station was initially supported by a grant from the U.S. Public Health Service, National Institute of Mental Health (MH-6). Over the years other grants have been received from the U.S. Public Health Service (MH-1513, MH-11211) and also from the Carnegie Corporation of New York, the Rockefeller Foundation, the Commonwealth Fund, the Association for the Aid of Crippled Children, the National Science Foundation (GS-116), and the University of Kansas. Data processing at the

University of Kansas Computation Center has been done as a part of the Center's service to research.

This report has been in preparation for a long time, and parts and versions of parts of it have been previously published; parts of Chapters 2 and 6 have appeared in *Big School, Small School* (Stanford University Press), parts of Chapters 1, 3, and 4 are revised from *Midwest and Its Children* (Harper & Row), and versions of Chapter 6 were first reported in the *Nebraska Symposium on Motivation* (Nebraska University Press), in the *American Psychologist* (American Psychological Association), and in the *Journal of Social Issues* (Society for the Psychological Study of Social Issues).

We note in Chapter 1 that the book deals with only a part of the whole field of ecological psychology. A specialized title is, therefore, desirable. The part we have considered will surely have a special designation in the future, but *Ecological Psychology* as specified by the subtitle is the best we can do today. This book and *Recording and Analyzing Child Behavior* by Herbert F. Wright encompass most of the field of ecological psychology as we now conceive of it.

R.G.B.

February 1968

Contents

ECOLOGICAL PSYCHOLOGY

1

Problems of Ecological Psychology

THE MIDWEST Psychological Field Station was established to facilitate the study of human behavior and its environment *in situ* by bringing to psychological science the kind of opportunity long available to biologists: easy access to phenomena of the science unaltered by the selection and preparation that occur in laboratories. The Field Station provided promising opportunities. But it also raised problems that were new to psychology: How does one collect specimens of behavior? What are the parts of the continuing stream of a person's behavior, and how does one enumerate and describe them? Among the limitless attributes of a person's surroundings, which ones are relevant to his behavior, and how does one identify and measure them?

These new methodological and conceptual problems arose in connection with a wide spectrum of psychological phenomena, for ecological psychology is concerned with both molecular and molar behavior, and with both the psychological environment (the life-space in Kurt Lewin's terms; the world as a particular person perceives and is otherwise affected by it) and with the ecological environment (the objective, preperceptual context of behavior; the real-life settings within which people behave). In this book we are concerned with only some of these issues, namely, *methods and concepts for dealing with the ecological environment of molar human behavior.*

Psychology has been predominantly an experimental science. The first psychologists were experimenters who worked in laboratories. Even clinical and industrial psychologists have, in their research, usually worked as experimenters, arranging and varying the conditions of behavior in order to test hypotheses and hunches. The descriptive, natural history, ecological phase of investigation has had a minor place in psychology, and this has seriously limited the science. Experimental procedures have revealed something about the laws of behavior, but they have not disclosed, nor can they disclose, how the variables of these laws are distributed across the types and conditions of men. Experimental work has produced a host of "if ..., then" statements:

If a one-inch red cube is placed on a table before an eight-month-old infant, then he will attempt to grasp the cube (Halverson, 1943).

If a person is frustrated, then he will exhibit aggressive and regressive behavior (Barker, Dembo, Lewin, 1941; Dollard, Doob, Miller, Mowrer, Sears, 1939).

If four-year-olds are asked, "Why do we have houses?" then they will give answers of the following kinds: "To go in," "Cause it won't rain on us," "To cook in," "To stay in," "To go in and sleep," "To play in," "Because we want to set down," "To play with them," "This is a house," "Houses," "In houses we have stoves and we have carpets, too, and we have tinkertoys and we have lots of things, too" (Terman, Merrill, 1937, p. 212).

Psychology knows how people behave under the conditions of experiments and clinical procedures, but it knows little about the distribution of these and other conditions, and of their behavior resultants, outside of laboratories and clinics.

It is different in other sciences. Chemists know the laws governing the interaction of oxygen and hydrogen, and they also know how these elements are distributed in nature. Entomologists know the biological vectors of malaria, and they also know much about the occurrence of these vectors over the earth. In contrast, psychologists know little more than laymen about the distribution and degree of occurrence of their basic phenomena: of punishment, of hostility, of friendliness, of social pressure, of reward, of fear, of frustration. Although we have daily records of the oxygen content of river water, of the ground temperatures of cornfields, of the activity of volcanoes, of the behavior of nesting robins, of the rate of sodium iodide absorption by crabs, there have been few scientific records of how human mothers care for their young, how teachers behave in the classroom (and how the children respond), what families actually do and say during mealtime, or how children live their lives from the time they wake in the morning until they go to sleep at night. Because we have lacked such records, we have been able only to speculate about many important questions such as these: What changes have occurred over the generations in the participation of children in community life? How does life differ for members of large and small families? How frequently is success achieved in everyday life, and what are its consequences for subsequent behavior? How does the environment differ for rural, town, and urban residents? Are American children disciplined differently from English and French children? If so, does this affect the national character of Americans, Englishmen, and Frenchmen? Before we can answer these kinds of questions, we must know more than the laws of behavior. We must know how the relevant conditions are distributed among men.

Moreover, the lack of ecological data limits the discovery of some of the laws of behavior. It is impossible to create in the laboratory the frequency, duration, scope, complexity, and magnitude of some important human conditions. In this, psychology has something in common with meteorology. Some of the principles of the whirlwind and the thunderbolt can be studied in the laboratory, but to extend the curves into the high values, and to include all complicating factors, it is necessary to go to the plains and to observe these events as they occur under natural conditions. This is true for psychology, too; some conditions that are frequent in daily life are difficult to create experimentally; but experiments in nature are occurring every day, and they will instruct us if we have the techniques and facilities to record and analyze them.

Our first approaches to these tasks of ecological psychology are reported in the volume *Midwest and Its Children* (Barker & Wright, 1955); other publications report special findings, methods, and theories.* We believe that it is very important to present a systematic account of the methods and concepts for investigating the ecological environment at this time, for the ecological environment is a more important phenomenon for the behavior sciences than it has been hitherto. When environments are relatively uniform and stable, *people* are an obvious source of behavior variance, and the dominant scientific problem and the persistent queries from the applied fields are: What are people like? What is the nature and what are the sources of individual differences? How can people be selected and sorted into the slots provided by bureaucracies, schools, businesses, armies? What are the needs and capacities of people to which highways, curricula, and laws must be adapted? But today *environments* are more varied and unstable than heretofore, and their contribution to the variance of behavior is enhanced. Both science and society ask with greater urgency than previously: What are environments like? How does man's habitat differ, for example, in developed and underdeveloped countries, in large and small schools, in glass-walled and windowless office buildings, in integrated and segregated classes? How do environments select and shape the people who inhabit them? What are the structural and dynamic proper-

* All Field Station publications are listed in the bibliography of this book.

ties of the environments to which people must adapt? These are questions for ecological psychology, and in particular, they pertain to the ecological environment and its consequences for men.

One might think that psychology would have become informed about the fundamental nature of the ecological environment in the course of its study of the context of behavior. But this is not the case. It is not the case because psychology has attended almost exclusively to those elements of the environment that are useful in probing the behavior-relevant circuitry within the skins of its subjects. Psychology knows much about the physical properties of the environmental probes it uses for this purpose: of distal objects of perception, for example, and of energy changes at receptor surfaces. But in accordance with the principles of experimental design it has excised these environmental elements from the complexities of the real-life settings in which they occur, from ball games, from symposia meetings, from turnpikes, from arithmetic classes. The result is, inevitably, that the science of psychology has had no adequate knowledge of the psychologist-free environment of behavior. The view is not uncommon among psychologists that the environment of behavior is a relatively unstructured, passive, probabilistic arena of objects and events upon which man behaves in accordance with the programming he carries about within himself (Brunswik, 1955; Leeper, 1963; Lewin, 1951). But research at the Midwest Field Station and elsewhere indicates that when we look at the environment of behavior as a phenomenon worthy of investigation for itself, and not as an instrument for unraveling the behavior-relevant programming within persons, the situation is quite different. From this viewpoint the environment is seen to consist of highly structured, improbable arrangements of objects and events which coerce behavior in accordance with their own dynamic patterning. When, early in our work at the Field Station, we made long records of children's behavior in real-life settings in accordance with a traditional person-centered approach, we found that some attributes of behavior varied less across children within settings than across settings within the days of children. We found, in short, that we could predict some aspects of children's behavior more adequately from knowledge of the behavior characteristics of the drugstores, arithmetic classes, and basketball games they inhabited than from knowledge of the behavior tendencies of particular children (Ashton, 1964; Barker & Gump, 1964; Raush *et al.*, 1959, 1960). It was this experience that led us to look at the real-life environment in which behavior occurs, with the methodological and theoretical consequences that are reported in this book.

2

The Ecological Environment

ONE OF THE OBVIOUS characteristics of human behavior is its variation. Every day of a person's life is marked by wide fluctuations in almost every discriminable attribute of his behavior: in the intelligence he exhibits, in the speed with which he moves, in the emotion he expresses, in the loudness with which he speaks, in the goals he pursues, in his friendliness, his humor, his energy, his anxiety. Even geniuses think ordinary thoughts much of the time; they, too, have to count their change and choose their neckties. Continuous records of the behavior of children show that the ever-changing aspect of the child's stream of behavior is one of its most striking features: trouble and well-being, quietude and activity, success and failure, dominance and submission, correct answers and wrong answers, interest and boredom occur in bewildering complexity (Barker & Wright, 1955). Laymen know of this dimension of human variation from their own experiences and observations; novelists, dramatists, and biographers have described it. But it is not prominent in scientific psychology.

Scientific psychology has been more concerned with another dimension of behavior variability, namely, with differences between individuals. It is one of the great achievements of psychology that in spite of the variation of every individual's behavior, methods have been devised for identifying and measuring individual behavior constants. An important part of scientific psychology is concerned with the great number of behavior constants that have been measured and with the relations between them.

It is unfortunate that these accomplishments have not been accompanied by equal progress in studying naturally occurring, individual behavior variation. But there is an incompatibility here: to achieve stable behavior measurements, stable conditions must be imposed upon the person, and the same conditions must be reimposed each time the measurement is repeated. This method provides measures of individual constancies (under the designated conditions), but it eliminates individual variations (under different conditions), and it destroys the naturally occurring contexts of behavior.

The problem is not peculiar to psychology. The strength of a beam can be measured only under specified conditions, and under the same conditions each time the measurement is made. But a beam has many strengths depending especially upon its structural context. The same is true, too, of the meaning of words. Words have a range of meanings, the precise one being determined by the context in which it occurs. A good dictionary gives a number of these meanings, the modal meanings; but for greatest precision it uses the word in revealing contexts. A person is like a beam or a word: he has many strengths, many intelligences, many social maturities, many speeds, many degrees of liberality and conservativeness, and many moralities.

The general sources of intra-individual behavior variation are clear. A person's behavior is connected in complicated ways with both his inside parts (with his neurons, his muscles, his hormones, for example) and with his outside context (with the school class where he is a pupil, the game in which he is a player, the street on which he is a pedestrian). The *psychological person* who writes essays, scores points, and crosses streets stands as an identifiable entity between unstable interior parts and exterior contexts, with both of which he is linked, yet from both of which he is profoundly separated. The separation comes from the fact that the inside parts and the outside contexts of a person involve phenomena that function according to laws that are different from those that govern his behavior. Brain lesions, muscle contraction, and hormone concentration are not psychological phenomena. In the present state of our understanding, they involve laws that are utterly incommensurate with those of psychology. The same is true of the environment with which a person is coupled. The school class where he is a pupil, the game in which he plays, and the street where he walks all function according to laws that are alien to those that govern his behavior as a person. This is the inside-outside problem which Allport (1955) has discussed. The outside context constitutes the *molar ecological environment*. It consists of those naturally occurring phenomena (1) outside a person's skin, (2) with which his molar actions are coupled, but (3) which function according to laws that are incommensurate with the laws that govern his molar behavior (Barker, 1960a). The ecological environment differs from the psychological environment (or life space) and from the stimulus, as the following discussion will make clear. The fact that behavior varies under the influence of the alien, incommensurate outside contexts of the psychological person places psychology in a serious dilemma. How is a unified science to encompass such diverse phenomena? Neither physics, nor astronomy, nor botany has to cope with psychological inputs to the systems with which it deals. How can psychology hope to cope with nonpsychological inputs? This is the core problem of ecological psychology.

THE TAUTOLOGICAL PROBLEM

In order to study environment-behavior relations on any level, the environment and the behavior must be described and measured independently; otherwise one becomes entangled in a tautological circle from which there is no escape. Thus, for example, three children who were each observed an entire day were found to interact with 571, 671, and 749 different objects; the total number of interactions with these objects were 1,882, 2,282, and 2,490, and each of these interactions had a number of attributes (Schoggen, 1951; Barker & Wright, 1955). But these objects did not constitute the ecological environments of the children, for the behavior of the children provided the sole criteria for identifying and describing the objects. When one uses a person's behavior as the only evidence of what constitutes his environment, one deals with psychological variables, i.e., with life-space phenomena. The naturally occurring life-space deserves investigation, but it is not the ecological environment, and the latter cannot be discovered by using the person's behavior as sole reference point. This is true not because it is impossible to see all the behavior that occurs, but because the ecological environment comprises a different class of phenomenon and can only be identified and understood independently of the behavior with which it is linked.

This confronts us with the essence of the ecological environment in its relation to people. One can easily conceive of the problems of students of light perception if they had no physical description of light, or only a physical description of light at the precise point of contact with the receptor. To understand this point of intersection, it is essential to know the structure of light, for the point of intersection takes part of its characteristics from the total matrix of which it is a part, and this cannot be known from the point of contact, i.e., the stimulus, alone.

This is a general problem in science. When we are concerned with the outside context of any entity, whether a behaving person, a supporting

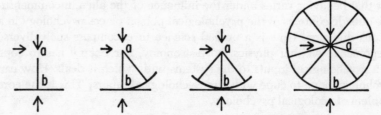

Fig. 2.1. A supporting beam (a,b) and its momentary context.

beam, or a word in a sentence (a product of behavior), this context cannot be described in terms of the points of contact with the entity alone. The properties of the points depend upon the structure of which they are parts. Take the word "brought" in the succeedingly more inclusive contexts in which it occurs.

brought
were brought under
provisions were brought under cover
fresh provisions were brought under cover of darkness*

The immediate points of contact between the word "brought" and its context are clearly insufficient to define this context; the properties of the contact points "were" and "under" depend upon the total sentence. That is, "were" and "under" are not the context of the word "brought"; the whole sentence is the context. The contexts of all words in Stevenson's writings, and in all meaningful writings, occur in organized units that are larger than the preceding and succeeding connecting words. Fig. 2.1 is a physical example of this. The supporting beam (a,b) and its momentary context are shown in the succeeding diagrams. The instantaneous behavior of the beam can be completely described in terms of the internal and external structural arrangements and forces existing for it at a particular instant without regard for what is outside of points a and b. However, if more than an infinitely small time interval is involved, more is required: it is essential to know the structural and dynamic contexts of the intersection points a and b. The properties of contact point b, in this case, can be defined in terms of its position on the rim of a wheel of a certain diameter and motion, and the properties of point a by its position as the center of the wheel. Knowing, for example, that b is on the rim of a wheel moving forward at 50 miles an hour tells

* From R. L. Stevenson, *The Pavilion on the Links.*

us immediately that there will be a cyclical change in the forward movement of b between zero and 100 miles an hour, with corresponding changes in the strength and direction of the forces and in the behavior of the beam.

This is true of the ecological environment of persons too. A person's momentary behavior is completely determined by his life-space, but if we wish to understand more than the immediate cross section of the behavior stream, knowledge of the ecological environment is essential. For example, giving and receiving love between mother and child is an important variable in some theories of psychological development. From the developmental viewpoint, such an exchange takes part of its significance from the total context of the mother's and the child's life. It is important to know the larger ecological situation within which this type of contact occurs, because this is often, technically, the only way to understand what actually happens at the momentary intersection between the person and the ecological environment. But, more important, knowledge of the ecological context is essential because development is not a momentary phenomenon (in fact, most behavior in which we are interested is not momentary), and the *course* of the life-space can only be known within the ecological environment in which it is embedded.

PROBLEM OF STRUCTURE

The most primitive and simple thing we know about the ecological environment is that it has structure; it has parts with stable relations between them. One task is to describe this structure. It is clear that structure cannot be discovered by observing a single part, such as the point of intersection of the environment with a particular person, or by considering the parts separately, one by one. For example, a complete description of a player's behavior in a ball game, or the complete statistics of all the plays occurring in the game does not reveal the game of baseball. It is the rules of the game, and the arrangement of things and people according to the rules, which constitute the essential, unitary ecological environment of the players; it is these that shape the life-space of each player. By dealing with such contexts in terms of their discriminable parts, and processing them by probability statistics, we destroy what we are searching to discover. This approach has the value of a filing system, or of a concordance; but we cannot understand a book from its concordance. By these methods, the structure of the context is dismantled and rearranged; the structure is destroyed.

This does not mean, of course, that such investigations are without value. Important information about one level of a functioning system can be obtained when the system is dismantled. All sciences have structure-destroying methods and make valuable use of them. Essential components of the brain can be determined by excising and macerating brain tissue and analyzing it by physical and chemical techniques, even though this ignores or destroys the brain's macrostructure. But most sciences have, also, special nondestructive techniques for studying the structure of their phenomena. X-ray analysis and electrical, magnetic, and resonance techniques are instances. A primary concern of geologists, oceanographers, cytologists, mineralogists, geneticists, and astronomers is precisely with the naturally occurring, unrearranged structure of things: from chromosomes to the solar system and beyond. So it is important for psychology to discover tender-minded, nondestructive techniques for preserving intact naturally occurring behavior and its ecological environment. Here are some guides for this discovery from general ecological methodologies translated into terms of behavior phenomena.

The behavior with which one is concerned must be identified. There are many levels of behavior, each of which has a special environmental context. In the present case we are interested in molar behavior, in the behavior of persons as undivided entities; we are not interested in the behavior of eyelids or glands.

The problem of identifying and describing the ecological environment of behavior is an empirical one. It is necessary to observe and describe the environment in order to develop theories that later can guide further empirical investigation.

The identification of the ecological environment is aided by the fact that, unlike the life-space, it has an objective reality "out there"; it has temporal and physical attributes.

Since the physical-temporal world is not homogeneous but exists in natural parts with definite boundaries, the ecological environment occurs in bounded units. Arbitrarily defined physical-temporal units will not, except by chance, comprise an environmental unit. Furthermore, the boundaries and characteristics of the ecological environment cannot be determined by observing the persons within it.

The individual persons within a bounded unit of the ecological environment differ in psychological attributes; their behavior in the same environment will, therefore, differ.

However, since people en masse can be expected to have common attributes, the inhabitants of identical ecological units will exhibit a characteristic overall extra-individual pattern of behavior; and the inhabitants of different ecological units will exhibit different overall extra-individual patterns of behavior.

The ecological environment of a person's molar behavior, the molar environment, consists of bounded, physical-temporal locales and variegated but stable patterns in the behavior of people en masse. These characteristics of the ecological environment and behavior are familiar to laymen. The dictionary defines common ecological units in terms of both their physical-temporal and their extra-individual behavior coordinates, thus,

> road: a track (physical attribute) for travel or for conveying goods (extra-individual pattern of behavior)
> store: any place where goods (physical attribute) are kept for sale (extra-individual behavior pattern)
> park: a piece of ground (physical attribute) kept for ornament or recreation (extra-individual pattern of behavior).

An analysis of all descriptions of behavior occurring in one newspaper revealed that about 50 per cent of the reports were in terms of ecological units, including their extra-individual behavior patterns (Barker & Wright, 1955). Examples, "Ellson Drugstore will hold a sale on Friday and Saturday," "The Midwest High School commencement was held last Tuesday." Such physical-behavioral units are common phenomenal entities, and they are natural units in no way imposed by an investigator. To laymen they are as objective as rivers and forests, and they can be defined by denotation; they involve, in the beginning, no theories or concepts; they are parts of the objective environment that are experienced directly as rain and sandy beaches are experienced.

ECOLOGICAL UNITS

An initial practical problem of ecological research is to identify the natural units of the phenomenon studied. The essential nature of the units with which ecology deals is the same whether they are physical, social, biological, or behavioral units: (*a*) they occur without feedback from the investigator, they are self-generated; (*b*) each unit has a time-space locus; (*c*) an unbroken boundary separates an internal pattern from a differing external pattern. By these criteria, an electron, a person, and a waterfall are ecological units. This is true also of most towns and cities; and within a city it is true of a particular school, of the geometry lesson within the school, and of student Joe Doakes raising his hand to ask to recite. On the other hand, a square mile in the center of a city is not an ecological unit; its boundary is not self-generated. Neither are the Republican voters of the city or the school system ecological units; they have no continuously bounded time-space locus.

Many ecological units occur in circumjacent-interjacent series, or assemblies. A chick embryo, for example, is a nesting set of organs, cells, nuclei, molecules, atoms, and subatomic particles. In these assemblies the number of included levels is sharply restricted (in the 14-day chick embryo, for example, there are nine or ten levels of units); at each level there are a limited number of discriminable varieties of units (at the level of organs in the chick embryo there are about 40 varieties of units); and within each variety there are differing numbers of individual units(within the organ variety *heart* there is a single unit). Within this arrangement, each circumjacent assembly is reciprocally linked with the interjacent units it is composed of. This is clearly exemplified by the relation between words, punctuation marks, and sentences: words and punctuation marks form sentences from which, in turn, the words and punctuation marks derive their precise meanings.

This raises the theoretical problem, mentioned above, of accounting within a univocal explanatory theory for the reciprocal relations between different levels of phenomena. How, for example, can we account for the fact that a gas molecule behaves according to the laws of molecular motion, and at the same time according to the entirely different laws of the jet of gas of which it is a part? How can the explanations of the movement of a train of wheat across the Kansas plains by an economist (a scientist of circumjacent assemblies) and by an engineer (a scientist of interjacent units) ever be incorporated into a single theory? Both the laws of economics and the laws of engineering are true; both operate in predictable ways upon the train, but they are as utterly incommensurate as the price of wheat in Chicago and the horsepower of the engine. How can we ever subsume the laws of individual motivation and the principles of institutional operation within one system of concepts?

The difficulty in all of these cases resides in the fact that the "laws" that govern individual units are different from those applicable to the compound, circumjacent series or assemblies of units; yet units and unit assemblies are closely coupled. Behavioral ecology is concerned with molar behavior and the ecological contexts in which it occurs. The problem can be illustrated by an example.

Anne Matson was 10 years and 11 months of age and in the sixth grade of the Midwest public school. It was 2:09 P.M. and time for the daily music lesson with Miss Madison. The first three minutes of the record, made at the time (March 8, 1951), reported Anne's behavior as follows (Barker *et al.*, 1961):

Mrs. Nelson said in a businesslike manner, "All right, the class will pass."

Anne picked up her music book from her desk.

She stood.

Anne motioned urgently to her row, indicating that they should follow her around the front of the room.

The class filed out, carrying their music books.

Anne walked quickly to the music room; she was near the end of the single-file line.

2:10. The children seated themselves in a semicircle across the front of the music room.

Anne sat with Opal Bennet directly on her right and Rex Graw on her left. Alvin Stone was one seat over from Rex.

Miss Madison said briskly, "All right, let's open our books to page 27."

Anne watched Miss Madison solemnly.

Anne licked her finger.

She turned to the correct page.

Miss Madison asked the class, "How would you conduct this song?"

Immediately Anne raised her hand urgently, eager to be called on.

2:11. Miss Madison called on Ellen Thomas to show how she would conduct this song.

Ellen waved her right arm in three-four ryhthm.

Miss Madison watched Ellen critically.

With her hand still partway in the air, Anne watched earnestly.

Someone in the class objected that Ellen's beat wasn't quite right.

Persistently, Anne put her hand up higher wishing to be called on.

Miss Madison called on Stella Townsend.

Anne put her hand down with disappointment showing in her facial expression.

Intently she watched Stella demonstrate the pattern for conducting the song.

Miss Madison called on Opal Bennet.

Anne didn't raise her hand.

(*There was really no opportunity for hand-raising.*)

She turned toward her right.

With interest she watched Opal demonstrate the way to lead the song.

Miss Madison demonstrated how three-four time should be led.

Anne watched with an interested expression.

2:12. She started to practice, moving her arms in the demonstrated pattern.

Some of the other children also started practicing.

Miss Madison said pedagogically, "All right, let's all do it together."

She stood sideways in a businesslike way so that the children could see her hands.

She led the children as they all practiced conducting three-four time.

Anne let her fingers hang loosely in a consciously graceful manner.

With restraint and enjoyment she moved her arm up, down, and across in the correct pattern.

2:13. Miss Madison said, "Now we want one person to get up in front of the class and conduct."

Anne immediately raised her hand very eagerly straight up into the air.

On her face was a look of expectancy.

She held her hand in the air until Miss Madison called on Ellen Thomas.

This is an example of the dependent variable with which we are concerned, namely, a child's molar actions, e.g., watching teacher demonstrate three-four time, practicing three-four time, raising hand to be called on, looking at Opal. We have raised the question: What are the ecological contexts of such behavior?

There are an infinite number of discriminable phenomena external to any individual's behavior. In the case of Anne Matson during the music class there were, for example, her neighbors Opal and Rex, the music book, the song on page 27, the piano, the fifth and sixth grade classroom across the hall, the cool overcast day, the town of Midwest, the country of U.S.A.; there were Anne's hand, the windows of the room, Andrea

French sitting five seats away, Ellen's smile, and so on without limit. With which of these innumerable exterior phenomena was Anne's behavior linked? And were these phenomena related only via their links with Anne, or did they have a stable independent structure; were they an ecological assembly of units independent of Anne and her behavior?

How does one identify and describe the environment of behavior? Students of perception have been centrally concerned with this problem, and they have had some success in dealing with it. When perception psychologists have turned from the nature of perception to the preperceptual nature of light and sound, they have discovered something very important about the ecological environment of vision and hearing: it is not random; it involves bounded manifolds of individual elements with varied and unusual patterns. The environment of vision and hearing has a structure that is independent of its connections with perceptual mechanisms. All science reveals that nature is not uniform; the environments of atoms and molecules, of cells and organs, of trees and forests are patterned and structured, and this greatly facilitates their identification.

It would appear that students of molar behavior might profitably emulate students of perception, and consider the ecological environment of the behavior with which they are concerned entirely aside from its connection with behavior. This requires, in fact, a new science which stands with respect to molar behavior as the physics of light and sound stand with respect to vision and hearing. An analogy may help to make the problem clear.

If a novice, an Englishman, for example, wished to understand the environment of a first baseman in a ball game, he might set about to observe the interactions of the player with his surroundings. To do this with utmost precision he might view the first baseman through field glasses, so focused that the player would be centered in the field of the glasses with just enough of the environment included to encompass all the player's contacts with the environment, all inputs and outputs: all balls caught, balls thrown, players tagged, etc. Despite the commendable observational care, however, this method would never provide a novice with an understanding of "the game" which gives meaning to a first baseman's transactions with his surroundings and which, in fact, constitutes the environment of his baseball-playing behavior. By observing a player in this way, the novice would, in fact, fragment the game and destroy what he was seeking. So, also, he might by observations and interviews construct the player's life-space during the game: his achievements, aspirations, successes, failures, and conflicts; his judgments of the speed of the ball, of the fairness of the umpire, of the errors of his teammates. But this would only substitute for the former fragmented picture of "the game" the psychological consequences of the fragments, and thus remove the novice even further from the ecological environment he sought. Finally, the novice might perform innumerable correlations between the first baseman's achievements (balls caught, players tagged, strikes and hits made, bases stolen, errors, etc.) and particular attributes of the ecological environment involved (speed of balls thrown to him, distance of throw, weight of bat, curve of balls, etc.). But he could never arrive at the phenomenon known as a baseball game by this means.

It would seem clear that a novice would learn more about the ecological environment of a first baseman by blotting out the player and observing the game around him. This is what the student of light and sound does with elaborate instrumentation, and it is the approach we have taken in the present studies.

It is not easy, at first, to leave the person out of observations of the environment of molar behavior. Our perceptual apparatus is adjusted by our long training with the idiocentric viewing glasses of individual observations, interviews, and questionnaires to see *persons* whenever we see behavior. But with some effort and experience the extra-individual assemblies of behavior episodes, behavior objects, and space that surround persons can be observed and described. Their nonrandom distribution and bounded character are a crucial aid. If the reader will recall school class meetings, some of the characteristics of environmental units will be clearly apparent:

It is a natural phenomenon; it is not created by an experimenter for scientific purposes.

It has a space-time locus.

A boundary surrounds a school class meeting.

The boundary is self-generated; it changes as the class changes in size and in the nature of its activity.

The class meeting is objective in the sense that it exists independent of anyone's perception of it, *qua* class; it is a preperceptual ecological entity.

It has two sets of components: (*a*) behavior (reciting, discussing, sitting) and (*b*) nonpsychological objects with which behavior is transacted, e.g., chairs, walls, a blackboard, paper, etc.

The unit, the class meeting, is circumjacent to its components; the pupils and equipment are *in* the class.

The behavior and physical objects that constitute the unit school class meeting are internally organized and arranged to form a pattern that is by no means random.

The pattern within the boundary of a class meeting is easily discriminated from that outside the boundary.

There is a synomorphic relation between the pattern of the behavior occurring within the class and the pattern of its nonbehavioral components, the behavior objects. The seats face the teacher's desk, and the children face the teacher, for example.

The unity of the class is not due to the similarity of its parts at any moment; for example, speaking occurs in one part and listening in another. The unity is based, rather, upon the interdependence of the parts; events in different parts of a class meeting have a greater effect upon each other than equivalent events beyond its boundary.

The people who inhabit a class are to a considerable degree interchangeable and replaceable. Pupils come and go; even the teacher may be replaced. But the same entity continues as serenely as an old car with new rings and the right front wheel now carried as the spare.

The behavior of this entity cannot, however, be greatly changed without destroying it: there must be teaching, there must be study, there must be recitation.

A pupil has two positions in a class; first, he is a component of the supra-individual unit, and second, he is an individual whose life-space is partly formed within the constraints imposed by the very entity of which he is a part.

Such entities stand out with great clarity; they are common phenomena of everyday life. We have called them *K-21 behavior settings* (frequently shortened to *behavior settings* and *settings* in the text). Studies of K-21 behavior settings provide evidence that they are stable, extra-individual units with great coercive power over the behavior that occurs within them (Barker & Wright, 1955; Gump & Sutton-Smith, 1955; Gump, Schoggen & Redl, 1957; Raush, Dittmann & Taylor, 1959 & 1960; Barker, 1960a; Jordan, 1963; Gump, Schoggen & Redl, 1963; Soskin & John, 1963; Ashton, 1964; Barker & Gump, 1964; Wicker, 1967).

In the next chapter we shall describe behavior settings in terms of concepts that have issued from our empirical studies. But there are other sources of information about behavior settings, for they are ubiquitous phenomena of everyday life; they are frequently portrayed in nonscientific writings, pictorial representations, and photographs. Chapter 5 contains examples of behavior settings as represented by photographers, news reporters, and encyclopedists. The reader may wish to turn to this exhibit for laymen's views of the phenomena with which we shall be concerned.

3

Behavior Settings: Defining Attributes and Varying Properties

A BEHAVIOR SETTING has both structural and dynamic attributes. On the structural side, a behavior setting consists of one or more standing patterns of behavior-and-milieu, with the milieu circumjacent and synomorphic to the behavior. On the dynamic side, the behavior-milieu parts of a behavior setting, the synomorphs, have a specified degree of interdependence among themselves that is greater than their interdependence with parts of other behavior settings. These are the essential attributes of a behavior setting; the crucial terms will now be defined and elaborated (the comments refer to the italicized words).

(1) A behavior setting consists of one or more *standing patterns of behavior*. Many units of behavior have been identified: reflex, actone, action, molar unit, and group activity are examples. A standing pattern of behavior is another behavior unit. It is a bounded pattern in the behavior of men, en masse. Examples in Midwest are a basketball game, a worship service, a piano lesson. A standing pattern of behavior is not a common behavior element among disparate behavior elements, such as the twang in Midwestern speech or the custom in small American towns of greeting strangers when they are encountered on the street. A standing pattern of behavior is a discrete behavior entity with univocal temporal-spatial coordinates; a basketball game, a worship service, or a piano lesson has, in each case, a precise and delimited position in time and space. Furthermore, a standing pattern of behavior is not a characteristic of the particular individuals involved; it is an extra-individual behavior phenomenon; it has unique characteristics that persist when the participants change.

(2) It consists of standing patterns of behavior-*and-milieu*. The behavior patterns of a behavior setting are attached to particular constellations of nonbehavioral phenomena. Both man-made parts of a town (buildings, streets, and baseball diamonds) and natural features (hills

and lakes) can comprise the milieu, or soma, of a behavior setting. Often the milieu is an intricate complex of times, places, and things. The milieu of the setting 4-H Club Meeting is a constellation of a particular room in a particular residence at a particular time with particular objects distributed in a particular pattern. The milieu of a behavior setting exists independently of the standing pattern of behavior and independently of anyone's perception of the setting. Between sessions, and when no one is thinking about it, i.e., when the behavior setting 4-H Club Meeting is nonexistent, its constitution, minute book, roll of members, meeting place, gavel, printed programs, etc., are in existence.

(3) The milieu is *circumjacent* to the behavior. Circumjacent means surrounding (enclosing, environing, encompassing); it describes an essential attribute of the milieu of a behavior setting. The milieu of a setting is circumjacent to the standing pattern of behavior. The temporal and physical boundaries of the milieu surround the behavior pattern without a break, as in the case of a store that opens at 8:00 A.M. and closes at 6:00 P.M.

(4) The milieu is *synomorphic* to the behavior. Synomorphic means similar in structure; it describes an essential feature of the relationship between the behavior and the milieu of a behavior setting. The synomorphy of the boundary of the behavior and of the boundary of the milieu is striking and fundamental: the boundary of a football field is the boundary of the game; the beginning and end of the school music period mark the limits of the pattern of music behavior. But the synomorphy of behavior and milieu extends, also, to the fine, interior structure of a behavior setting. In the case of a worship service, both the pews (milieu) and the listening congregation (behavior) face the pulpit (milieu) and the preaching pastor (behavior). The behavioral and somatic components of a behavior setting are not independently arranged; there is an essential fittingness between them; see, for example, Fig. 3.1.

(5) The *behavior-milieu parts* are called synomorphs. The physical sciences have avoided phenomena with behavior as a component, and the behavioral sciences have avoided phenomena with physical things and conditions as essential elements. So we have sciences of behavior-free objects and events (ponds, glaciers, and lightning flashes), and we have sciences of phenomena without geophysical loci and attributes (organizations, social classes, roles). We lack a science of things and occurrences that have both physical and behavioral attributes. Behavior settings are such phenomena; they consist of behavior-and-circum-

© United Feature Syndicate, Inc., 1966

Fig. 3.1. Charlie Brown deals with a problem of synomorphy.

jacent-synomorphic-milieu entities. We call these parts of a behavior setting behavior-milieu synomorphs, or, more briefly, synomorphs. Structurally a behavior setting is a set of such synomorphs.

(6) The synomorphs have a specified *degree of interdependence*. It is understood in Midwest that behavior-milieu synomorphs are more or less interdependent. Functionaries of the Methodist Church Evening Guild Food Sale know that this affair should not be arranged for the same day as the 4-H Club Food Sale; they know that its standing pattern of behavior would not be vigorous. It is common knowledge, too, that the Boy Scout Pop Stand thrives when it coincides in time with the Old Settlers Reunion Midway. On the other hand, the Pintner Abstract and Title Company Office is not affected by the occurrence or nonoccurrence of the Parent-Teacher Association Carnival. Merchants, preachers, teachers, and organization leaders of Midwest are astute judges of these interrelations.

The fact that the synomorphs of Midwest constitute a more or less interconnected network makes it possible to identify those with any specified degree of interdependence. This may be clarified by an analogy. The climate of a country can be described in terms of climatic areas and the economy in terms of economic regions. There are two common ways of defining the extent of such areas and regions: (a) in terms of a defined amount of intra-area variability, e.g., an average annual rainfall differential of two inches might be established as the limit of the territory to be included in a climatic area; (b) in terms of a defined degree of interdependence, e.g., a correlation of 0.70 between indices of economic change might be fixed as the limit of the domain included in an economic region. We have used the second kind of criterion as a basis for identifying unitary sets of synomorphs.

The nature of this interdependence criterion was stated with precision by Lewin (1951). He pointed out that in all interdependent systems, whether they involve behavior settings or physiological, physical, or economic systems, a unit can be defined in terms of any degree of interdependence desired. Thus, we might divide the population of Midwest into economic units on the basis of financial interdependence. Such an economic unit can be defined as follows: individuals $A, B, C, \ldots N$ make up an economic unit if a change in the economic state of A of x amount is accompanied by a change of Kx in the economic state of B, $C \ldots N$. An interdependence index, K, of 0.9 would divide the town into many economic units, for only immediate family units as highly interdependent as husband, wife, and minor children would fall into so close an economic unit. An interdependence index of 0.5 would undoubtedly combine some immediate family units with extended family units, and perhaps some business associates and their families would fall within the same unit; hence the town would have fewer economic units. If the degree of interdependence were placed very low, e.g., 0.01, the community might turn out to be a single economic unit.

This can be exemplified by the hypothetical case of Mr. Joe Lamprey, and what might happen if he were to inherit an annuity of $500 a month.

	Previous Monthly Income	Subsequent Monthly Income	Per Cent Change
Mr. Joe Lamprey	$ 500	$1,000	100
Mrs. Joe Lamprey	300	575	92
George Lamprey, son	10	20	100
Mary Lamprey, daughter	5	15	200
Mrs. Ella Lamprey, mother	200	250	25
James Hill, business partner	400	424	6
Jack Rolf, insurance agent	300	312	4
Ten Midwesterners (average) ..	200	206	3
115 Midwesterners (average) ..	1,500	1,500	0.3

Detailed study of the monthly income of a number of people might reveal information contained in the tabulation. In terms of an interdependence index, K, of 0.90, the economic unit with reference to Joe Lamprey contains the first four persons of the list, since an increase of 100 per cent in Joe's income is accompanied by an increase of 90 per cent or more in their income. If this relationship were mutual for all the members of this group of four, and if this were the average number of persons with an economic interdependence index of 0.90, there would be 187 such economic units in a total population of 750. An interdependence index of 0.25 would increase the unit centering about Joe to five persons; and again if this were general, it would reduce the number of economic units to 150. An interdependence index of 0.03 would, according to the data of the tabulation, include 17 in Joe's economic unit, making 44 such units in the town. With an index of 0.003 there would be only six economic units in the community.

The same principles of interdependence can be used to define such diverse community units as friendship groups, ground water or air pollution units, information units, and sets of behavior-milieu synomorphs.

(7) The synomorphs have a greater degree of interdependence *among themselves than with parts of other behavior settings.* One of the dynamic criteria of a behavior setting is internal, namely, that the degree of interdependences, K, among its synomorphs be equal to or greater than a specified amount. An example of the required degree of internal unity is found in the Drugstore. The Fountain, the Pharmacy, and the Variety Department are separate synomorphs interjacent to the Drugstore. Structurally they are discrete, but dynamically they are so *inter*dependent in their functioning that, by the criteria used, they are parts of the single behavior setting Drugstore. On the other hand, the Junior High Class, the Intermediate Class, and the Primary Class, which are also structurally separate synomorphs interjacent to Vacation Church School, are so *in*dependent in their functioning that, by the criteria used, they are discrete behavior settings. A fundamental property of a behavior setting is internal unity. However, Midwest's Vacation Church School does not have this unity; it is a multisetting synomorph.

There is, also, an external dynamic criterion of a behavior setting. An example is found in the behavior setting Chaco Garage and Service Station. Structurally Chaco Garage and Chaco Service Station are separate synomorphs; and, unlike the Fountain, Pharmacy, and Variety Department, they are interjacent to no other synomorph. But dynamically they are not independent; small changes in the functioning of the garage (e.g., the number of its customers) are accompanied by changes in the functioning of the service station, and vice versa. These two structurally separate synomorphs are so interdependent that by the index we have used they become the single synomorph, or behavior setting, Chaco Garage and Service Station. On the other hand, the synomorphs Chaco Garage and Eastman Garage, which are also structurally separate, are dynamically almost completely independent. Even quite large changes in the functioning of Chaco Garage are accompanied by only small changes in the functioning of Eastman Garage. These two synomorphs are so independent in their operations that they are separate behavior settings.

Implicit in the structural and dynamic attributes of a behavior setting are three tests for evaluating any part, *Pt*, of a community as a possible behavior setting.

Structural test. Is *Pt* a behavior-milieu synomorph? This criterion serves to exclude as behavior settings such discriminable community features as mores and customs, social classes, organizations, ethnic groups, geographical areas, roles, legal codes, educational systems.

Internal dynamic test. Does *Pt* have the specified degree of interdependence, *K*, among synomorphs that are structurally interjacent to it? This test is applied to a community part that has passed the structure test, i.e., that it is a synomorph. If *Pt* contains synomorphs with *less* than the specified degree of *inter*dependence, i.e., if any of *Pt*'s structural parts are too *in*dependent of other parts of *Pt*, or too independent of the total synomorph *Pt*, then *Pt* is by definition more than a single behavior setting. This criterion serves, in Midwest, to exclude as behavior settings such synomorphs as the churches, the schools, and the courthouse; these behavior-milieu structures are not behavior settings, but multiple-setting synomorphs.

External dynamic test. Does *Pt* have the specified degree of *in*dependence, or dynamic separation, from synomorphs that are structurally external to it? This test is applied to a community part that has passed the structure test and the internal dynamic test (if it contains synomorphs). If *Pt*, or any part of *Pt*, has a degree of *inter*dependency with synomorphs structurally external to it that is *equal to or greater than* the specified amount, i.e., if *Pt* is not sufficiently *in*dependent of all other community parts, then *Pt* is by definition a constituent part of a more inclusive setting. This criterion serves, in Midwest, to exclude as a discrete behavior setting the Presbyterian Church Worship Service on June 19; this worship service is, by the criterion used, a part (a single syno-

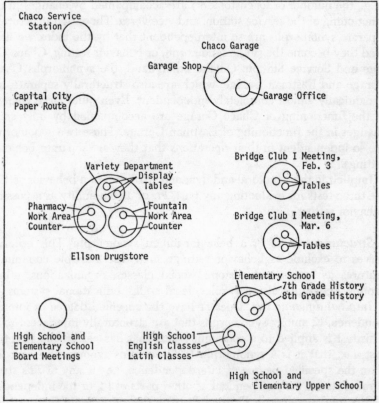

Fig. 3.2. Synomorphic structure of a part of Midwest.

morph) of the recurring, multiple-synomorph behavior setting Presbyterian Church Worship Service.

When research was initiated in Midwest, we were confronted with the discouraging task of selecting from the countless parts of the town those which were relevant to our efforts to describe the living conditions of the residents. The endless list included such varied features of Midwest as the weather vane on the Courthouse, the upper social class, Delaware Street, the Methodist Church, the Old Settlers Reunion Amateur Show, the County Commissioners Meeting on February 3, the Negro residents, the Culver family, the Stop-for-Pedestrians signs, the Volunteer Fire Department, a school tax of 12 mills, May Day, the North Precinct Polling Place, Mrs. Arla Grainger, a bonded indebtedness of $8,500, the *Midwest Weekly,* and the prevailing southwest wind. Behav-

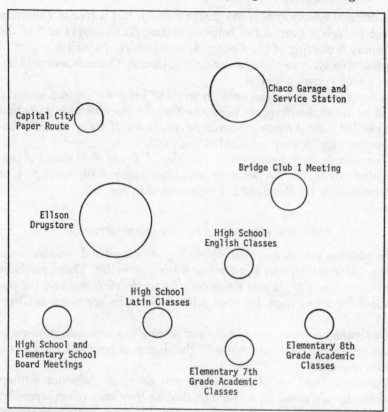

Fig. 3.3. Behavior setting structure of the part of Midwest shown in Fig. 3.2.

ior settings made the environment of Midwest manageable. For example, the three tests reduce this sample list of community parts to two behavior settings: Old Settlers Reunion Amateur Show and North Precinct Polling Place. Some parts are excluded because they are not behavior-milieu synomorphs with circumjacent milieu (Test *a*); this is true of the weather vane, the upper social class, the Negro residents, the Culver family, the Stop-for-Pedestrians signs, the Volunteer Fire Department, the school tax, May Day, Mrs. Grainger, the bonded indebtedness, the *Midwest Weekly*, and the prevailing winds. Another part is excluded because there is less than the requisite degree of interdependence with and among its structurally interjacent synomorphs (Test *b*), namely, the Methodist Church. Still other potential settings on the list are excluded because their interdependence with structurally external synomorphs is too great (Test *c*); this is true of Delaware Street (which is part of the behavior setting Trafficways) and of the February 3 meeting of the County Commissioners (which is a part of the multiple-synomorph behavior setting County Commissioners Meeting (which occurs weekly).

A description of a community in terms of behavior settings includes all of its discriminable parts, because either the discriminable parts that are not behavior settings are parts or attributes of more inclusive behavior settings, or they are multisetting units.

The complicated *synomorphic* structure of a part of Midwest is represented in Fig. 3.2; the *behavior setting* structure of the same part, as determined by the three tests, is represented in Fig. 3.3.

VARIABLE PROPERTIES OF BEHAVIOR SETTINGS

In addition to their essential, unvarying, structural and dynamic attributes, behavior settings have many other properties. Those we have studied will now be briefly described; detailed definitions and the operations for rating these behavior setting properties are given in Chapter 4.

Geographical locus. Every behavior setting has a precise position in space which can be designated with the degree of precision the investigation requires.

Temporal locus, serial occurrence, and duration. Behavior settings may occur only once, on a specified day, or they may recur according to some temporal schedule of days. The behavior setting Northeast Kansas County Officials Meeting occurred in Midwest on September 24, 1963, from 9:00 A.M. to 12:00 noon; it had not occurred previously in the year and it did not occur subsequently, but Boy Scout Troop Meeting occurred regularly on most Mondays from 7:30 to 9:00 P.M. Whether recurring or nonrecurring, behavior settings have a definite day or days of occurrence and a definite duration at each occurrence; from this information, the total number of occurrences, the total hours of duration, and the mean duration per occurrence of a behavior setting within a stated period of time can be determined. The Northeast Kansas Officials Meeting had one occurrence of 3 hours in the year 1963–64; the Boy Scout Troop Meeting had 43 occurrences for a total duration of 64.5 hours and a mean duration per occurrence of 1.5 hours.

Population. A behavior setting has a definite number of inhabitants at each occurrence. This population can be identified with respect to whatever attributes are relevant, such as age, sex, social class, town residents, nonresident inhabitants.

Occupancy time. The number of person-hours a behavior setting is occupied over a designated period of time is the occupancy time of the setting for that period; it is the product of the mean population per occurrence and the duration in hours of all occurrences. Occupancy time can be determined separately for population subgroups. The total occupancy time of the Boy Scout Troop Meeting in 1963–64 of 816 hours was divided between four adult leaders (125 hours), 17 adolescent members (468 hours), and 15 child members and visitors (224 hours); occupancy by males was 816 hours, by females 0 hours.

Functional position of inhabitants. Behavior settings have an internal structure, and individuals and categories of individuals occupy the various parts to different degrees. An important feature of the internal structure of a behavior setting is the power that different parts exercise over its functioning. This power can be determined with some precision; it ranges from parts with virtually no power over the setting (e.g., the parts that the "sidewalk superintendents" occupy in the setting High School Construction Project) to the part with control over the entire behavior setting (e.g., the part occupied by the single teacher of the setting Fourth Grade Music Class). We have called this dimension of the internal structure of behavior settings the *penetration* dimension; and we have called those parts of a setting with some direct power over all or a part of its functioning the *performance zones*; persons who inhabit performance zones are *performers*.

Action patterns. The pattern of behavior of a setting has limitless attributes. We have identified and investigated the degree of occurrence of 11 attributes which we have named action patterns, namely, aesthetic, business, educational, governmental, nutritional, personal appearance, physical health, professional, recreational, religious, and social action patterns.

Behavior mechanisms. The behavior pattern of a setting involves different effector systems to various degrees. The degree of involvement of the following mechanisms has been systematically studied: affective, gross motor, manipulation, verbal, and thinking mechanisms.

Pressure. Behavior settings differ in the degree to which they bring pressure upon different population subgroups to enter and participate in them. The setting High School English Class possesses forces, via two other behavior settings, High School Principal's Office and County Court, to require adolescents to become its inhabitants; the setting Pearl Cafe, on the other hand, can only issue more or less seductive invitations; and the North Precinct Polling Place exerts strong negative pressure on adolescents, restricting them to the most superficial zones of penetration.

Autonomy. Behavior settings differ in the extent to which their functioning is influenced by occurrences originating within and outside the community. The setting Bridge Club I Meeting is subject to no influence from outside Midwest, but the functioning of the behavior setting Midwest Bank is strongly influenced by regulations originating at state and national levels.

Welfare. Settings differ in the degree to which they cater to the needs of different population subgroups. The Boy Scout Troop Meeting is devoted exclusively to the welfare of boys 11 to 17 years of age, whereas Kanes Grocery Store serves the nutritional needs of all ages.

SOURCES OF OUR KNOWLEDGE OF BEHAVIOR SETTINGS

The structural attributes of behavior settings are directly perceived. One sees that the behavior of the Saturday Night Dance (ticket-taking, dancing, conversing, eating, playing musical instruments, etc.) occurs inside, not outside, the setting (of which the hall is part); one sees that the geographical arrangement of the chairs, the open floor area, the refreshment counter, the drums, etc., is congruent with the pattern of behavior. But the dynamic attributes of behavior settings, their internal unity, and the forces patterning persons, behavior, and objects into the shape and order required by the setting are indirectly apprehended. The evidence initially available to us on the dynamics of behavior settings will now be presented.

Influence of behavior settings upon the behavior of inhabitants. The influence of behavior settings upon behavior is exhibited in natural experiments that occur in Midwest. In these experiments, behavior settings are the independent variable and the behavior of Midwest inhabitants the dependent variable. Data of one such experiment are presented in Table 3.1, where some aspects of the behavior of the children of the second grade are summarized as they passed from one behavior setting to another during the school day. The same children exhibit these different patterns of behavior day after day; and the experiment

TABLE 3.1. *Behavior of the Same Children in Different Behavior Settings*

	Behavior Setting		
	Second-Grade Academic Class	Playground	Second-Grade Music Class
Behavior pattern	Organized activity; little change in position; slow tempo; serious mood; limited variety of behavior, with sitting, reading, writing, and reciting predominant.	Unorganized or partly organized activity; fast tempo; exuberant mood; large variety of behavior, with games predominant.	Organized activity, variation in tempo; medium cheerfulness; little variety of behavior, singing predominant.

is repeated each year with a new group, with the same results. The changes observed in the behavior of children as they change from one setting to another can only be ascribed to forces operating within the behavior settings.

However, some aspects of the behavior of different persons within the same behavior setting may differ widely: one person may enter a drugstore to buy medicine for a friend, another may enter to buy poison for an enemy; one person may go to church for spiritual satisfaction, another for social advantage; one patient in the doctor's office may have his anxieties allayed, another may have his worst fears confirmed; one pupil in a class may experience great success, another profound failure. Yet all of these people will conform to the standing pattern characteristic of behavior in the setting. In other words, the content and structure of a person's own psychological world, his life-space, are by no means determined by the behavior setting.

Sources of behavior-milieu synomorphy. Evidence of the internal unity and coerciveness of behavior settings, and of some of the mechanisms involved, is revealed when the sources of the behavior-milieu synomorphy are considered. Eight possible sources of the synomorphy of standing patterns of behavior and nonpsychological milieu are as follows:

(1) *Physical forces.* Physical arrangements can enforce some patterns of behavior and prevent others. School corridors, for example, allow locomotion in certain directions only, their narrowness prevents the playing of circle games, and the absence of chairs or ledges encourages

standing and walking and discourages sitting or lying. The layout of streets and sidewalks, the size and arrangement of rooms, and the distribution of furniture and equipment are often important factors in coercing certain features of standing patterns of behavior and in restricting others. The physical forces impelling and hindering behavior do not have to be absolute, like a wall that cannot be breached; they can be effective by making actions of some kinds easier than others. It is physically easier to walk on the streets and sidewalks of Midwest than to cut across lots; even dogs follow the streets and sidewalks to a considerable degree. In these cases, physical forces from the milieu mold behavior to conform to its shape.

(2) *Social forces.* Social forces can be strongly coercive. The power attaching to a teacher, organization president, or store manager to enforce a particular pattern of behavior is well known. In addition, social forces to conform to the standing pattern issue from the behavior pattern itself. Thus, a child who "holds back" as the third and fourth grades rush pell-mell through the school halls to the playground for recess is pushed along by the tide of behavior: by physical forces in the form of crowding and shoving, but also by social forces in the form of threats and promises.

(3) *Physiological processes.* Without question there are built-in behavior mechanisms in men that respond with mechanical compulsiveness to some features of the nonpsychological milieu. In Kerrs Locker (for frozen food storage), where the temperature is maintained near zero, behavior is brisk, and movements stiff and ungraceful.

(4) *Physiognomic perception.* An important factor in molding standing patterns of behavior is the coercive influence upon perception of some configurations of stimuli originating in the nonpsychological milieu. The children of Midwest appear to see a smooth, level area free of obstructions, such as the football field, the courthouse lawn, the school gymnasium, or the American Legion hall, as a place for running and romping in unorganized, exuberant activity. These milieu features appear via perception to demand this kind of behavior. Open spaces seduce children. Midwest is loaded with these perceived, seductive characteristics. The displays and arrangements of the stores, the order of the church services, the ceremony at weddings, the guide lines painted on the streets, the furnishings of homes are all calculated to coerce behavior to the appropriate pattern.

It is our impression that the social milieu is even more seductive. The forces upon an individual to rise when the congregation rises, to sit when it sits, and to be silent when it is silent are strong indeed. The social pressures to be gay at a carnival, businesslike at the annual school meeting, and sad at a funeral are strong.

(5) *Learning*. The learning of behavior suitable for particular behavior-milieu synomorphs is an important source of the conformity of individuals to the standing patterns of behavior. The process of teaching children to conform, to be quiet in church, to eat at mealtime, to sit still in school proceeds continually.

(6) *Selection by persons*. There is an affinity between the standing pattern of a behavior setting and the behavior repertoires of the persons who enter it. This occurs partly via the discriminative and selective behavior of individuals. An adolescent boy who finds the behavior pattern of a Sunday school class intolerable will refuse to attend. Those who remain will, therefore, be self-selected for their ability to conform to the standing pattern of behavior.

(7) *Selection by behavior settings*. Some behavior settings have entrance requirements that exclude persons whose behavior does not readily conform to that of the standing pattern and to the requirements of the milieu. Boys younger than 11 years cannot join the Boy Scouts; candidates for membership in the Masonic Lodge are examined to make sure that they can abide by the behavioral requirements of the lodge. Furthermore, many settings eject persons who do not conform to the standing pattern of behavior; a member of a bridge club who insisted on playing poker would soon be dropped, "incorrigible" boys are expelled from school, "inactive" members are dropped from the church rolls.

(8) *Influence of behavior on the milieu*. The channels so far mentioned by which the synomorphy of behavior pattern and milieu arises have been via direct physical and social forces acting on behavior, via the native or learned reactions to the milieu through perception, or via selection of persons with appropriate behavior possibilities. Another source is the effect of behavior on milieu. This can occur as an incidental resultant of the behavior. The path from the south entrance of the Midwest schoolhouse to the corner of the yard is a prominent behavior-milieu synomorph; a great part of the going to and coming from the school is associated with this path. In this case the milieu was created by the feet of many children taking the shortest way home. At the present time it coerces travelers not to stray from its physically smooth and perceptually demanding course, but in the beginning the path was created by behavior.

The synomorphy of milieu and behavior arises, too, from the explicit demand of behavior for a particular milieu. The boys of Midwest want to play basketball. This requires a particular milieu, including special behavior objects. Midwest boys have, therefore, created the necessary milieu and assembled the necessary behavior objects, and in consequence Howells Hayloft is a behavior-milieu synomorph of Midwest. Similarly, when preparations are made for the Senior Class festivities, the school gymnasium is transformed into a banquet hall and the behavior-milieu synomorph Junior Class Banquet for Seniors occurs in Midwest. As a matter of fact, a great amount of behavior in Midwest is concerned with creating new milieu arrangements to support new standing patterns of behavior, or altering old milieu features to conform to changes in old patterns of behavior.

Initiation and termination of behavior settings. Still other evidence of the internal unity and coerciveness of behavior settings is found in the functional interconnectedness of their parts. When any principal part of a setting is changed, for example, when the teacher is absent from the setting Fourth Grade Music Class, all aspects of the setting are affected; this is true, too, if the heat or the lights fail. The internal interdependence of behavior settings is nowhere shown more clearly than in the beginning and end of a behavior-setting occurrence. Characteristically, all parts of a setting begin and cease simultaneously. Midwest's Department Store ceases to exist, *in toto*, at 5:30 P.M.; and it recurs, fully accessible, at 8:00 the following morning. The Drugstore is open until 6:30 P.M., when it suddenly ceases; it rejoins the public behavior areas at 7:30 A.M. Different behavior settings of Midwest have different schedules of opening and closing, and the schedules combine in such a way that the town slowly expands in the morning and slowly closes down at night. But almost every setting opens and closes as a unit; in this respect settings almost always function in an all-or-none manner, i.e., as units.

Nontransposability of standing patterns of behavior. The unity and coerciveness of behavior settings is further demonstrated by the fact that behavior frequently cannot be transposed between them. Midwest residents cannot telephone at the behavior setting Post Office or deposit mail in the setting Telephone Booth; they cannot weld a bearing in the Latin Class or recite a Latin lesson in the setting Machine Shop. The conditions obtaining in particular settings are as essential for some kinds of behavior as are persons with the requisite motives and skills. Behavior settings are not neutral, geographical-temporal regions to which any behavior can be freely added; the behavior pattern and the milieu are dynamically inseparable.

CATEGORIES OF BEHAVIOR SETTINGS

Behavior settings can be classified in as many ways as they have discriminable attributes; they can be classified into settings of short and long duration, settings with male, female, and mixed sex population, settings where work predominates, and settings where play predominates. However, anyone who deals regularly with behavior settings classifies them in terms of more general similarities. Laymen do this as a matter of course: attorneys' offices, auction sales, banks, barbershops, baseball games, billiard parlors, and card parties, for example, are common names for categories of behavior settings, and the settings included in each of them are similar with respect to many behavior setting attributes and properties. In Midwest, the four attorneys' offices all have the essential attributes of behavior settings, and in addition they have a surprising degree of equivalence with respect to the form and content of their standing patterns of behavior and milieu, their temporal occurrences and durations, their kinds of inhabitants, their population densities and occupancy times, their action patterns, their behavior mechanisms, their degrees of autonomy. In fact, they are so similar in so many respects that, like automobiles of the same make and model, most of their parts are interchangeable (books, secretaries, office machines), and particular courses of action (e.g., cases) could be, and are, smoothly transposed from one attorney's office setting to another.

Methods of identifying categories of equivalent behavior settings, called genotypes, are presented in Chapter 4. The interdependence of behavior-milieu synomorphs is one of the grounds for identifying behavior settings; it is also the basis of an important relationship between settings. This relationship occurs when one behavior setting has the power to alter the standing pattern of another setting. The behavior setting High School Principal's Office, for example, can modify—it can even eliminate—the behavior setting High School Dance. One behavior setting may have this power over a number of other settings, and its power may operate via subordinate settings to form chains of superordination-subordination. These chains of interdependence we have called authority systems, and we have categorized them according to the most powerful settings in the systems.

NOMENCLATURE OF BEHAVIOR SETTINGS

The nomenclature of behavior settings presents difficulties. While a behavior setting is the total, extra-individual pattern of behavior and milieu, the common names of settings often refer to only one of these aspects. Although the name of the behavior setting Midwest Lake specifies its physical side, the pattern of the behaving persons and objects is an essential part of the setting. The physical lake, per se, without the behavior and objects is not a behavior setting. On the other hand, the name of the setting Presbyterian Sunday School Exercises stresses the behavior, when actually this setting is comprised of the integrated functioning of the members, superintendent, auditorium, piano, song leader, pews, songbooks, etc. Again, the name of the behavior setting County Superintendent of Schools Office implicates at any particular time a particular person; in fact, this setting is the behavior-milieu complex associated with a number of different individuals over a period of time and certain persisting parts of the community (a suite of offices labeled "County Superintendent of Schools," a certificate of election, etc.). The inhabitants of a community understand this verbal shorthand.

This completes our general consideration of ecological psychology and of the defining attributes and varying properties of behavior settings. In Chapter 4 we deal with technical problems involved in the identification, assessment, and classification of behavior settings. The reader who is not concerned with detailed applications of behavior setting methods may wish to turn next to Chapter 5, where the methods are exemplified by means of data for one community.

4

Behavior Setting Survey

A BEHAVIOR SETTING SURVEY is an inventory and description of the behavior settings of a town or institution. Three operations are involved: identifying and listing all potential behavior settings; discarding potential settings that upon closer examination do not meet the criteria of behavior settings; and describing the behavior settings.

The identification of behavior settings is a precise operation, and a detailed technical exposition is required to describe the procedures involved. The seeming complexity of the procedures should not discourage one from undertaking a behavior setting survey, however, for experience with the procedures soon teaches a fieldworker to recognize most community units that possess the structural and dynamic properties of behavior settings. This is facilitated by the fact that behavior setting criteria are chosen, in part, so that they will identify commonly perceived community units. In questionable cases a few calculations usually eliminate uncertainties. However, this should not obscure the fact that behavior settings are precisely defined, that there are reliable procedures for identifying behavior settings, and that even an experienced fieldworker has regularly to make detailed judgments and computations.

IDENTIFYING POTENTIAL BEHAVIOR SETTINGS

The first task is to discover every possible setting. The best way to begin is to walk the streets and halls of the community or institution and observe and record the walled, fenced, and otherwise bounded areas; almost all of these are the exoskeletons of behavior-milieu synomorphs and many of them are the loci of behavior settings. Frequently the name of the setting is inscribed on a door or window. Detailed maps and plans of areas and buildings are useful, too.

Excellent sources of potential settings are the local newspaper, tele-

TABLE 4.1. *Sample List of Potential Settings*

Category	Setting
Business	1. *Drugstore
	2. Fountain of Drugstore
	3. Pharmacy of Drugstore
	4. Variety Department of Drugstore
	5. *J. Wiley, Attorneys Office
	6. *Barber Shop
	7. *J. Wiley, Music Lessons
Church	8. Methodist Church
	9. *Joash Worship Service at Methodist Church
	10. *Adult Choir Practice at Methodist Church
	11. Presbyterian Church
	12. *Worship Service at Presbyterian Church
	13. Anthem by Presbyterian Church Choir
Government	14. *County Treasurers Office
	15. *Payment of Taxes at County Treasurers Office*
	16. *Courthouse Square
	17. *Sitting on Benches of Courthouse Square*
Voluntary	18. *Boy Scout Troop 72 Meeting
Association	19. Tenderfoot Test at Scout Meeting
	20. Beaver Patrol Activities at Scout Meeting
	21. *4-H Club*
	22. *Skating Party of 4-H Club
	23. *Regular Meeting of 4-H Club
	24. Election of 4-H Club Officers
	25. *Achievement Banquet of 4-H Club
	26. *Hopscotch Games*
	27. March 3 Meeting of Couples Bridge Club
	28. April 1 Meeting of Couples Bridge Club
	29. May 2 Meeting of Couples Bridge Club
School	30. High School
	31. *High School Senior Class*
	32. *Box Social by Senior Class
	33. Bingo Game
	34. Walk for a Cake
	35. *High School Gym*
	36. *Girls Locker Room
	37. *Brick-paved Area in Front of High School*
Miscellaneous	38. *Trafficways
	39. *State Highway*

* Behavior settings, i.e., community parts that pass both structure and dynamic tests.

Items in italics are not behavior-milieu synomorphs according to the structure test; they are not tested by the dynamics tests.

The *structural* relationships of these potential behavior settings are indicated by the indent, as follows:

phone and other classified directories, school schedules, organization programs, church bulletins, placards, handbills. They report many potential settings for inclusion in a preliminary list. Here is an example of an item from the Midwest Weekly of the sort that provides a number of potential settings:

Box Social
Wednesday, October 15, at 7:30 P.M. the Senior Class of
M.H.S. will sponsor a Box Social in the high school gym.
Come and play Bingo, walk for a cake, eat pie and ice cream.
Girls: Be sure to bring a box!
Boys: Be sure to bring plenty of money!

In this item there are the following possible settings: Box Social, Senior Class, Midwest High School, High School Gym, Bingo, Walk for a Cake.

Informants selected for their knowledge of particular community areas and institutions can be extremely useful. Most behavior settings of a community are in the public domain and are well known to many citizens. Complicated definitions of behavior settings are not required to give an informant a sufficiently adequate idea of what is wanted; a sample list is usually enough.

The initial inventory should aim to include all parts of the community that might fit the definition of a behavior setting, and it should be organized into an efficient working list. In the first Midwest survey the items of the inventory were classified into six broad categories: Business, Church, Government, Voluntary Association, School, and Miscellaneous, as shown in Table 4.1. This classification had no systematic significance, but it served as a convenient way to locate items in the inventory.

DISCARDING NONSETTINGS

The second step of the survey is to eliminate items from the initial inventory that do not fit the definition of a behavior setting. To be included, a community part must pass the three behavior setting tests (Chap. 3, p. 23). First it must pass the structure test; it must be a behavior-milieu synomorph, i.e., (*a*) a standing pattern of behavior (a

---

11. Presbyterian Church (a community part that stands alone, that is interjacent to no other potential setting in the list)

12. Worship Service at Presbyterian Church (first nesting level; a part that is interjacent to a community part that stands alone)

13. Anthem by Presbyterian Church Choir (second nesting level; a part that is interjacent to an interjacent part)

bounded pattern in the behavior of men en masse which occurs independently of the particular persons involved), (*b*) anchored to a particular milieu complex, (*c*) at particular time-space loci, (*d*) with behavior and milieu synomorphic, (*e*) and with milieu circumjacent to behavior.

Characteristics (*a–c*) are especially important for the process eliminating nonsynomorphs. If a community part involves a pattern of behavior-in-general, i.e., is *not* bounded, or if a bounded behavior pattern is not anchored to a denotable milieu complex, or if a bounded behavior-milieu pattern does *not* have univocal time-space loci, the part is not a behavior-milieu synomorph and hence not a potential behavior setting. One scans the list of potential settings and asks if for each item on the list there is a corresponding entity with all of the essential structural characteristics. On this basis some items are eliminated from the original list. This is true of the following items in Table 4.1 (the main structural inadequacies of these items are indicated in the parentheses):

15. Payment of taxes at County Treasurers Office ((*a*) there is no bounded pattern of behavior distinct from the total pattern of the County Treasurers Office)

17. Sitting on benches of Courthouse Square ((*e*) the milieu, i.e., the benches, is not circumjacent to the behavior)

21. 4-H Club ((*a*) the 4-H Club exhibits highly varied patterns of behavior, (*b*) it is anchored to many different milieu complexes, (*c*) at unpredictable times and places. The 4-H Club appears in many disguises in meetings, parties, banquets, cooking classes; it turns out to be a multisetting phenomenon)

26. Hopscotch Games ((*c*) occur at almost any time and place. A particular game would be a synomorph)

31. High School Senior Class (see comments for item 21)

35. High School Gym ((*a*) a great variety of behavior patterns are anchored to the Gym: basketball games, dances, banquets, PTA meetings)

37. Brick-paved Area in front of High School ((*d*) no synomorphic pattern of behavior and milieu; the boundary of the bricked area is not the boundary of any pattern of behavior. The bricked area is a behaviorally nonsignificant part of the behavior setting Trafficways)

39. State Highway (see comments for item 37)

After applying the structure test to the items of the initial inventory, those that pass are behavior-milieu synomorphs; of the 39 items in the exemplifying list, Table 4.1, 31 synomorphs remain (i.e., those not in italics); they are next tested by the internal dynamics test.

The internal dynamics test requires that synomorphs structurally interjacent to other synomorphs be tested for their degree of interdependence. In the present example, this means testing the degree of interdependence of:

(2) Fountain, (3) Pharmacy, and (4) Variety Department and of each with (1) Drugstore;

(9) Joash Service and (10) Adult Choir Practice (and of each with (8) Methodist Church);

(12) Worship Service with (11) Presbyterian Church);

(13) Anthem with (12) Worship Service;

(19) Tenderfoot Test and (20) Beaver Patrol Activities (and of each with the (18) Boy Scout Meeting);

(24) Election of 4-H Club Officers with (23) Regular Meeting of 4-H Club;

(32) Box Social and (36) Girls Locker Room (and of each with (30) High School);

(33) Bingo Game and (34) Walk for a Cake (and of each with (32) Box Social);

(39) State Highway with (38) Trafficways.

Of these, the following pass the internal dynamics test, i.e., their interjacent synomorphs have the degree of internal unity specified for behavior settings: (1) Drugstore, (12) Worship Service at Presbyterian Church, (18) Boy Scout Troop 72 Meeting, (23) Regular Meeting of 4-H Club, (32) Box Social, and (38) Trafficways. The following are not behavior settings because their interjacent synomorphs do not have the specified degree of interdependence; the synomorphs are too independent: (8) Methodist Church, (11) Presbyterian Church, (30) High School; they are multiple setting synomorphs.

The potential settings remaining are finally tested by the external dynamics test, i.e., for their degree of interdependence with synomorphs structurally external to them. In the present example all the remaining potential behavior settings are sufficiently independent of each other except the three monthly meetings of the Couples Bridge Club (27, 28, 29); they are interdependent synomorphs, and comprise the behavior setting Couples Bridge Club Meeting.

Those potential behavior settings marked with an asterisk in Table 4.1 are K-21 behavior settings according to the structure, internal dynamics, and external dynamics tests.

The Index of Interdependence, K

The degree of interdependence of behavior-milieu synomorphs is a crucial test of a behavior setting; it is equal in importance to the structural test. The operations for determining the interdependence index K of pairs of synomorphs are based upon two sets of assumptions: (1) that interdependence between synomorphs occurs (a) via behavior, which has effects across synomorphs, (b) via inhabitants, who migrate between synomorphs, and (c) via leaders, who are common to synomorphs; and (2) that the amount of interdependence that occurs via these channels is a direct function of (a) the amount of behavior, the number of inhabitants, and the number of leaders that span the synomorphs, (b) the closeness of the synomorphs in space and time, and (c) the similarity of the synomorphs with respect to behavior objects and behavior mechanisms.

In consequence, the value of K for a pair of synomorphs consists of ratings of the degree to which:

(1) behavior or its consequences span the synomorphs;
(2) the same inhabitants enter the synomorphs;
(3) the same leaders are active in the synomorphs;
(4) the synomorphs use the same physical space or spaces that are near together;
(5) the synomorphs occur at the same time or at times that are near together;
(6) the synomorphs use the same or similar behavior objects;
(7) the same kinds of behavior mechanisms occur in the synomorphs.

Two meetings of a card club on consecutive months are structurally discrete synomorphs, which have the same inhabitants and leaders, occupy the same space, and use the same behavior objects by means of the same behavior mechanisms; i.e., they are identical with respect to five of the seven measures of K. Two meetings of different card clubs, on the other hand, are identical with respect to only two of the measures, i.e., behavior objects and behavior mechanisms. Therefore, according to the assumptions upon which the index K is based, the two meetings of the same card club have greater interdependence than the two meetings of different card clubs. In fact, according to the rating of K, the two monthly meetings of the same card club constitute two occurrences of a single behavior setting, whereas the two meetings of the different card clubs are single occurrences of entirely different behavior settings.

The degree of interdependence of two synomorphs is estimated by rating them with respect to each of the seven measures on 7-point scales. A rating of 1 represents the greatest and a rating of 7 the least commonality, similarity, or connectedness between the settings on the measure in question. The interdependence index of the pair of settings equals the sum of the ratings of the seven measures. The total interdependence scale, then, ranges from a score of 7, indicating maximal interdependence, to a score of 49, indicating minimal interdependence. The interdependence scales are presented below.

SCALE 4.1

Rating	Per Cent of Molar Actions Beginning in A That Is Complete in B, or Vice Versa (Highest Per Cent Counts)	Per Cent of Behavior in A Having Physical Consequences in B, or Vice Versa (Highest Per Cent Counts)
1	95–100	95–100
2	67–94	67–94
3	34–66	34–66
4	5–33	5–33
5	2–4	2–4
6	trace–1	trace–1
7	none	none

(1) *Behavioral interdependence:* the degree to which behavior in synomorph A has direct consequences in synomorph B. Behavior may interconnect synomorphs in two ways: (*a*) Molar actions begun in A may be completed in B, and vice versa. The mechanic in Chaco Garage may take an engine part to Chaco Service Station in order to clean it with compressed air; a customer at the Drugstore Fountain may speak directly to a customer in the Drugstore Pharmacy. (*b*) The physical resultants of behavior in A may spread to B, and vice versa. Cooking vapors may diffuse via the air from the kitchen to the dining room of the Pearl Cafe; traffic vibrations may spread from the Highway to the Presbyterian Church Worship Service through the air or the ground. Scale 4.1 provides for both kinds of behavioral interdependence. The highest per cent that applies is used; if both kinds of behavioral interdependence occur, the average of the two ratings is the final rating.

(2) *Population (inhabitant) interdependence:* the degree to which the people who enter synomorph A also enter synomorph B. The per cent of population overlap is determined by the following formula:

$$\text{Per cent overlap} = \frac{2P_{ab}}{P_a + P_b},$$

where P_a = Number of people who enter synomorph A, P_b = Number of people who enter synomorph B, P_{ab} = Number of people who enter both A and B. See Scale 4.2 for converting the per cent overlap to an interdependence rating.

(3) *Leadership interdependence:* the degree to which the leaders of synomorph A are also the leaders of synomorph B. Judge for persons who penetrate to zones 4, 5, and 6 (p. 49) in the same way as for population interdependence.

(4) *Spatial interdependence:* the degree to which synomorphs A and B use the same or proximate spatial areas (see Scale 4.3). In case both "same" and "proximate" scales apply, use the one that indicates the greater interdependence.

SCALE 4.2

Rating	Per Cent Overlap
1	95–100
2	67–94
3	33–66
4	6–32
5	2–5
6	trace–1
7	none

SCALE 4.3

Rating	Same Space — Per Cent of Space Common to A and B	Proximate Space
1	95–100	
2	50–94	
3	10–49	or A and B use different parts of same room or small area
4	5–9	or A and B use differents part of same building or lot
5	2–4	or A and B use areas in same part of town
6	trace–1	or A and B use areas in same town but different parts of the town
7	none	or A in town, B out of town

(5) *Interdependence based on temporal contiguity:* the degree to which synomorphs A and B occur at the same time, or at proximate times. Settings may occur temporally close together on some occasions and be temporally separated at other times. For example, the American Legion meets monthly, whereas the Boy Scout Troop meets weekly; once a month, therefore, their meetings occur during the same week and once a month their meetings are more than two weeks apart. Rate temporal contiguity via the scales below. The closest temporal proximity of synomorphs A and B determines the column to enter (simultaneous, same part of day, same day, etc.). The per cent of all contacts with "closest temporal proximity" is the number of such contacts for A plus the number for B divided by the total number of occurrences of both behavior settings multiplied by 100 (see Scale 4.4 for rating temporal interdependence).

SCALE 4.4

Interde-pendence Rating	Per Cent of Contacts with Closest Temporal Proximity					
	Simulta-neous	Same Part of Day	Same Day	Same Week	Same Month	Same Year
1	75–100					
2	50–74	75–100				
3	25–49	50–74	75–100			
4	5–24	25–49	50–74	75–100		
5	0–4	5–24	25–49	50–74	75–100	
6		0–4	5–24	25–49	50–74	75–100
7			0–4	0–24	0–49	0–49

For example, the Boy Scout Troop met every Monday night during the survey year. The American Legion met the first Wednesday of every month. The closest temporal proximity of these settings was Same Week in Scale 4.4. The 12 Scout and the 12 Legion meetings that occurred in this close contact are added and the sum divided by the sum of the 12 Legion meetings and the 52 Scout meetings, as follows:

$$\frac{12 \text{ Scout Meetings} + 12 \text{ Legion Meetings}}{52 \text{ Scout Meetings} + 12 \text{ Legion Meetings}} = 24/64 = .37 \times 100 = 37\%.$$

In column Same Week 37 falls at scale point 6. The temporal contiguity score then is 6.

(6) *Interdependence based on behavior objects:* the extent to which

SCALE 4.5

Rating	Identical Objects		Similar Objects
1	Identical objects used in A and B; i.e., all behavior objects shared		
2	More than half of the objects shared by A and B	or	Virtually all objects in A and B of same kind*
3	Half of the objected shared by A and B	or	More than half of the objects in A and B of same kind*
4	Less than half the objects shared by A and B	or	Half the objects in A and B of same kind*
5	Few behavior objects in A and B identical	or	Less than half the objects of A and B of same kind*
6	Almost no objects shared by A and B	or	Few behavior objects of same kind* in A and B
7	No objects shared	or	Almost no similarity between objects in A and B

* Objects of the same kind are objects that have the same dictionary definition; e.g., spoons are used in the behavior setting School Lunchroom and the setting Cliffords Drugstore Fountain, but they are different spoons.

SCALE 4.6

Interdependence Rating	Number of Mechanisms Present in One Setting and Absent in the Other
1	0–1
2	2–3
3	4–6
4	7–8
5	9–10
6	11
7	12

synomorph A and synomorph B use identical or similar behavior objects. See Scale 4.5. In case both scales apply, use the scale that indicates the greater interdependence.

(7) *Interdependence based on similarity of behavior mechanisms:* the degree to which behavior mechanisms are similar in synomorphs A and B. The interdependence score is determined by the number of

the following behavior mechanisms that are present in one setting and absent in the other.

Gross Motor Actions	Writing	Eating
Manipulation	Observing	Reading
Verbalization	Listening	Emoting
Singing	Thinking	Tactual Feeling

The interdependence rating is given in Scale 4.6.

The K-21 Cutting Point: Behavior Settings

A set of synomorphs with K values, *inter se*, of 20 or less constitutes a single behavior setting; synomorphs with K values of 21 or greater are discrete behavior settings, or parts of discrete settings.

The reliability of the interdependence scale was investigated by having three judges compute K values for a stratified sample of 100 synomorph pairs. The sample was selected to represent every kind of relation between synomorphs. In the case of 79 of these pairs, the K values of all judges were 21 or above, and for 10 of the pairs the K values of all judges were 20 or below; i.e., the three judges agreed that 89 per cent of the synomorphs were or were not behavior settings. This agreement was better than chance at the .001 level of confidence. Correlations between the ratings of pairs of judges were .93, .93, and .92.

It has been pointed out (Chap. 3) that when the units of a system are defined in terms of degree of interdependence, the units can be made larger or smaller by varying the degree of interdependence by which the units are defined. The critical value of K for identifying separate behavior settings was originally set at 21 on an empirical basis; this value appeared to identify community parts with phenomenal reality and with dynamic significance for behavior. Evidence that the K-21 cutting point does identify community units of fundamental significance will be considered later. Higher or lower values of K would identify units with different properties, and might be appropriate for particular problems. A higher critical K value would identify fewer community units with a lower degree of internal interdependence. A cutting point between 30 and 31, for example, would place together in the same unit all garages and service stations of the town; similarly the grocery stores and other classes of businesses and professions would become community units. A lower cutting point would identify more community units with a higher degree of internal interdependence. A critical K value of

14 would separate the Fountain, Pharmacy, and Variety Department of the Drugstore into separate units; it would detach Chaco Service Station from Chaco Garage.

In view of the less-than-perfect reliability with which the value of K is judged, synomorph pairs with K values between 18 and 22 are always reconsidered in practical fieldwork and compared with previous judgments for similar synomorph pairs. If the obtained K value is not in accord with the previous determinations, the scale ratings are inspected and new ratings made if errors are discovered. K values less than 18 and greater than 22 are not reconsidered.

Here are examples of sets of synomorphs with different ranges of K values, *inter se*, and the behavior settings they form.

Synomorph Sets	K Values	Behavior Settings
Third Grade Reading Class Third Grade Writing Class Third Grade Arithmetic Class	14–16	Third Grade Academic Subjects
Drugstore Fountain Drugstore Pharmacy Drugstore Variety Department	19–20	Drugstore
Twelve Monthly Meetings of Womens Club I	18–20	Womens Club I Meeting
Third Grade Academic Subjects Fourth Grade Academic Subjects Fifth Grade Academic Subjects	28–30	Third Grade Academic Subjects Fourth Grade Academic Subjects Fifth Grade Academic Subjects
Presbyterian Church Worship Service Presbyterian Church Sunday School Opening Exercises Presbyterian Church Members Meeting Presbyterian Church Martha Circle Study Group	22–37	Presbyterian Church Worship Service Presbyterian Church Sunday School Opening Exercises Presbyterian Church Members Meeting Presbyterian Church Martha Circle Study Group

DESCRIBING BEHAVIOR SETTINGS

The final step in making a behavior setting survey is to describe the settings. There are limitless possibilities; and for the purposes of the Midwest survey we selected the behavior setting attributes defined in the remainder of this chapter.

Occurrence

The occurrence (O) of a behavior setting is the number of days in a year it occurs for any period of time. The maximum occurrence of a setting is 366 in 1963–64 (a leap year), i.e., one occurrence a day. This is true for behavior settings that function for less than an hour, for those that continue for 24 hours, and for settings that suspend operations for a period during a day (the Midwest Bank and many offices cease for an hour at noon; a court session may convene for an hour in the morning, be dismissed for three hours, and reconvene in the afternoon). In all of these cases, a setting is credited with a single occurrence per day. Behavior settings that can be initiated by anyone at any time without special arrangement have an occurrence of 366 even though there *may be* days when they are uninhabited, e.g., telephone kiosks, cemetery, park.

Duration

The duration (D) of a behavior setting is the total number of hours it functions during a year. In the ordinary case, duration in hours per occurrence (d) and number of occurrences (O) are stable and well-known attributes of behavior settings, so that duration (D) is the product of hours per occurrence and number of occurrences (Od); this is true of school classes, church worship services, grocery stores, for example. But when the length of the occurrence varies (e.g., auction sales, fashion shows), and when the setting is available at any time but is actually occupied only intermittently (e.g., cemetery, telephone kiosks), detailed information must be obtained or estimates made of separate occurrences and their durations.

Data concerning the occurrence and duration of most behavior settings are readily available; they are often posted on the doors of businesses and offices, announced in newspapers and organization bulletins, and recorded in minutes of meetings. The occurrence and duration of settings with irregular schedules such as auction sales are obtained from informants or by observation.

Population

The population (P) of a behavior setting is the total number of different persons who inhabit it for any length of time during a year. Population may be determined for any population subgroup; those identified in the Midwest research are:

Residence Subgroups:

Town residents	Persons whose homes are within the boundaries of Midwest
Out-of-town residents	Persons whose homes are not within the boundaries of Midwest

Age Subgroups:

Infants (Inf)	Under 2 years of age
Preschool children (PS)	2 to 5:11 years of age
Younger School ages (YS)	6 to 8:11 years of age
Older School ages (OS)	9 to 11:11 years of age
Children	For some purposes all persons under 12 years are grouped together as children
Adolescents (Adol)	12 to 17:11 years of age
Adults (Adu)	18 to 64:11 years of age
Aged (Aged)	65 years and over

Sex Subgroups:

Males (M)
Females (F)

Social Class Subgroups:

Social Class I (SC I)	Social Classes I, II, and III correspond fairly
Social Class II (SC II)	well to Warner's Upper Middle, Lower
Social Class III (SC III)	Middle, and Upper Lower Classes (Warner, Meeker, and Eells, 1949). The identification of these population categories in Midwest is based upon the reconciled judgments of three resident staff members who used Warner's criteria.

Race Subgroups:

White (W)
Negro (N)

Occupancy Time

The occupancy time (OT) of a behavior setting is the total number of person-hours inhabitants spend in it during a year. OT is the product of the number of occurrences of a setting (O), the average number of inhabitants per occurrence (p), and the average duration per occurrence in hours (d). This product, *Opd*, person-hours-per-year is the occupancy time of the behavior setting. Examples of behavior setting occupancy times are given in Table 4.2.

In our studies, separate estimates of occupancy time have been computed for the 14 divisions of the population listed in Table 4.3. This table illustrates the computation of occupancy time of Midwest resi-

TABLE 4.2. *Behavior Setting Occupancy Times, 1963–64*
(*Person-hours-per-year*)

Behavior Setting	Midwest Residents OT	Total OT
Elementary School Third Grade Academic Subjects...	7,280	18,430
Burgess Beauty Shop	12,750	15,750
Elementary Lower School Lunchroom	10,103	15,500
Chaco Garage and Service Station	9,542	14,000
Blanchard Hardware Store	6,822	8,322
High School A Team Football Game	2,710	7,467
Presbyterian Church Worship Service	4,015	5,918
Keith Barber Shop	1,540	4,290
Rotary Club Meeting	2,083	2,341
Presbyterian Church Funeral	320	605
Halloween Dance...............................	150	213
Methodist Church Kindergarten Sunday School Class.	111	146

dents for the behavior setting Mother-Daughter Banquet. In the analyses, occupation times are coded via the code given in Appendix 1.

The total occupancy time of Midwest settings varied from 94,145 person-hours-per-year for Trafficways to 6 for Cemetery Board Meeting.

Precise records of occurrence, duration, and population are available for a considerable number of settings. This is true of most school and Sunday school settings and of many social organization settings. Data for other behavior settings must be secured from informants or by means of observation by fieldworkers. Such data are not private in the case of almost all community settings.

Penetration of Behavior Settings

Not only do inhabitants enter settings for different amounts of time, but they enter and participate in them in different capacities and with different degrees of involvement and responsibility. One index of the involvement and responsibility of a person in a behavior setting is the depth or centrality of his penetration. Six zones of centrality are defined. The more central the zone, the deeper the penetration and the greater the involvement and responsibility of its occupants. These zones with their number designations and descriptive titles are as follows (see Fig. 4.1 for a schematic presentation).

Zone 1. Onlooker. This is the most peripheral zone. Persons in this zone are within the behavior setting but take no active part in the standing pattern of behavior; at most they are onlookers. They are tolerated

TABLE 4.3. *Methodist Church Mother-Daughter Banquet Occupancy Times of Subgroups of Midwest Residents, 1963–64*

Population Subgroup	Occur-rence O	Popu-lation p	Duration in hours d	Occu-pancy Time Opd
Infant (under 2 yrs.)	1	1	2	2
Preschool (2:0–5:11)	1	5	2	10
Younger School (6:0–8:11)	1	11	2	22
Older School (9:0–11:11)	1	7	2	14
Adolescent (12:0–17:11)	1	17	1.75*	29
Adult (18:0–64:11)	1	51	2.1*	109
Aged (65:0 and over)	1	20	2.5*	60
Male	1	7	1*	7
Female	1	105	2	237
Social Class I	1	20	2	40
Social Class II	1	81	2.2	176
Social Class III	1	11	2.75	30
White	1	112	2.2	246
Negro	1	0	0	0
Total	1	112	2.2	246

* The male adolescents waited on tables only. Some of the adult and aged women cooked the dinner and prepared the tables.

but not welcomed; they have no power. Examples: the infant who accompanies his mother to Kanes Grocery; loafers at the Post Office; a child waiting in the Dentists Office while her friend has a tooth filled.

Zone 2. Audience or Invited Guest. The inhabitants of this zone have a definite place; they are welcome, but they have little power in the setting; at most they can applaud or express disapproval. Examples: spectators at a ball game; those in the church congregation who are not members of the church; the mothers invited to the Cub Scout Den Meeting when the Christmas party is scheduled.

Zone 3. Member or Customer. Occupants of zone 3 have great potential power, but usually little immediate power. They are the voting members, the paying customers who ultimately make or break the setting. Examples: member at Rotary Club Meeting; pupil in First Grade Academic Activities.

Zone 4. Active Functionary. Inhabitants of this zone have power over a part of a setting, but they do not lead it. The people in this zone have direct power over a limited part of the setting. Examples: cast of the Junior Class Play, witness at Court Session, church deacon at Worship Service.

Zone 5. Joint Leaders. Persons who enter zone 5 lead the setting jointly with others in this zone. Persons in zone 5 have immediate authority over the whole setting, but their power is shared with others. Examples: Mr. and Mrs. Cabell who jointly own and operate Cabell Department Store, the president of the High School Drama Club and the teacher who sponsors it.

Zone 6. Single Leader. Zone 6 is the most central zone. Here are included the positions of all persons who serve as single leaders of behavior settings. These single leaders may have helpers or subordinate leaders in zone 4. Persons in zone 6 have immediate authority over the whole setting. Examples: the teacher in Second Grade Academic Activities, the scoutmaster at a Boy Scout Troop Meeting, the band leader at the Summer Band Concert.

The maximum depth of penetration into behavior settings can be rated for individuals or for population subgroups. The maximum depth of penetration of a subgroup is the most central position any member of a population subgroup enters during the survey year. If one pre-

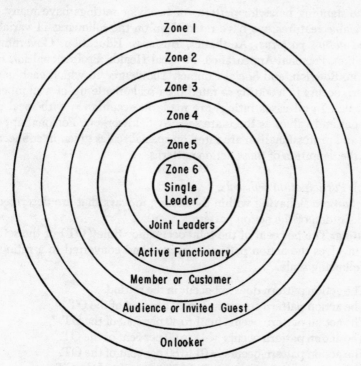

Fig. 4.1. Zones of penetration into behavior settings.

school child sings in the program of the setting Parent-Teachers Association Meeting, and no preschool child penetrates further, preschool children are rated as having a maximum penetration rating of 4, i.e., active functionary, for the behavior setting Parent-Teachers Association Meeting. Persons penetrating to zone 4, 5, or 6 are called *performers* in a behavior setting.

The maximal depth of penetration of individuals and of members of population subgroups is available from the records of many behavior settings, such as school and Sunday school settings, some behavior settings connected with government agencies (e.g., court sessions, committee meetings), and some voluntary organization settings (e.g., Boy Scout Troop Meeting). Some penetration data are published in newspapers and other publications (e.g., church bulletins, school yearbooks); in other cases penetration data are secured from informants or by observation within behavior settings.

Action Patterns: Rating Scales

The standing behavior patterns of behavior settings have many discriminable features; we have rated them on the following 11 variables called *action patterns*: Aesthetics, Business, Education, Government, Nutrition, Personal Appearance, Physical Health, Professionalism, Recreation, Religion, and Social Contact. The degree to which each action pattern occurs in a setting is rated on a scale made up of a number of subscales. In all cases ratings are made in accordance with local perceptions and values as these are seen by fieldworkers. Personal appearance and professionalism are rated on special scales given in connection with the definition of these action patterns.

(1) *Participation Subscale.*
Definition: Behaving within the setting in ways that are described in the definition of the action pattern.
Rating: The per cent of the total occupancy time (OT) of the setting that involves the action pattern is judged and converted to a rating on the following scale.

0   The action pattern does not occur in the setting.
1   The action pattern occurs in 1 to 20 per cent of the OT.
2   The action pattern occurs in 21 to 40 per cent of the OT.
3   The action pattern occurs in 41 to 60 per cent of the OT.
4   The action pattern occurs in 61 to 80 per cent of the OT.
5   The action pattern occurs in 81 to 100 per cent of the OT.

Example: It is judged that normally 81 to 100 per cent of all the occupancy time of the setting Mrs. Wiley, Music Lesson involves the action pattern Education, i.e., formal teaching by Mrs. Wiley and learning by the pupil. This setting is, therefore, rated 5 (maximum) for participation in the action pattern Education.

(2) *Supply Subscale.*

Definition: Providing materials for carrying out the action pattern in another setting. To receive a rating for Supply, there must be either (*a*) a product that is exported to another setting or (*b*) a person especially prepared within the setting for contributions to the action patterns of another setting. Examples of the latter are choir practice and play practice, which contribute specially trained persons to Worship Service and Play. General education does not count as contributing to another setting.

Rating: Rate as on Participation subscale. But note that the same behavior pattern does not receive a rating for both Participation and Supply. The OT of both Participation and Supply cannot be greater than 100 per cent, but the maximum rating is 6, e.g., from a Participation rating of 5 for 82 per cent OT, and Supply rating of 1 for 10 per cent OT. In other words, Participation and Supply activities are mutually exclusive.

Examples: Buying and eating a milkshake at the Drugstore Soda Fountain is judged on the participation subscale of the action pattern Nutrition, but buying ice cream to take home is judged on the Supply scale. The occupancy time of Kanes Grocery Store is mostly devoted to obtaining food for use in other settings (judged 81–100 per cent); only a small amount of the time is devoted to eating or preparing food for eating in the setting (judged 1–20 per cent).

(3) *Evaluation and Appreciation Subscale.*

Definition: Refers to behavior that explicitly recognizes the values of the action pattern, whether good or bad, or tests its effectiveness. Applauding at a play is an evaluation of the action patterns Aesthetics and Recreation; presenting attendance pins in Sunday school for a year's perfect attendance is a recognition of the action pattern Religion; giving tests in school is evaluation of the action pattern Education.

Appraisal that is *merely conventional* or part of the general conversation is not rated. This is necessary, for in every setting there is some evaluation of action patterns; but, unless open and explicit, it cannot be rated. To receive a rating, there must usually be a place in the program for appreciation and evaluation; a vote of thanks, an examination, a prayer, applause, a cheer.

In settings such as Church Worship Service, where it is inappropriate to openly express appreciation, a rating for evaluation can, nevertheless, be made if there is clear evidence of evaluation that is more than the merely polite thing to do. In other settings, too, where it is clear from the comments of individuals that the evaluation is more than casual, a rating is indicated.

This comes down to the rule that conventional or polite evaluation of a setting receives no rating; there must be evidence of greater evaluative involvement in the setting by the participants:

Rating:

0   No behavior in the setting explicitly evaluates or appreciates the action pattern.
1   Less than half of the OT of the setting is devoted to evaluation or appreciation of the action pattern.
2   More than half of the OT of the setting is devoted to evaluation or appreciation of the action pattern.

Example: Public recognition of educational achievement is judged to constitute less than half of the occupancy time of the setting Eighth Grade Graduation; Education is, therefore, rated 1 on this subscale.

(4) *Teaching and Learning Subscale.*

Definition: Explicit learning and teaching of the action pattern; does not include incidental learning.

Rating: Rate as on Evaluation and Appreciation subscale.

Example: Teachers Institute in Midwest is a place where teachers not only participate in being educated but learn how to educate. This is rated 2 (maximum) for learning about the action pattern Education.

The rating of an action pattern of a setting is the sum of the ratings on the Participation, Supply, Appreciation, and Learning subscales. The total rating varies from 0 to 14. Sample ratings of a number of behavior settings on the action pattern Recreation are given in Table 4.4.

An action pattern rating is, in most cases, an indication of the proportion of the total OT of a behavior setting that is devoted to the action pattern. However, this basis is not appropriate with Personal Appearance and Professionalism, and the basis of the rating is, accordingly, modified. In these cases, however, the rating values appear to be harmonious with the interpretation of action pattern ratings as indicating the importance of action patterns relative to their total possible range of importance in the setting.

TABLE 4.4. *Sample Ratings of Selected Behavior Settings on the Action Pattern Recreation*

Behavior Setting	Rating on Subscale				
	Partici-pation	Supply	Appreci-ation	Learning	Total
Cemetery Board Meeting..	0	0	0	0	0
Trafficways	2	0	0	0	2
Midwest Theater	5	0	1	1	7
Wesley Lumber Yard	1	0	0	0	1
Midwest Town Team Baseball Game	5	0	2	2	9

Action Patterns: Definitions

(1) *Aesthetic Action Pattern:* Any artistic activity; any behavior aimed at making the environment more beautiful, as this is locally defined.

Participation: Doing artistic work of any kind (painting, decorating, landscaping, singing, dancing, etc.) and removing the unsightly. A purely functional setting such as a machine shop is rated zero. A setting such as a store, where there is even a minimal effort to make it attractive, is rated 1 (OT 1–20 per cent).

Supply: Supplying art, cleaning, landscaping, musical materials and equipment. Key question: Does the setting provide materials for beautifying another setting? The setting Dent and Company, Decorators, besides doing artistic things itself, provides beautification of other settings.

Evaluation and appreciation: Assessing products of art or persons with aesthetic talents or accomplishments.

Learning: Teaching art, learning art. Key question: Is music, home decoration, china painting, etc., formally taught here? Incidental learning about art is not considered.

Beautifying the self (Personal Appearance) is *not* included under Aesthetics. For example, in rating a beauty shop, beautification of the customers is not included as aesthetics. This applies to Worship Service, to Parties, and to other settings where both "dressing up" and making the setting beautiful occur. In other words, the action patterns Aesthetics and Personal Appearance can be summed to get the total hours for all beautification.

If time is spent making a setting beautiful *before* the setting officially begins, e.g., decorating for a party, these hours are included in the total occupancy time, and they are counted as aesthetic participation. When the setting has permanent beauty, the process of keeping it in a beautiful state contributes to participation in aesthetics. There will often in this case be time spent in evaluation, too. In fact, the *choice* of a beautiful rather than an unbeautiful locus for a setting in itself constitutes an evaluation.

Putting things in order, or in accordance with an accepted or established standard (such as spacing of a letter on a page), is *not* included under Aesthetics.

Some patterns of behavior are purely utilitarian or functional, e.g., making a tool box; other patterns are purely aesthetic, e.g., painting a picture, singing a song; still other activities are a mixture, e.g., making bookshelves or tables. In rating aesthetics, judge the proportion of the OT concerned with aesthetic aspects of the activity.

At a concert, the audience is included as participating in aesthetic behavior. In addition, there are often some hours for evaluation.

(2) *Business Action Pattern:* The exchange of goods, services, or privileges where *payment is obligatory.* Does not include gifts of money or service or hiring out for wages (see Professionalism).

Participation: Exchanging merchandise, services, or privileges for money; transporting persons or goods for a fee; processing raw materials into salable form. That part of the OT of a setting that is occupied with the *sale* of goods, services, or privileges.

Supply: Supplying objects and materials necessary for the execution of business in other settings. That part of the OT of a setting that is involved in supplying goods to support business in other settings within or outside of the town.

Evaluation and appreciation: Examining and appreciating the achievements or values of business, businessmen, or business institutions.

Learning: Learning and teaching how to do business; serving as an apprentice where there is explicit instruction in business practices; the extent to which the OT of the setting is devoted to instructing and learning the methods and skills of business.

Buying and selling means that payment is obligatory, whether or not payment is made on the spot. However, it must be understood that a "business" transaction has been made and obligation to pay assumed by the buyer. This does *not* include time spent in working for wages, but it does include the time spent in "hiring out" and collecting wages. The highest participation in Business is found in an efficient store where practically all the behavior is concerned with trying to sell and buy. Low participation is found in a football game where payment of the entrance fee is almost incidental to watching and playing. School Classroom and Church Worship Service receive no rating for Business. The hiring of teachers and preachers occurs in the School Board Meeting and in the Church Committee Meetings.

In rating, estimate the time involved in actual transactions of buying and selling. If time is spent in the setting, thereafter, using what has been purchased, do not include this. Thus, when admission is charged to a cinema, only the short time in purchasing tickets is included in the OT of Business participation, not the time spent in watching the film.

Every commercial setting, where prices are set competitively, receives some rating for Evaluation. A bookkeeper who looks after payment of accounts is rated as participating in buying and selling, as are clerks when they are stocking shelves and preparing goods. Business is not merely waiting on customers. The purpose of the buying and selling is not taken into consideration. A church Bazaar gets as high a rating for Business as a Grocery. Any social organization with a *regular* obligatory entrance fee rates 1–20 per cent for Business. Any business meeting that pays bills, authorizes salaries, etc., receives rating for Business. This is true of a school board meeting that hires teachers and of a meeting of a church congregation that sets the pay of a minister. But a church committee that deals only with "stewardship," i.e., collecting gifts from the members, is not a business setting.

(3) *Education Action Pattern:* Formal education of any kind; does not include incidental learning or teaching. The crucial question is: Does someone take the role of teacher and others the role of pupils, with the intent to teach in the first case and to learn in the second?

Participation: Teaching individuals or classes of students, and learning in individual or group lessons. The OT of both teacher and pupils is included in the participation rating.

Supply: Supplying materials for teaching or learning in other settings.

Evaluation and appreciation: Approving of education or of persons who have completed a course of study, evaluating educational achievements, e.g., examinations, graduations.

Learning: Teaching or learning procedures of education or stimulating people to increase education.

In almost every setting there probably is teaching by someone, and learning by someone. At a Bridge Club someone may say, "Tell me how to count this hand according to Goren"; and the one addressed may reply, "I would be glad to." This is not included in the action pattern Education. The teaching position and the learning positions have to be regular parts of the setting. For this to occur there usually is someone with professional training (a teacher, a doctor, a pastor), though in some settings, such as Home Demonstration Units, members take turns filling the role of teacher. But there is always someone in a teaching position and there is always a pupil or a class.

Adolescent apprentices are pupils and their supervisors are teachers; a setting with apprentices receives a rating for Education. But a store with a shop assistant does *not* receive an Education rating. Giving information about coming events is not Education. Lectures and cinemas at cultural and religious meetings are often instructional, but for the present purpose they do not count as Education. On the other hand, a driving school and an adult Sunday school class are Education, for people enter them in the roles of pupils and teachers. A class that involves much individual work, such as a woodwork or typing class, in which the teacher walks about giving individual instruction is rated as 81–100 per cent participation in Education; i.e., the teacher is teaching and the pupils are learning all the time.

(4) *Government Action Pattern:* Behavior that has to do with government at any level.

Participation: Engaging in civic affairs or in behavior that is controlled by government regulations. Key question: What proportion of the total occupancy time is devoted to carrying out governmental orders or governmental functions? Note that Government activities are defined very strictly as law making, law interpretation, and law execution; they do not include, for example, using the streets and sidewalks (which are entirely government-controlled) or getting mail at the post office. Only the OT of the performers in these settings contributes to the Government rating.

Supply: Supplying materials for governing activities; e.g., printing ballots at print shop.

Evaluation and appreciation: Recognition of patriotic people or events; evaluating laws.

Learning: Teaching or learning about government or legal procedures.

The essential question: To what degree does this setting involve activities directly controlled by a *primary* government agency? A store that collects a state tax on each sale carries out a governmental activity, with low OT, however. The meeting of an elected or appointed School Board is a setting with almost 100 per cent governmental occupancy time. But the school that the Board sets up and turns over to administrators to operate is *not* a primary government agency, and it receives no rating for participation in the Government action pattern. However, if the School Board makes special demands at the level of behavior settings *in the schools*, e.g., requires fire drills or particular courses of study, or sets the dates of opening and closing, it takes this behavior out of the hands of the intermediary administrator, and this behavior *is* governmental. Settings requiring a license from a primary governmental agency which must be regularly renewed are rated at least one per cent governmental behavior. This is true, too, if there are any legal restrictions such as that which prohibits the presence of dogs in a cafe.

However, regulations that influence behavior only once, and then become a permanent part of the background of the setting, are *not* rated. This is true of building requirements, e.g., standards of electrical wiring, fire-door regulations. The argument is that these do not influence the ordinary behavior pattern of the setting. All businesses with hired help will receive minimum Government rating because of government controls on wages and working conditions. But this is not true of family businesses.

Behavior settings where Government is involved in instigating or restraining behavior to no greater extent than that required to cope with illegal activity receive no Government rating. These behavior settings start, stop, and function without any government participation or reference to government at any level.

The behavior settings of organizations with government charters, as the Red Cross and Boy Scouts, do *not* for this reason receive a Government rating; neither do the settings of voluntary professional associations of government employees such as School Custodians County Association Meeting. If evaluation of Government occurs in these behavior settings, some Government rating will be required.

Behavior settings that *may* occur at a location that has government regulations, e.g., Past Matrons Club Meeting at Country Kitchen where taxes were paid, receive no Government rating. The Government rating goes to the Country Kitchen and not to the Past Matrons Club. This applies to organization dances that occur in buildings with occupancy regulations, for example.

The difference between Government ratings 0 and 1 is crucial. Rating 0 means that government activities are not involved in any degree in the action pattern of the setting, whereas ratings 1 and above mean that there is a minimum of government involvement (greater than the general police powers that apply to all settings). The minimum is exemplified for Church Worship Services where there is regularly a prayer for government officials, and by 4-H Cooking Class which is instigated by a government organization.

Note that behavior settings without government employees may require Government rating. This is true of lawyers' offices, for example, where almost all the OT is concerned with influencing the making, execution, enforcement, and interpretation of government activities for clients.

Note, too, that the Government rating makes no distinction between public and private settings. A lawyer's office (private) receives a Government rating of 6, whereas the City Park (public) receives a rating of 1. This is true because in the lawyer's office almost 100 per cent of the OT of the lawyer and his clients is spent attempting to influence, i.e., participate in, and evaluating the operation of government laws and regulations; in the setting City Park, the OT of the one government employee who carries out the regulations of the City Council is less than 20 per cent of the total OT of the park, most of whose occupants are concerned not with government regulations but with picnicking, playing, etc.

(5) *Nutrition Action Pattern:* Behavior that has to do with eating or drinking for nutritional purposes (including soft drinks and alcoholic beverages).

Participation: Eating, drinking, preparing, or serving food. Key question: Does anyone eat or drink or prepare food or drink in the setting?

Supply: Acquiring food, drink, eating utensils, or preparing food for use in another setting.

Evaluation and appreciation: Judging or appreciating the values of nutrition, of ways and means of serving food, or recognizing persons who excel in the preparation of meals.

Learning: Teaching or learning ways and means of preparing and serving meals.

Here are some nutritional properties of behavior settings receiving different total ratings for Nutrition, and some examples of such settings.

Nutrition rating 0: no eating, and no involvement with nutrition via supply, evaluation, or learning. Examples: Music Classes, Executive Committees, Plays and Programs, Machine Shops, Sunday School Classes, Post Offices, Scout Meetings.

Nutrition rating 1: snacks, coffee, tea consumed, or small amount of supply, evaluation, and learning. Examples: Academic Classes, Games, Trafficways.

Nutrition rating 2: light refreshments served. Examples: Lodge Meetings, Parties, Fellowship Meetings, Bridge Clubs, Receptions.

Nutrition rating 3: meetings with supper and/or continuous light eating—Bowling Club Matches, Ice Cream Socials with Concert, Picnics.

Nutrition rating 4: meetings with meals. Examples: Easter Service with Breakfast, Rotary Club Meeting, Alumni Reunion with Dinner, Dramatic Society Dinner-Dance.

Nutrition rating 5: dinners with meetings. Example: Annual Dinners of Organizations.

Nutrition rating 6: food supply and/or consumation 80 per cent plus of OT. Examples: Food Sales, Restaurants, Cooking Classes, Groceries, Market Day.

(6) *Personal Appearance Action Pattern:* Behavior concerned with improving personal appearance via clothing, grooming, adornment.

Participation: Getting well dressed, well groomed, looking one's best.

Supply: Supplying materials for personal adornment and grooming.

Evaluation and appreciation: Recognizing well-groomed persons; appreciating clothing or equipment for grooming.

Learning: Teaching or learning ways and means of proper grooming and personal appearance.

The action pattern Personal Appearance is concerned with adornment, not with utility. Dress that is purely for functional purposes, as wearing warm clothing for cold weather, receive no rating for Personal Appearance. However, many work clothes have some aesthetic aspects. In any case, Personal Appearance is concerned with aesthetics applied to personal appearance; in this connection see note under Aesthetics.

The basic or zero level for Personal Appearance is house clothing, i.e., what is acceptable within the privacy of home. The following scale is applicable:

0 House clothing and adornment
1 Street, school, ordinary work clothing
2 Clothing for church, Sunday school
3 Dress for semiformal party
4 Formal dress affairs
5 Fancy dress ball, ceremonial dress

Jewelry and adornments count as Personal Appearance. But insignia that only identify a person's role (e.g., police badge) do not count.

Often, of course, insignia have adornment properties; in this case, judge the beauty of the insignia. Uniforms and ceremonial and symbolic dress and adornment are evidence of participation in Personal Appearance. The rating varies with the elaborateness, elegance, and care devoted to the costume and adornment. In general, wearing uniforms and ceremonial or formal dress receives a rating 1 or 2 points above a similar setting without uniforms or ceremonial dress. Thus, school settings where uniforms are worn receive a rating of 2 instead of 1. A police station where elaborate uniforms are worn and carefully cared for receives a rating of 3 instead of 1. A confirmation service with the girls in veils and the bishop in robes receives a rating of 4 instead of 2, as for a church service. To receive the extra bonus, the number of specially dressed persons must be substantial. In cases where only some people in a setting are specially dressed, as at a church service where only the minister and choir wear robes, or a fashion show, a proportional allowance must be made. In some of these cases there may be some rating for evaluation and appreciation, too. The highest ratings for Personal Appearance are for fancy dress balls and lodge meetings where ceremonial costumes are worn and admired by everyone.

(7) *Physical Health Action Pattern:* Behavior that promotes or evaluates physical health or the healthy. Applies specifically to physical, not mental health.

Participation: Caring medically for people in any way, promoting physical health; includes athletic activities concerned with improving physical health.

Supply: Supplying medicines and medical or athletic equipment; books and money for promoting physical health elsewhere are included.

Evaluation and appreciation: Recognizing healthy people, judging health; e.g., physical examinations, athletic awards.

Learning: Teaching or learning ways and means of being healthy, stimulating healthful ways of living, learning medical skills; e.g., Home Economics Class, Red Cross Home Nursing Course.

Physical Health does not include sale of food for ordinary nutrition, but it includes special foods such as vitamins. It refers only to the active promotion of health, not to prevention of accidents or illness. Behavior settings that operate under government health regulations, such as restaurants, barber shops, grocery stores, do not receive a Health rating. Only human health is rated; animal health is not included. Fund drives for particular health purposes (Heart, Cancer, etc.) are rated for Health, but those behavior settings concerned with general welfare, with health only implicit, are not rated, e.g., Red Cross, Children's Service League. Types of behavior settings receiving high health ratings are Physical Education Classes, Medical Services (Doctors and Dentists Offices, Medical Inspectors), Fund Drives for Health Causes, Chemists (in England).

(8) *Professionalism Action Pattern:* The degree to which the performers in the setting are paid rather than voluntary. All ratings are based upon the occupancy times of *performers,* i.e., inhabitants of penetration zones 4, 5, and 6.

Participation: Receiving wages or profits for performing in the setting; the proportion of the occupancy time of *all the performers* of the setting that is *paid* time, paid by wages or by profits. The occupancy time of the *performers* is judged on the usual participation scale, namely:

0   the performers receive no pay.
1   1 to 20 per cent of the OT of the performers is paid.
2   21 to 40 per cent of the OT of the performers is paid.
3   41 to 60 per cent of the OT of the performers is paid.
4   61 to 80 per cent of the OT of the performers is paid.
5   81 to 100 per cent of the OT of the performers is paid.

Supply: Providing materials for paid work by performers in another setting. Judge on above scale; the performers in feed stores spend some per cent of their time supplying materials for farmers to make a profit in other settings.

Evaluation and appreciation: Evaluating paid performers. But note that evaluation by members, customers, and audience is *not* counted as professional evaluation; only evaluation by superiors is counted, i.e., by persons with power to determine the future employment of a performer (chairman of a committee, employer, headmaster). Judge on usual evaluation scale with *total* OT as base.

Learning: Providing education in classes or via apprenticeship for eventual paid work; e.g., school typewriting classes; garage with apprentices. Judge on usual Learning and Teaching scale with *total OT* as base.

In cases where the performers get only a nominal fee, much of the occupancy time is voluntary; therefore the occupancy hours should be reduced accordingly, e.g., jurors are semivoluntary, also firemen in volunteer fire departments. Paying transportation for entertainers is *not* considered payment. Every business with employees receives some rating for evaluation, i.e., the employer judges his employees as paid performers.

Teaching and learning that involve progress toward a certificate or examination for entrance to or promotion in a profession or vocation receive some rating under evaluation and appreciation. Where the professional is not a performer, as the church pastor at a church bazaar, even though he is present in all his dignity, he does not count as a professional. A performer "performs" during the whole setting even though he actually acts only a part of the time; e.g., the church organist is in the role of performer at all times during the worship service. But in the case of repeated settings, if a performer is present in only some of the occurrences, his performance time is reduced accordingly. Also, if there is a single *performance period* after which the performer leaves, then only the time of the period is counted. But when a person is in the role of performer for the whole time, as is the organist, but is active only a part of the time, the whole period is counted.

(9) *Recreation Action Pattern:* Behavior that gives immediate gratification; consumatory behavior; play, sport, games.

Participation: Playing, having fun, reading for enjoyment, relaxing, being entertained. Recreational behavior is guided by the person's own needs; there is little compulsion. The Recreation rating is decreased to the degree that such serious action patterns as Business, Education, Government, and Religion share the OT of a setting.

Supply: Supplying materials and objects for recreation in other settings.

Evaluation and appreciation: Recognizing or appreciating entertainment or entertainers.

Learning: Teaching or learning about ways and means of recreation, stimulating the use of facilities for entertainment.

Not all behavior that is enjoyable is Recreation. Social contacts that are incidental to a business or religious setting may be enjoyable but do not count as recreation unless recreation is the purpose of the social contact. *Immediate gratification* must be the primary function of the behavior. This means that to receive a rating for Recreation (*a*) a setting must have a time, e.g., a tea break, or (*b*) a setting must have a place, e.g., reading nook, expressly for Recreation, or (*c*) the standing pattern of the setting must be free enough that it can be shifted from serious to recreational behavior at any time, e.g., Snack Bar. The whole setting may, of course, be a time and place for recreation (as a party); in this case the participation rating is 81–100 per cent.

Films in a cinema are Recreation; instructional films are not. Selling gasoline for recreational use of cars is Supply for Recreation. A concert of sacred music in a church is not Recreation; a concert of secular songs in a church is recreational. One symptom of whether a setting is a recreational setting is the presence of joyful applause, not applause for achievement; i.e., applause that indicates "I am enjoying myself."

Behavior settings in which 80 per cent of the OT is concerned seriously and purposefully with reality, and with no supply, evaluation, or learning of Recreation receive a 0 rating for Recreation, e.g., most Laundry Services, Building Construction and Repair Services, Lumberyards, Real Estate Agents, Government Records and Business Offices, Banks, Attorneys' Offices, Court Sessions, Elections, Academic School Classes, Standardized Tests, Religion Study Groups, and Worship Services.

Behavior settings with 80 per cent plus of the OT devoted to enjoyment, relaxation, consumatory behavior, and in addition with some evaluation of Recreation, receive high (6+) ratings for Recreation, e.g., most Parties, Moving Picture Shows, Dances, Swimming Trips, Hikes and Camps, Organization Dinners and Banquets, Golf Games, Parades, Track Meets, Picnics, Bowling Games, and Football Games and Practices. Behavior settings rated intermediate (1 to 5) in Recreation are Restaurants, School Classrooms, Free Time, Hardware Stores, and Religious Fellowship Meetings.

(10) *Religion Action Pattern:* Behavior that has to do with worship.

Participation: Engaging in religious exercises.

Supply: Supplying religious artifacts or materials for purposes of worship.

Evaluation and appreciation: Criticizing and appreciating religion and religious behavior.

Learning: Teaching or learning about religion or ways to practice religion. It must be formal teaching in classes.

Behavior settings with no religious behavior whatever, either participation, supply, evaluation, or learning, receive 0 rating; settings with perfunctory, often formal religious behavior, e.g., saying Grace at an otherwise nonreligious setting, receive 1 rating. Behavior settings with combination of substantial religious behavior and substantial nonreligious behavior, e.g., Youth Fellowship Meetings, Easter Sunrise Service with Breakfast, receive 2–5 rating. Settings with 80 per cent plus OT devoted to religious behavior and with some evaluation receive 6+ rating. This includes church committees that open with a prayer and then consider church problems exclusively.

(11) *Social Contact Action Pattern:* Having interpersonal relations of any kind.

Participation: Engaging in social interactions.

Supply: Supplying materials and equipment for engaging in social interaction.

Evaluation and appreciation: Recognizing sociable persons or values of sociability.

Learning: Teaching and learning social techniques.

Calculate the proportion of the total OT in which there is actual social interaction. When a teacher calls a school class to order and all the pupils respond, all are engaging in social contact. If the pupils are doing individual desk work and the teacher is speaking to one child and only he is listening, the proportion engaging in social contact is $2/N$, where N is the number in the class.

A concert involves social contact to the degree that the musicians are communicating with the audience. In Midwest there are no behavior settings that receive an overall 0 rating on Social Contact. Ratings of 1 to 3 include behavior settings with some occupants who function for considerable periods of time in isolation; nonsocial functioning is possible in these settings, and in some cases it is enforced. Ratings 1, 2, and 3 include small, single-man shops; settings where there are mechanics who must do much work alone; offices with routine, single-person jobs, e.g., Typing, Filing, Examinations, Delivery Routes. High Social Contact ratings occur in Meetings, Classes, Card Clubs, Worship Services, Pubs, Weddings, Lodge Meetings, Concerts and Plays.

Behavior Mechanisms: Rating Scales

The standing behavior patterns of behavior settings have been rated on five variables called behavior mechanisms: Affective Behavior, Gross Motor Activity, Manipulation, Talking, and Thinking. The extent to which these mechanisms occur in a behavior setting is judged by a rating method similar to that used with the action patterns. There are three subscales.

(1) *Participation Subscale:* The degree of occurrence of the mechanism in the standing behavior pattern of the setting; it is rated according to the following scale:

0   The mechanism occurs in less than 10 per cent of the OT of the setting.

1   The mechanism occurs in 10 to 33 per cent of the OT of the setting.

2 The mechanism occurs in 34 to 66 per cent of the OT of the
   setting.
3 The mechanism occurs in 67 to 90 per cent of the OT of the
   setting.
4 The mechanism occurs in more than 90 per cent of the OT of
   the setting.

Example: Talking, including singing, was judged to be involved in 34
to 66 per cent of the total OT of the setting Primary School Music Classes; hence, it was rated 2 for the mechanism Talking.

(2) *Tempo Subscale:* The maximum speed with which the mechanism normally occurs in the setting; the unusual, abnormal burst of
speed is not rated. In rating tempo and also intensity, consider the
average maximum speed or degree of occurrence in the setting. An analogy may help here: a single index of the height of the range of moun-
tains is the average height of the peaks of the range. A curve representing the tempo or intensity of a behavior setting is in most cases a fluctu-
ating curve, and the "height" of the curve can similarly be indicated by
a single index—the average height of its peaks. This is what is meant by
the maximum normal speed and intensity.

In the behavior mechanism ratings, ratings of the peak speeds with
which the mechanisms occur (during the time that they do occur) and
ratings of the peak intensities with which they occur (when they do
occur) are added to ratings of the extent to which the mechanisms occur in the standing patterns of behavior. These are not, therefore, "volu-
metric" ratings. A mechanism that is expressed in only one per cent of
the OT of the setting but that is expressed at top speed and intensity
when it does occur receives a rating only 40 per cent less than if it occurred at those high speeds and intensities during the whole time, i.e.,
it would in the latter case receive a rating of 10 and in the former case
a rating of 6. There are other combinations that add to 6; e.g., the mechanism occurs in 100 per cent of the OT (rating 4) at average speed (rating 1) and average intensity (rating 1). Tempo is rated as follows:

0 When the mechanism occurs, its maximal normal speed is slow;
   reaction times are long.
1 The maximal normal speed of the mechanism is in the median
   range, neither fast nor slow.
2 The maximal normal speed of the mechanism is above the median range.
3 The maximal normal speed of the mechanism is near the physiological limit.

Example: In the setting Pearson Dairy Route, the maximal speed of Gross Motor Activity is regularly more rapid than the median rate of gross motor movement, the milkman hurries, rated 2. High School Boys Basketball Practice involves Gross Motor Activity at top speed, rated 3.

(3) *Intensity Subscale:* The usual, maximal rate of energy expenditure via the mechanism, rated as follows:

0   When the mechanism occurs, the maximal normal rate of energy expenditure is very low.
1   Maximal normal energy expenditure is in the median range.
2   Maximal normal energy expenditure is above the median range.
3   Maximal normal energy exerted is near the physiological limit.

Example: The events in the High School Track Meet regularly involve a maximal energy expenditure via Gross Motor Activity, rated 3.

A behavior setting mechanism rating is the sum of the rating on these three subscales. The range of ratings is from 0 to 10.

Behavior Mechanisms: Definitions

(1) *Affective Behavior:* Overt emotional behavior of any kind.

Participation: The per cent of the total OT of the setting in which overt emotionality occurs.

Tempo: Refers to rate of change in emotionality, to speed of mood changes, to swiftness of alteration in emotional expression. Rate the highest, *normal* rate of variation in affective behavior.

Intensity: The greatest normal intensity of overt emotionality that regularly occurs in the setting.

To receive a rating for participation in the case of Affective Behavior, the emotional aspect of behavior must deviate from the degree of expressiveness that occurs when behavior is described as calm, placid, unemotional. Deviation from this norm may be shown by (*a*) unusual quietness, restraint, self-control, (*b*) excessive expressiveness, e.g., cheering, yelling, hearty singing, kicking, running, and (*c*) verbal description of feelings, e.g., "we are profoundly saddened . . . ." The degree of deviation via any of these routes is the basis of the rating of *intensity*.

In church services the prayers and singing are means of expressing emotion overtly. An organ concert in a church where there is no overt emotional expression, except by the organist as performer, receives additional rating for Affective Behavior insofar as the audience is attentive, i.e., participates in the mood of music.

(2) *Gross Motor Activity:* Involvement of the large muscles, limbs, and trunk of the body in the standing behavior pattern of a setting; opposed to sedentary behavior.

Participation: Degree to which movements involving the large muscles occur in the standing behavior pattern of the setting.

Tempo: Maximal, normal speed of large muscle, limb, and trunk movements in the setting.

Intensity: Greatest force regularly used in gross motor activity when it occurs.

With athletic events, note that the number of spectators in relation to the players is an important factor. Usually, only the players participate in Gross Motor Activity of any intensity. Standing is counted as a gross motor behavior of 0 speed and 0 intensity.

(3) *Manipulation:* Involvement of the hands in the standing behavior pattern or setting.

Participation: The proportion of the total OT in which the hands are used to grasp, manipulate, push, pull, tap, clap, etc.

Tempo: Maximal normal rate of hand movement.

Intensity: Maximal, regular force exerted by the hands in behavior.

(4) *Talking:* All forms of verbalizing, including singing, yelling, crying, cheering.

Participation: Per cent of the total OT of a setting that involves verbalization of any kind.

Tempo: Maximal, normal speed of verbalizing.

Intensity: Maximal, ordinary loudness of verbalizing.

At a cocktail party where almost everyone talks most of the time, Talking is rated 67 per cent to 90 per cent of OT; during a normal conversation between two people, Talking is 100 per cent of OT. This is reduced as the conversing group becomes larger. In a formal lecture only the lecturer talks. In a committee meeting of five, about two-fifths will be talking, usually.

(5) *Thinking:* Problem solving and decision making; does not include routine motor behavior or emotional behavior.

Participation: Per cent of the OT of a setting occupied with problem solving or decision making.

Tempo: Maximal speed with which problems are normally solved and decisions made.

Intensity: The maximal level of Thinking that typically occurs in the setting.

Thinking OT is reduced in proportion to the length of time it takes to carry out decisions that are made.

The listeners at a sermon or lecture think to the degree that they evaluate and criticize what is said; to the degree that they only record what is said, they do not think.

Participation is low, 0–9 per cent, (*a*) if few participants make decisions or (*b*) if the participants could be thinking about something else most of the time.

Richness of Behavior Settings

In general, the richness of a behavior setting refers to the variety of behavior within its pattern of behavior. Many different categories of persons responsibly participating in a behavior setting via many action patterns and many behavior mechanisms, many of them with high ratings, are the mark of a setting with great behavioral richness. A General Richness Index is computed for a behavior setting by summing (*a*) the penetration ratings of the 14 population subgroups, (*b*) the ratings of the 11 action patterns, and (*c*) the ratings of the five behavior mechanisms, and by weighting the sum for the OT of the setting. The General Richness Index (GRI) can be defined as follows:

$$GRI = \frac{(\Sigma PenR + \Sigma ApR + \Sigma BmR)cOT}{100},$$

where GRI is the General Richness Index of setting X, PenR are the Penetration Ratings of setting X, ApR are the Action Pattern Ratings of setting X, BmR is the Behavior Mechanism Rating of setting X, and cOT is the Code number of Occupancy Time of setting X. (See Appendix 1.) General Richness Indexes of Midwest behavior settings vary from 57 for Ellson Drugstore to 1 for Farm Bureau District Delegates Meeting.

Pressure

The pressure of a behavior setting is the degree to which foreign forces act upon a person to approach and enter or to withdraw from and avoid it. Pressure does *not* refer to the positive or negative valence (attractiveness or repulsiveness) of a setting for a person himself; it refers to the outside forces that bear upon him. The pressure of a behavior setting can be rated for a particular individual or for a population subgroup. The following scale refers to the pressure of behavior settings on children:

1   *Required:* children are required to enter the setting; they have no choice, e.g., school classes. This rating is made *for the setting's eligible children.* Three-year-old children for example, do not have to attend school; they are not eligible.

2   *Urged:* eligible children are pressured but not required to attend the setting; they have some choice, e.g., boys are urged to participate in the setting Boy Scout Cub Pack Meeting.

3   *Invited:* eligible children are welcomed to the setting; they are asked to attend, e.g., Methodist Church Kindergarten Class.

4   *Neutral:* children are free to enter this setting equally with others; there is no positive or negative discrimination with respect to children, e.g., City Park.

5   *Tolerated:* children are not welcomed to the setting; others can enter more freely than children; there is resistance to children, but it is not strong, e.g., County Clerks Office.

6   *Resisted:* children are pressured not to enter the setting, but they are not forbidden. There must be strong reasons (counterpressures) to allow a child to enter, e.g., Married Couples Bridge Club.

7   *Prohibited:* children are excluded, e.g., an organization meeting with age limits, Masonic Lodge Meeting.

If a setting is scheduled at a time when children cannot inhabit it, e.g., during school hours, this signifies some resistance to school-age children. When a behavior setting simultaneously involves forces upon children both to attend and to avoid the setting, a decision has to be made as to which pressure is most significant for the setting. Thus, six-year-old children receive strong forces (rated 1) to attend First Grade Academic Activities; at the same time children under six years receive strong forces (which would be rated 7) not to attend this setting. A court session may require the attendance of some children as witnesses, for example, and exclude others. At the installation of new members in a club, the newly elected members are urged to attend, whereas the attendance of those not elected is resisted. There is usually little difficulty in choosing the most salient pressure for the setting. In the above cases it seems clear that for the wide age-range of children it is crucial that schools require children to attend, that courts require child witnesses to be present, that clubs urge child members to come to installation meetings (even though schools also prevent *some* children from attending, courts may reject some children from its proceedings, and clubs may exclude children who are not members).

The pressure of a setting upon children to enter it is not rated on an absolute scale; it is rated *relative to* the pressure of the setting upon other age groups. The central pressure-rating category is 4. A rating of 4 means that children are not singled out in any way for greater pressure to enter or not enter the setting than other age groups. Both Trafficways and Country Kitchen, for example, receive a pressure rating of 4; but the pressure on any age group to enter or not enter Trafficways is very low, whereas the setting Country Kitchen brings much greater pressure via signs, advertisements, etc., on people of all ages to enter it.

The forces that operate upon children to enter settings rated 2 and 3 are greater than those that operate upon some other age groups, but the forces are not irresistible; children have a choice of entering or not entering. Children are invited, urged, encouraged to enter these settings to a greater degree than some other age groups; children are singled out as a focus of the forces into these settings. But a setting *does not* receive a pressure rating of 2 or 3 for children if the pressure is on a particular person who happens to be a child. It is sometimes difficult to determine, for example, if the proprietor of a store has searched for and secured "a child helper" or John Doe who happens to be a child. To avoid this difficulty in the most frequent case, family businesses in which children (and adolescents) are involved as helpers are *not* rated 2 or 3 on pressure, but 4.

The basis of rating 1, Required, is the same as that for ratings 2 and 3 except that here the forces are irresistible. In the case of Pressure 2 or 3 the setting suffers, and may cease to operate, if the forces from the setting are not sufficiently strong to bring the necessary children into it. This regularly occurs with Cub Scout Packs, school clubs, and Sunday school classes, for example. But in the case of some behavior settings this is not allowed to happen; outside forces from the community require that these settings continue to function at an effective level. Community forces are added to behavior setting claim forces to overcome all child resistance to entering these settings. Children "have to go" to settings rated 1; all the pressure of the family in most cases, and if necessary the police force of the community, requires child attendance. These are, in Midwest and Yoredale, almost exclusively school settings.

Settings are rated 5 or 6 when the forces that operate on children *not to enter* them are stronger than those that operate upon some other age groups, but the forces are not irresistible. Children are discouraged from entering these settings; impediments are placed in their paths; doors are closed; the "Not Welcome" sign is displayed in many ways. The programs of these settings are disturbed and delayed by children more than by the presence of some other age groups; the removal of children and their replacement by people-in-general contributes to the smooth operation of these settings.

The basis of rating 7 is the same as that of rating 5 or 6, except that here the forces upon children are much stronger; they are irresistible, and children are prohibited (except temporarily, in emergencies). In the case of rating 5 or 6 the behavior setting programs continue to function with more or less disturbance and drag when children are present. This regularly occurs in Midwest in such settings as Presbyterian Senior Choir Practice and Study Club, where children are more or less in the way. But there are some settings that cease functioning if children are regularly present. In these cases there is usually an arbitrary cut-off, or safety factor, which stops operations when children are present; this may be an article of the constitution, or a bylaw of the organization that operates the setting.

There is almost always an exception to the absolute exclusion of children from behavior settings. Emergencies arise such as when an essential person cannot attend the setting without bringing a child; in these cases, the setting will usually continue temporarily with the offending child more or less isolated from the operation of the setting.

The "No Admittance" signs on these settings take many forms via rules and regulations, meeting times when children cannot attend, etc. One common bit of evidence is that a member of such a setting will usually not attend the setting if he has to take a child with him, unless it is so essential that he be present that an emergency must be declared.

It should be noted that the occurrence of pressure upon children does not mean that the same behavior setting does not exert pressure upon other age groups. There is pressure upon adults (teachers) to enter First Grade Academic Activities, for example. But at the same time, there is no pressure upon adolescents or aged persons to enter this setting. If the First Grade Academic setting would function without noticeable disruption with a random sample of 30 Midwest inhabitants, the pressure rating on children would be 4. But this is not true, of course; the program of First Grade Activities requires children as one of its components.

There are in general two sources of evidence regarding the forces on children to enter behavior settings: children are actually observed to receive more and/or stronger forces than other groups in the way of requests, invitations, urgings, orders, etc.; and the behavior setting is observed to falter more in its functioning if its child inhabitants are removed (and replaced by people-in-general) than if some other age groups are removed.

An effective procedure for rating behavior settings on Pressure is to answer the following questions in order:

(1) Are children *required* to enter this behavior setting? If there are laws requiring it; or (*a*) if the setting would cease to function if it had no child inhabitants and (*b*) if the community would not allow this to happen, rate 1. If these statements are *not* true, consider question #2.

(2) Are children *prohibited* from entering this behavior setting except in emergency? If children are such foreign bodies in this setting that the program ceases if they are regularly present, rate 7. In practice, the following classes of behavior settings receive a rating of 7.

—Behavior settings inhabited by trained professionals with training and/or experience requirements that preclude children, e.g., Teachers Association Meeting, Insurance Salesmens Meeting.

—Boards and Committees of adult organizations (even when children are not excluded from the organization meeting), e.g., PTA Executive Committee Meeting.

—Business and Vocational Association Meetings, e.g., Chamber of Commerce Meeting.

—Adult Lodge Meetings.

—Adult organization special settings (even when children attend regular meetings), e.g., Home Demonstration Unit Trip to Capital City.

—Meetings of adult organization delegates from a large area (even if children are not excluded from local meetings), e.g., Farm Bureau District Meeting.

—Children excluded by law, e.g., Oil Tank Truck and Storage Area.

—Behavior settings that are age-graded (especially when age-appropriate setting occurs simultaneously), e.g., High School Latin Class.

If children are not prohibited, consider question 3.

(3) Is this behavior setting neutral to children? Would people-in-general be as effective to the program of this behavior setting as children? If the answer is Yes, rate 4; if No, consider question #4.

(4) Is the program of this behavior setting benefited by children? Does the setting welcome and invite children? Does the absence of chil-

dren interfere with the functioning of this behavior setting? If the answer is Yes, rate 2 or 3.

(5) If none of the above questions are answered Yes, rate 5 or 6.

Welfare

The *raison d'être* of a setting with respect to any class of inhabitants is the welfare attribute. The following scale illustrates a setting's welfare vis-à-vis children:

0   The setting is not concerned with children; this rating applies to all behavior settings not clearly covered by rating 1, 2, or 3.

1   *Serves child members:* the setting serves the welfare of its child inhabitants; its product or output is children processed in a particular way, educated, recreated, strengthened, fed, bathed, etc.

   A setting may be given a welfare rating 1 for both its child and adolescent members, for example, simultaneously; but the output of the setting must be processed children and/or adolescents, not just processed people-in-general. Thus a moving picture show that entertains everyone does not receive a Welfare rating of 1; but a Sixth Grade Party does receive a rating of 1 for child welfare.

2   *Serves children in other settings:* the setting instigates and supports *other* settings that are primarily for the welfare of children; it has no child members itself. The setting fosters settings that are for the benefit of child members, settings that receive a rating of 1 on Welfare. The setting does not, itself, have child output; it has power to create and/or support settings that do have child products.

   Rating 2 does not include behavior settings that have as *one* function among others the fostering of children's behavior settings; e.g., Women's Institute that arranges a children's Christmas party. Rating 2 is given only if the adult setting would cease if the child setting it fosters should cease, e.g., Elementary School Board Meeting.

3   *Children serve other members:* the setting has child performers who operate the setting for the benefit of the members of other age groups. Children in this case operate settings that recreate, educate, feed people of other age groups (adults, aged, infants, etc.).

   Rating 3 does not apply to business behavior settings where

children are minor staff members, i.e., where their contribution at any time is minor; but it does apply to behavior settings where children occasionally have important parts in the program, e.g., PTA Meeting, where perhaps twice a year children provide the program.

Rating 0 includes settings that entirely exclude children from their area of concern, i.e., settings rated 4, 5, 6, or 7 on Pressure receive a rating of 0 on Welfare. Also, settings that do *not* fall in rating 1, 2, or 3 are rated 0.

Local Autonomy

The local autonomy of a behavior setting is a rating of the degree to which four decisions regarding the operations of the setting, namely,

appointment of performers,
admittance of members,
determination of fees and prices, and
establishment of programs and schedules

occur within five geographical areas with differing proximities to the setting, as follows:

within the town,
outside the town but within the school district,
outside the district but within the county,
outside the county but within the state,
outside the state but within the nation.

The highest local autonomy rating is 9; it indicates that the four decisions are made entirely within the boundaries of Midwest; that the setting has complete local autonomy. Ratings vary between 9 and 1; a rating of 1 means that the four decisions are made at the national level. Ratings between 9 and 1 signify that the decisions are made at state (rating 3), county (rating 5), and district (rating 7) levels.

The local autonomy of each decision is rated on a rating form illustrated in the several examples that follow. The proximity ratings (PR) are the same for all decisions and settings and therefore are entered on the form. The rating problems that vary are (*a*) to determine the loci of all persons or agencies involved in the decision under consideration, and (*b*) to judge the *relative* weight (RW) with respect to this decision of all of the involved loci, and enter the weights in the appropriate

BS: Bridge Club I, 1963–64
Decision: appointment of performers

Locus of Decision	Proximity Rating of Locus (PR)	Relative Weight of Locus (RW)	Weighted Rating of Locus (PR × RW)
Within town	9	1.00	9
Within school district	7	0	0
Within county	5	0	0
Within state	3	0	0
Within nation	1	0	0

Local autonomy: Σ(PR × RW) 9

BS: Presbyterian Church, Quarterly Presbytery Meeting
Decision: appointment of performers

Locus of Decision	Proximity Rating of Locus (PR)	Relative Weight of Locus (RW)	Weighted Rating of Locus (PR × RW)
Within town	9	0	0
Within school district	7	0	0
Within county	5	0	0
Within state	3	0.75	2.25
Within nation	1	0.25	0.25

Local autonomy: Σ(PR × RW) 2.50

BS: Presbyterian Church, Quarterly Presbytery Meeting
Decision: finances; programs and schedules

Locus of Decision	Proximity Rating of Locus (PR)	Relative Weight of Locus (RW)	Weighted Rating of Locus (PR × RW)
Within town	9	0.15	1.35
Within school district	7	0	0
Within county	5	0	0
Within state	3	0.85	2.55
Within nation	1	0	0

Local autonomy: Σ(PR × RW) 3.90

spaces under RW. Some examples follow. The rating form for each of the examples is shown on p. 77.

Bridge Club I. The performers in this behavior setting are all chosen within the borders of Midwest; no person or agency in the district, county, state, or nation has any influence over the decision regarding who shall be the performers (President, Host, etc.). In connection with performers, therefore, the locus "within town" receives a relative weight of 1.00, and all other loci a weight of 0. Bridge Club I in Midwest has complete local autonomy in the appointment of performers. Similar processes with respect to admission of members, financial policies, and club programs and schedules produce the same result; the autonomy rating is 9 for each of them. The local autonomy rating for the club, therefore, is the mean of the local autonomy ratings for the four decisions, i.e., $36/4 = 9$.

Presbyterian Church, Quarterly Presbytery Meeting. The main decisions concerning appointment of performers in this behavior setting are at the state level; but national committees and nationally determined policies have some weight; relative weight of these loci is judged to be .75 and .25. Decisions regarding admission of members are judged to be the same as for performers, and its rating form duplicates the one above.

Decisions about the finances of this behavior setting and about its programs and schedules are made almost entirely at the state level, but with some influence within the town, e.g., regarding the price of the meal served the delegates and the scheduling of the program. State and town loci are judged to have weights of 0.85 and 0.15 in these decisions. So the form for decisions regarding fees and prices (and also programs and schedules) is as shown in the final example on p. 77.

The local autonomy of the Presbyterian Church Quarterly Presbytery Meeting is computed as follows:

Decisions	Autonomy Rating
Appointment of performers	2.5
Admittance of members	2.5
Determination of fees and prices	3.9
Establishment of programs and schedules	3.9
Mean autonomy rating	$12.8/4 = 3.2$

Examples of the local autonomy ratings of a number of Midwest behavior settings are given below (autonomy ratings are rounded to the nearest integer):

Setting	Autonomy Rating
Garland Lanes Bowling Exhibitions	8
High School Senior Car Wash	9
American Legion Auxiliary Card Party for March of Dimes	9
U.S. Corps of Engineers Office	2
U.S. Farmers Home Administration Office	3
U.S. Post Office	1
State Primary Election South Midwest Polling Place	4
County Engineers Office	5
County Superintendent of Schools Office	6
High School Award Assembly	7

Each behavior setting is, of course, local; it is located within the town under investigation. Almost every behavior setting has within it zone 5/6 performers, who exercise control over the program of the setting. (See zones on p. 50.) But people become zone 5/6 performers via power that has a locus. The locus may be (*a*) within the 5/6 zone itself (e.g., a proprietor "opens" a real estate office); (*b*) outside of zone 5/6 but within the setting (e.g., the president of PTA Meeting is elected by the members); (*c*) outside of the setting but within the town (e.g., the City Council appoints the Fire Marshal, who presides over the City Firemens Meeting); all of these loci receive an autonomy rating of 9. However, zone 5/6 performers may be appointed by powers that reside (*d*) outside the town but within the immediately surrounding district (e.g., Sixth Grade Teacher), (*e*) outside the district but within the county (e.g., Manager of County Cooperative Feed Mill), (*f*) outside the county but within the state (e.g., Judge of District Court), (*g*) and outside the state but within the nation (e.g., Manager, U.S. Army Corps of Engineers Office). Loci (*d*) to (*g*) receive local autonomy ratings of 7 to 1, respectively, as per rating instructions.

The zone 5/6 performers operate the programs of the settings. But one can ask: What power establishes the programs? The performer, himself, may do so, as in the case of the proprietor of a privately owned store; but this power may reside at any location. In our rating scale, three attributes of behavior setting programs, namely, membership regulations, finances, and other policy matters, are rated according to the same directives that govern the appointment of 5/6 performers.

In judging power over any of these attributes of behavior settings, only the next most inclusive area is considered, e.g., local service stations in Midwest get their gasoline prices, etc., from a "headquarters" at the state level; these are controlled by other centers outside the state. Only the first headquarters is considered in rating locus of power.

In the case of stores, the customers are the members. Here the question is: who determines what kind of customers will be catered to, males or females, elite or common, Negro or white?

Where a local merchant's main business is based upon a franchise granted by a firm outside the town, e.g., an auto agent or insurance salesman, the power to appoint 5/6 performers is shared equally within the town and at the locus of the firm's headquarters. Where an individual is hired and paid from a distance, e.g., a teacher or gas company representative, one should rate power as located solely at the agency's headquarters.

In the case of finances, where an out-of-town authority decides what the prices or fees are and the local people determine if they will pay them, one should count local and foreign power as equal.

In the case of games with distant schools, the performers, members, finances, and policies are decided jointly by the local and visiting schools; one should rate the power of each as equal.

BEHAVIOR SETTING GENOTYPES

The problem of classifying behavior settings poses difficulties comparable to that of classifying organisms or minerals. The outward appearance of the standing patterns of the settings Pintner Abstract and Title Company and of Wolf Attorney Office are so similar that a stranger might easily confuse them and attempt to transact lawyer's business in an abstract office, and vice versa. The surface aspect of the Midwest School Principals Office changed so much between 1954 and 1964 that a former student would be excused for thinking he had returned to the wrong school. It is widely recognized, however, that such superficial similarities and differences are adventitious, and that among the perplexing multiplicity of behavior settings on this level there are a smaller number of more fundamental types.

A community has common names, or code words, which identify types of behavior settings. Four people at a card table with cards before them do not know how to initiate the behavior setting until the code word is known: bridge, pinochle, poker, hearts, etc. A patron inquires if he is in a setting with the correct standing pattern by the appropriate code word: Is this a bank? No, this is a real estate office. Code words of these kinds identify behavior settings with such fundamental similarities that we have called them behavior setting genotypes.

Organisms of the same genotype have the same coded programs

stored in their nuclei, and behavior settings of the same genotype have the same coded programs stored in their most central zones (zone 6 if the most central region has a single inhabitant, zone 5 if it has multiple inhabitants). Sometimes this program is coded via written language; a print-out of the program of baseball games is available in a baseball rule book. In these cases, the programs of different settings can be compared, item by item, to determine their degree of equivalence. However, written programs are not usually available; for most behavior settings, therefore, other evidence of their genotypic equivalence is essential.

A central problem of behavior setting operation is to get the proper program stored within performance zone inhabitants, and especially within the occupants of zone 5/6. This is accomplished by formal training and/or experience in the setting, and it requires time. But when the program of a setting is incorporated within a person, it is one of his relatively permanent attributes, and he is branded with the code name of the program: Attorney, Postmaster, Grocer, etc. It is especially important in the present connection to note that a longer time is usually required for a person to become *the carrier of the program* of a setting than to become the *carrier of input* to the setting. A person can generate a problem for an attorney much faster than he can generate the know-how of an attorney.

These facts provide a practical basis for judging whether different behavior settings are of the same or different genotypes even when details of their programs are not known. If settings A and B continue to function without change when their zone 5/6 inhabitants are interchanged, then A and B have the same program and are identical in genotype. The behavior setting Wolf Attorney Office would continue to function effectively if Attorney Wiley displaced Attorney Wolf in zone 6, e.g., if Attorney Wiley purchased Attorney Wolf's practice. Transpositions of this kind occur not infrequently. And they can occur because the programs of general law offices are the same: the laws, the principles, the forms, the know-how are identical. It is the particular legal cases and the problems of particular clients that differ. These are the inputs. Attorney Wiley would have to be briefed on Attorney Wolf's cases, but the functioning of the setting would scarcely miss a beat. On the other hand, if Attorney Wiley were to transfer to zone 6 of County Engineers Office, the setting would stop short; the general law office program that has been incorporated within Attorney Wiley by long schooling and experience could not process the inputs to County Engineers Office.

So there are persons who carry the program brand of a particular behavior setting genotype upon them, and all behavior settings in which they function effectively as zone 5/6 performers are of the same genotype. In this connection it is important to recognize that some individuals store a number of programs, i.e., some people are versatile. The test, therefore, is not whether a particular person is interchangeable between zone 5/6 of settings but whether the program he possesses as performer in a particular behavior setting is transposable to other behavior settings.

The transposability of *programmed* performers between zone 5/6 of behavior settings is the most crucial evidence of their genotypic equivalence. But there is other evidence of considerable value in borderline cases.

(1) In judging the transposability of stored programs, the inhabitants of all zones are relevant, though their diagnostic significance increases with their depth of penetration. The part of a behavior setting program stored by a zone 2 inhabitant (audience, invited guest) is widely interchangeable among zone 2 of other behavior settings, the program of a zone 3 inhabitant (member, customer) is less widely transferable, the program of a minor functionary in zone 4 (bookkeeper, mechanic) has restricted transposability, whereas the total program stored by occupants of zones 5 and 6 (piano teacher, cafe operator) are transposable only between settings with the same total program. In marginal cases, the total picture of inhabitant transposability may be of diagnostic significance.

(2) The program of a behavior setting requires "hardware" (behavior objects, an exoskeleton) of a particular kind. When a program functions with inappropriate hardware, the result can be disastrous or ridiculous. Donkey baseball, with the players riding donkeys, is an example of the latter; the point of this amusing exhibition is that the baseball program cannot function effectively when donkeys are involved as behavior objects. Behavior settings with the same genotype have, in general, interchangeable classes of inhabitants, behavior objects, and milieu properties.

(3) The program of a setting is responsive to a limited range of input. The setting Dr. Sterne Dentist Office will not receive the input "Treat my sick dog," or "I want a quart of milk"; but for appropriate inputs the setting exhibits zero or minimum resistance, e.g., "I have a toothache." Settings with the same programs accept the same kinds of inputs.

Operations for Identifying Behavior Setting Genotypes

Whatever program criterion is used, the question arises: What degree of program difference places settings in different genotypes? Is the program of a baseball game sufficiently different from that of a softball game to signify that they are of different genotypes? A cutting point is obviously required, and we have set it as follows: *Two behavior settings are of the same genotype if, when their zone 5/6 performers are interchanged, they receive and process the same inputs as formerly, in the same way and without delay.*

The requirement "without delay" is important, for *given enough time* almost all behavior settings have interchangeable performers. A librarian could become the proprietor of a grocery store, and vice versa, if he devoted enough time to learning the new program; a dentist could operate a law office, and vice versa, if the dentist and the lawyer returned to school for some years. The rule is, therefore, that two settings are of the same genotype if both operate without delay when their most central inhabitants are interchanged. "Without delay" is interpreted as follows:

(*a*) if X is the time required to incorporate the program of behavior setting A into a naïve person, i.e., to make him a skilled, zone 5/6 performer, and

(*b*) if the time required to incorporate the program of behavior setting A into a person *who already has the program of setting B* is between 0 per cent and 25 per cent of X, and

(*c*) if statements (*a*) and (*b*), above, hold also for behavior setting B,

(*d*) then settings A and B are of the same genotype; the programs are transferable.

The 25 per cent delay in achieving effectiveness is allowed to accommodate differences in inputs and for some "retooling" of the transposed program.

Here are examples: An experienced zone 6 performer in the behavior setting Presbyterian Church Worship Service, i.e., a Presbyterian pastor, with no training or experience in the setting Methodist Church Worship Service, could, nevertheless, function efficiently in the latter with almost no delay. Evidence: (*a*) this has been observed to occur; (*b*) the training programs and curricula that imprint the programs of the setting Methodist Church Worship Service and the setting Presbyterian Church Worship Service within the respective pastors are almost identical. But

TABLE 4.5. *Genotype Comparator*

Setting A ———————————— vs. Setting B

(1) Synomorph Programs of A	(2) Time to Program Novice	(3) Time to Program B-Performer	(4) Per Cent of A's OT*	(5) Synomorph Programs of B	(6) Time to Program Novice	(7) Time to Program A-Performer	(8) Per Cent of B's OT*

Total per cent of OT devoted to nontransferable programs (9) ———

Total per cent of OT devoted to nontransferable programs (10) ———

* For nontransferable programs.

an experienced zone 6 performer in the setting Presbyterian Church Worship Service with no training or experience in the behavior setting Garland Lanes Monday Mens League Bowling Game could *not* transfer efficiently to the latter even with a full 25 per cent allowance; the worship service program he possesses would give him no saving over an entirely naïve person in becoming programmed for bowling. Evidence: (*a*) a Presbyterian pastor has been observed to bowl without any advantage over other naïve bowlers; (*b*) the curriculum for training a Presbyterian pastor has no elements in common with the lessons of a bowling school or the training of a bowling alley proprietor.

Some complications arise when the test is applied to behavior settings with more than one program, i.e., to settings with multiple synomorphs (see Chap. 3). Some programs of such paired settings may be interchangeable and not others. The variety store–programmed proprietor of Kane Variety Store could function effectively in only one of the three programs of Ellson Drugstore, namely, the variety department. Having the variety store program would give him no advantage in becoming programmed for the pharmacy or the fountain. On the other hand, the druggist, being programmed for the variety department of Ellson Drugstore, as well as the pharmacy and the fountain, could function effectively in zone 6 of Kane Variety Store. Since transferability must be mutual, the Kane Variety Store and Ellson Drugstore belong to different genotypes.

A standardized form (a comparator) has been prepared for identifying pairs of behavior settings with the same and different genotypes (see Table 4.5). The six steps are as follows:

(1) Determine via the interdependence index K the number of interjacent synomorph programs of behavior setting A and behavior setting B, and list them in columns (1) and (5), respectively, of the comparator. (In computing K between interjacent synomorphs, include as leaders all performers, zones 4 to 6.)

(2) Estimate the time required to incorporate each of these programs within a novice, i.e., estimate the time required to make a novice into an effective performer at deepest levels of penetration; record these times in columns (2) and (6).

The time required to incorporate some programs into performers is officially documented, e.g., nine months for a barber, three years to train a dentist. The course of training required for licensing these performers is prescribed. In cases where there is no recognized training curriculum, the time is estimated, e.g., for proprietor of a grocery store, for carrier of a paper route, for teacher of a Sunday school class. In all cases the incorporation time is the time required in addition to the essential general education.

(3) Estimate the time required to incorporate each program of setting A within an efficient performer of setting B, and vice versa; record these times in columns (3) and (7).

The first question in connection with step 3 is: What performers incorporate within themselves the total program of the synomorph? The second question is: What is the essential curriculum or training experience for mastering this program? Some performers must master specialized "content"; the mathematics teacher must know mathematics as well as teaching methods; he is *not* transferable to an English class. But the chairman of a golf club meeting does not need to know in detail about the "content" of golf club business (greens, membership, buildings); he must, however, know about conducting a business meeting, and part of this is making sure that the experts with the information are present. The same is true of the chairman of a city council meeting. It is the business meeting program that is essential, and this can be learned in any business meeting irrespective of the particular business transacted.

In judging transferability of a performer, the question is: How effective in behavior setting A would be a man programmed for behavior setting B, and vice versa? The program of setting A may be wide or narrow, simple or complex. The program of Third Grade Academic Subjects is wide and simple in comparison with Swine Producers School. A third grade teacher is able to transfer to the similarly wide and simple program of other elementary school academic classes; but the teacher of the swine class might or might not be effective in other animal husbandry courses; the general breadth of the training required for the particular course must be considered.

It is essential to be empirical in making these estimates. The best evidence is instances within the community where a similar transfer has occurred, and the time to "retool" is known. But there is other evidence. The amount of duplication in the training curricula of the two settings is one kind of evidence. Whether different licenses are required to function in the performance zones of setting A and setting B (e.g., chiropractor vs. school administrator), whether different examinations are set for performers of setting A than for performers of setting B (e.g., barbers vs. beauticians), and whether experience in performance zones of setting A is generally accepted as qualifying a person for the performance zones of setting B are other sorts of evidence.

(4) Identify nontransferable programs, i.e., programs for which

$$\frac{\text{time recorded in column 3 (and 7)}}{\text{time recorded in column 2 (and 6)}}$$

is between 0.26 and 1.0.

(5) Estimate the per cent of the total OT devoted to each nontransferable program and record in columns (4) and (8).

The occupancy time of a synomorph corresponding to one of the programs of a behavior setting is determined in the same way as the total OT of the setting, and it is then expressed as a per cent of the total OT. The OT of some synomorphs is available in official records, e.g., the dinner synomorph and the business meeting synomorph of Farm Bureau Annual County Dinner and Program. The OT of other synomorphs has to be estimated.

(6) Sum the per cents in columns (4) and (8) and record in spaces (9) and (10).

If the nontransferable programs recorded in space 9 *or* in space 10 amount to more than 25 per cent of the OT, settings A and B are *not* of the same genotype; if they amount to less than 25 per cent of the OT of *both* A and B, they are of the same genotype.

Variety Within and Difference Between Behavior Setting Genotypes

The fact that behavior settings of each genotype have transposable programs *inter se* does not mean that all genotypes have the same variety and complication within their programs, or that there is the same difference between programs of different genotypes.

A nonbehavioral example will illustrate this: Take two Briggs & Stratton one-cylinder gasoline motors, two Rolls Royce eight-cylinder automobile engines, and two IBM 7040 computers. The programs and parts involved in the operation of these pairs of machines are completely interchangeable; by this test each pair is of the same "genotype." But the variety and complication *within* the programs of each of the three genotypes is very different; each Briggs & Stratton motor may have 50 different parts, the Rolls Royce engine may have 500 parts each, and each computer may have 5,000 different parts. And the degree of difference *between* the different genotypes is very different; the Briggs & Stratton motors and the Rolls Royce engines have greater similarity than either one has with the computers. Some big engines of the Rolls Royce type incorporate small motors of the Briggs & Stratton type within them; in this respect they are identical.

So it is with behavior settings. Behavior setting genotypes are empirically determined classes of settings. One genotype may be limited and rigid in its programs (e.g., Refreshment Stands); another genotype may be much broader and, indeed, may incorporate subparts that, alone, are separate genotypes (e.g., Carnivals). The situation in these respects may be systematized as follows. If

   (1) zone 5/6 performers of setting A are interchangeable with 5/6 performers of setting B
   (2) zone 5/6 performers of setting C are interchangeable with 5/6 performers of setting D
   (3) zone 5/6 performers of setting E are interchangeable with 5/6 performers of setting F

and if

   (4) zone 5/6 performers of setting A are *not* interchangeable with 5/6 performers of setting C
   (5) zone 5/6 performers of setting C are *not* interchangeable with 5/6 performers of setting E
   (6) zone 5/6 performers of setting A are *not* interchangeable with 5/6 performers of setting E

and if

   (7) the genotype of A can be represented by ———
   (8) the genotype of C can be represented by ——— ◁
   (9) the genotype of E can be represented by ——— ◁o

then,

   (10) the genotype of B can be represented by ———
   (11) the genotype of D can be represented by ——— ◁
   (12) the genotype of F can be represented by ——— ◁o

and

   (13) ———   is genotype AB
   (14) ——— ◁   is genotype CD
   (15) ——— ◁o   is genotype EF

But the relations stated do not tell us (1) that genotypes AB and EF are *more* different than genotypes AB and CD, or than genotypes CD and EF; (2) that genotype EF is more varied than genotype CD and that CD is more varied than genotype AB; or (3) that genotype EF incorporates genotypes AB and CD within it. Still it is correct to say that there are three genotypes, namely

AB (———), CD (——— ◁), and EF (——— ◁∘).

This is the situation with respect to behavior setting genotypes, except that there are many genotypes without any overlap of part programs.

BEHAVIOR SETTING AUTHORITY SYSTEMS

The Elementary and High School Board Meeting is an important behavior setting in Midwest because it has great authority over a considerable number of the town's behavior settings, for example, over the Elementary School Principals Office, and through it over Sixth Grade Basic Subjects Class, and through it over Sixth Grade Hike. The School Board Meeting has some authority over 227 other behavior settings in Midwest. On the other hand, Burgess Beauty Shop is not under the authority of the School Board or of any other setting, and it has no authority over any other Midwest behavior setting. Both Elementary and High School Board Meeting and Burgess Beauty Shop are authority systems, the former involving 228 settings and the last involving a single behavior setting.

The test of the authority of a behavior setting is whether it determines the standing pattern of other settings via directed, intentional intervention either immediately or via intermediary settings. Excluded by this test are the nonselective interdependencies that diffuse settings without direction; the interdependencies involved in the index K are of this kind. Behavior settings within the same authority system may have lower interdependence indexes than settings in different authority systems. For example, there is almost no diffusion of influence between the Elementary School Principals Office and Sixth Grade Basic Subjects Class. The communications that do take place are of short duration, are irregular in occurrence, have in each case a particular content, are usually in one direction only, and are dominated by the Principals Office. But there is much more diffusion of influence between Sixth Grade Basic Subjects Class and Methodist Church Intermediate Sunday School Class, which is within a different authority system. The diffusion in this case is largely via many common inhabitants.

Arbitrarily excluded from consideration in connection with authority systems are controls by governmental behavior settings via legal regulations.

In some cases a behavior setting is within two authority systems; this is the case, for example, with Union Church Worship Service, which is within the authority system of the Methodist Church Official Board Meeting and the Presbyterian Church Session Meeting.

A behavior setting authority system is identified by the controlling setting, e.g., Elementary and High School Board Meeting, Baseball Association Committee Meeting. The controlling setting of an authority system is frequently a committee meeting.

The behavior settings of the different authority systems are grouped into five classes on the basis of the following characteristics of the controlling settings; these characteristics are based on Warriner and Prather (1965).

(1) *Business.* The controlling settings are operated by the owners or partners, acting as private citizens, in order to earn a living.

(2) *Churches.* The controlling settings are operated by the membership of a religious organization.

(3) *Government.* The controlling settings are city, county, state, or federal agencies. Excluded are Department of Education related settings (see category 4 below).

(4) *Schools.* The controlling settings are agencies of the city, district, county, state, or federal education departments.

(5) *Voluntary Associations.* The controlling settings are freely organized by the citizens for the pursuit of some interests in contrast to any of the above (e.g., Women's Club 1 Meeting, Bowling Association Womens Executive Meeting, Rebekah Lodge Meeting, Baseball Association Committee Meeting).

RELIABILITY OF BEHAVIOR SETTING RATINGS AND CLASSIFICATIONS

The degree of agreement between independent judges' ratings of the 11 action patterns, of the five behavior mechanisms, and of the *K* values, occupancy times, and depths of penetration of behavior settings has been investigated and reported (Barker & Wright, 1955). In all cases the degree of agreement is well above that usually accepted as adequate for studies of distributions of ratings and differences in central tendencies.

Reliability data have not been obtained for assessments of the occurrence, duration, population, pressure, welfare, local autonomy, genotypes, or authority systems of behavior settings. These data have not been obtained for a number of reasons: (*a*) When ratings are involved in these assessments, they are not more difficult to make than the ratings whose reliabilities have been investigated, and there is no reason to expect the former to be less reliably made than the latter. (*b*) A number of the assessments (occurrence, duration, population) are based wholly on census-type information obtained from public records, publications, informants, and direct observation. Maximal accuracy is obtained in these cases by double-checking clerical work, by obtaining information from more than one informant or observer, and by cross-checking the findings against other variables with known relations to the variable being assessed, e.g., if the duration and population of a setting are relatively high, the occupancy time must be relatively high, also. (*c*) The remaining assessments require the evaluation of less-than-complete information in terms of the judges' knowledge of their sources and of the community, e.g., assessing the direction and degree of pressure on children to attend or to avoid the behavior setting Kindergarten Parents Association Meeting requires careful fieldwork in the first place to secure information from inhabitants of this setting, and it requires judgment in evaluating what may be meager or perhaps contradictory information from fallible informants. Maximal accuracy in cases such as this is obtained by using multiple information sources and cross-checking against other variables.

Our efforts toward obtaining adequate data have been focused upon careful field and clerical work of the kinds mentioned under (*b*) and (*c*), above. In this connection, a permanent field station with staff members well informed about the community and with archives of verified community data has great advantages. Much research will be required to perfect the techniques of ecological psychology.

5

The Behavior Settings of Midwest, 1963–64

In THIS CHAPTER we shall present some data from the town of Midwest which illustrate behavior setting methodology. The chapter has three parts: (a) examples of Midwest's behavior settings as they occur among the common phenomena of daily life and as data in systematic studies; (b) a survey of the molar environment of Midwest in terms of behavior settings; and (c) a study of the behavioral output of the town's behavior setting resources.

Midwest is the county seat of an eastern Kansas county of approximately 400 square miles inhabited by 11,000 people. The region is almost purely agricultural; its chief products are wheat, corn, milk, and beef. Midwest had a population of 830 on January 1, 1964. Its inhabitants are overwhelmingly from family lines whose historical roots are in northern Europe; there are 26 Negro residents. The town is a geographically unified community spreading over 400 acres; it is surrounded by open fields. It is 20, 35, and 45 miles, respectively, from cities of 35,000, 100,000, and 800,000 population. Midwest is the business and educational center of the circumjacent part of the county. It is not an isolated community; it has open and busy channels of communication via roads, telephone, radio, television, newspapers, and mail with the larger society. Midwest is in no way atypical within its culture; it is a vigorous, thriving community.

The data refer to Midwest in the period September 1, 1963, to August 31, 1964, and they are concerned with the *public parts of the town*. The terms molar environment, molar behavior resources, behavior setting resources, refer in all cases to the non-family parts of Midwest.

EXAMPLES OF MIDWEST BEHAVIOR SETTINGS

The December 12, 1963, issue of *The Midwest Weekly* contained the following three items:

Midwest County Barracks and Auxiliary, Veterans of WW I, met Nov. 21 in the Legion Hall in Midwest. Fifty-eight members were there to enjoy Thanksgiving festivities. Officers elected will be installed next month. Owing to our regular meeting date being too close to Christmas, we will meet Dec. 19 at 6:30 in the Legion Hall at Midwest. The ladies auxiliary will serve two turkeys. You bring the trimmings and a 25¢ gift and we will have a Merry Christmas party.

On Saturday, Dec. 7, seventeen MHS Latin students and Miss Hoffer attended the Foreign Language Christmas Festival at Ellton State College. They began the day by registering in Albert Taylor Hall, the main building. They practiced Christmas carols in Latin, saw a motion picture in Latin, and listened to tapes of "Interviews on Mt. Olympus." They attended the Festival in the afternoon and sang their carols along with students of other languages. The program closed with the breaking of the pinata.

Watches—Diamonds
EXPERT REPAIR
Ruttley's Jewelry
Midwest, Kansas

These are glimpses of three behavior settings that occurred in Midwest during the year 1963–64, namely, American Legion World War I Barracks and Auxiliary Meeting and Dinner (of the genotype Dinners with Business Meetings), High School Latin Class Trip to Convention at State College (of the genotype Latin Classes), and Ruttleys Jewelry and Watch Repair Shop (of the genotype Jewelry Stores). The December 12, 1963, issue of *The Midwest Weekly* was in no way an unusual issue; it described the week in Midwest in terms of 106 behavior settings similar to the three above; the settings were of 60 genotypes. In 79 of the 106 behavior setting reports, one or more individuals were identified as participants (usually performers), as in the second and third items above; the other 27 reports describe standing patterns of settings, or fragments of them, without identifying any inhabitant, as in the first news item. In addition to the 106 items about behavior settings within the town, there were two reports of behavior in unspecified settings, 11 reports of out-of-town activities in the behavior settings of other communities, 26 reports of activities within behavior settings of private homes in town, and 14 reports of visits of residents to homes outside of Midwest.

The Midwest Weekly exemplifies the importance of behavior settings in the everyday lives of Midwest residents; settings are, in fact, their most common means of describing the town's behavior and environment. The hybrid, eco-behavioral character of behavior settings appears to present Midwest's inhabitants with no difficulty; nouns that combine milieu and standing behavior pattern are common, e.g., oyster supper, basketball game, turkey dinner, golden gavel ceremony, cake walk, back surgery, gift exchange, livestock auction, auto repair.

More detailed descriptions of two Midwest behavior settings as they occur in the town will now be given.

Basketball Game

Basketball games are common and popular behavior settings in Midwest. Five views of them are presented: (*a*) synopsis of the rules, i.e., of the program of the setting for the players; (*b*) photograph of a basketball game; (*c*) news report of a game; (*d*) précis of the behavior setting genotype Basketball Games; (*e*) copy of the data sheet of one basketball behavior setting, as prepared for the research.

(*a*) *Rules for High School Basketball Game (Program of Genotype 18 for Players).** Two teams of five players each play the game of basketball. The players work together in trying to score by throwing the ball through their own basket while preventing their opponents from scoring.

The *ball* is round, about 2.5 feet in circumference, and weighs 20 to 22 ounces. It has a leather or composition cover and is inflated with air.

The *baskets* hang 10 feet above the floor at opposite ends of the court. Each basket has a metal ring 18 inches in inside diameter, with a bottomless white cord net that hangs down 15 to 18 inches. The net slows down the flight of the ball as it goes through the basket. The baskets are firmly attached to backboards four feet inside the opposite ends of the court midway between the sidelines. They may be fastened solidly to a wall, hung by rigid supports from the ceiling, or anchored to the floor on supports beyond the playing court. The boards may be made of wood or any other flat, rigid material. Fan-shaped backboards are 35 inches high and 54 inches wide, with a 29-inch radius. They are mounted so the tops are 12 feet 8 inches above the court. Rectangular boards are 48 inches high and 72 inches wide; when mounted, the tops are 13 feet above the floor.

The *court* usually measures 50 by 84 feet.

* Adapted from *The World Book Encyclopedia* (Chicago: Field Enterprises Educational Corporation, 1964), II, 106–11.

A team consists of a center, two forwards, and two guards. The *forwards* play near their own basket, i.e., the basket their opponents are guarding, so they can maneuver into good positions for *shooting* (throwing the ball at the basket) and *rebounding* (grabbing the ball as soon as it bounces off the basket or backboard after a shot). The *center* plays near the basket or along the free-throw lane. He also concentrates on scoring and rebounding. The *guards* play closer to their opponents' basket. They bring the ball down the court for the center and forwards.

The game starts with a *jump ball*. The referee tosses the ball into the air in the center, and the opposing centers try to tap it to a teammate. During the game, a jump ball occurs whenever opposing players grab and hold the ball at the same time. The players move the ball by *passing* (throwing) it to a teammate or by *dribbling* it (bouncing the ball on the floor, tapping it with one hand; dribbling is the only means besides passing of advancing the ball down the court).

A player scores two points when the ball enters the basket from above and passes through it. When one team scores, the other team takes the ball beyond the end line of the court. A player passes it to a teammate on the court, who moves it toward the other basket. The offensive team must move the ball forward across the mid-court line within 10 seconds. This rule is set up to prevent *stalling* (deliberately slowing down the progress of the game).

A *free throw* is awarded to a player who has been fouled by an opponent. A successful free throw counts one point. The fouled player shoots the free throw from behind the free-throw line, 19 feet from the end line of the court.

Teams play four 8-minute quarters. They rest for one minute at the end of the first and third quarters, and for 10 minutes at the half.

If the opposing teams are tied at the end of the regulation time, they play one or more 3-minute *overtime* (extra) periods.

The Officials include two referees, one timer, and two scorers. The *referees* approve all the equipment before the game starts. A referee tosses the ball in the center to start the game. They decide all disagreements or problems not covered by the rules, notify the scorers when a team calls "time out," and call fouls. The *scorers* record all scoring and fouls. The *timer* operates the scoreboard clock to record playing time.

When a player holds, pushes, charges into, or trips an opponent, he commits a *personal foul*. The fouled player receives one free throw, unless he was in the act of shooting; in that case he receives two free throws. Teams are penalized, if they make more than four fouls in a half, by the fouled player on the other team being allowed an extra free throw if he scores on the first one. Players must leave the game if they commit five personal fouls.

A *technical foul* can be called for delaying the game, too many time-outs, leaving or entering the playing court illegally, or unsportsmanlike conduct. The opposing team receives one free throw.

A team loses possession of the ball for such violations as *traveling* (running or walking with the ball) and *double dribbling* (using both hands to bounce the ball, or stopping dribbling and starting again).

(*b*) *Photograph of Basketball Game.* The photograph is a 0.004-second record of the Midwest behavior setting High School Boys Basketball Game. In spite of its extreme brevity (0.0000015 of an occurrence), a number of the behavior setting attributes described in Chapters 3 and 4 are revealed. (See picture facing p. 102.)

(1) The picture demonstrates that this behavior setting is a preperceptual phenomenon; it is photographable. It indicates that, on a continuum from objects to concepts, High School Boys Basketball Game falls toward the object end of the scale.

(2) The two kinds of behavior setting components can be seen: humans and milieu objects (balls, goals, bleachers).

(3) Parts of the boundary of the setting are pictured.

(4) The ordered and organized nature of this setting's standing pattern of behavior and milieu are shown; it is unlikely indeed that the components of the setting would by chance fall into the pattern recorded by the photograph.

(5) The synomorphic relation between the standing behavior pattern and the pattern of the milieu is exhibited, e.g., the spectators face the court, the players face the ball.

(6) The circumjacency of the milieu of the game (walls, doors) to the standing pattern of behavior is shown; the players, spectators, officials, etc., are within the milieu.

(7) The picture shows that the parts of this behavior setting are not uniform and iterative but multiform and nonrepetitive; varied inhabitants and behavior (e.g., players playing, spectators watching, referee refereeing) and varied objects and events (e.g., lights illuminating, bleachers supporting spectators) are recorded.

(8) The interchangeable parts of the setting are represented; substitute players are on the bench.

(9) Inhabitants of different power positions can be identified: spectators (zone 2), players, officials, cheerleaders (zone 4), coaches (zone 5).

(10) The action patterns Personal Appearance and Social Contact and the behavior mechanisms Gross Motor Activities and Manipulation are clearly in evidence.

(c) *News Report of Basketball Game from the Midwest High School Cub Reporter.*

BEARS STUN PATTON

The slow, control Midwest team of last year turned run and gun, and showed promise for a good year with a stunning upset over the Kaws of Patton, 66–64.

The "stars" were abandoned for the first game, but Ken Kelcey and Ron Barton were the most formidable. Ken, whose great uncle was a kangaroo, poured in 24 points on his patented turnabout-explosion shot. He kept Midwest in reach at the first of the game as the Bears had a bad case of the jitters.

Patton took an early lead but couldn't hold the pace against the Bears' full court press and pressure offense. The Bears went to the lockers at half time down one point.

The fans were not downhearted and gave the Bears tremendous support.

In the second half the Bears turned it on and took a 10-point lead. About this time the reserves made their debut. Jim Auburn, who made three fouls in the first quarter, fouled out. Vern Day came in and made his presence known; Allen Bertram and Vern got nine points between them to keep the Bears in the lead. Coach substituted freely during this time as Ron Barton had four fouls and the Bears were weakening.

It looked as if Midwest was out of it when they were down four points with less than two minutes to play. The Bears put the pressure on and tied it when Ron Barton was fouled from behind with three seconds left. The 5'3" senior coolly stepped to the line and hit both tosses of a 1 and 1 to assure the Bears of the victory.

Frank Nading, who likes to rest his elbows on opponents' noses, was instrumental in the win. He and Ken rebounded with the taller Patton foes.

The game was a classic affair, and it pointed out the strength in Midwest this year.

(d) *Précis of Genotype 18, Basketball Games, Midwest, 1963–64.*
Milieu: located in residential area of Midwest (and of neighboring towns in the case of out-of-town games), within high school gymnasium; playing court as defined above; bleachers for spectators, pep clubs, and school band on one side of court; refreshment stand in hall;

behavior objects are basketballs, goal baskets, referee's whistle, uniforms, candy bars, popcorn, soft drinks, band instruments.

Standing pattern: consists of three behavior-milieu synomorphs, viz., basketball game, refreshment stand, and band performances.

Program (and penetration) of performers: coaches (5) arrange game, instruct players; referees (4) approve equipment, start game, enforce rules; scorers (4) keep scores and record fouls; timer (4) keeps time ball is in play and ends quarters, half, and game; players (4) play according to rules; cheerleaders (4) lead pep club and other spectators in cheers; band (4) plays music in intervals; salesmen (4) sell popcorn, candy, soft drinks, tickets. Program of spectators (2): watch, cheer, converse, eat.

Extent of molar environment devoted to Genotype 18: 14 behavior settings, 124 occurrences, 272 hours of duration; proportion of Midwest's total public environment, ERI (see p. 107), 0.64 per cent.

Extent of the behavior product of Genotype 18: 14,164 person-hours of occupancy by Midwest inhabitants, which is 1.26 per cent of the occupancy of all the town's settings by Midwest residents; 36,058 person-hours of occupancy by all persons, which is 1.92 per cent of the occupancy of all Midwest behavior settings by all persons.

Behavior settings:

18.1 Elementary Upper School Basketball Game
18.2 Elementary Upper School Basketball Game out of town
18.3 Elementary Upper School Basketball Practice
18.4 Elementary Upper School Basketball Tournament
18.5 High School Boys Basketball Game
18.6 High School Boys Basketball Game out of town including Tournament at Patton
18.7 High School Boys Basketball Practice
18.8 High School Freshman Boys Basketball Tournament out of town
18.9 High School Freshman and Sophomore Girls Basketball Game
18.10 High School Freshman and Sophomore Girls Basketball Game out of town
18.11 High School Girls Basketball Practice
18.12 High School Girls and Freshman Boys Basketball Game
18.13 High School Girls and Freshman Boys Basketball Game out of town
18.14 Midwest Town Team Basketball Game

(e) *Data Sheet of Basketball Game.* See Fig. 5.1.

Name: High School Boys Basketball Game							
Genotype # 1-3: 0 ' 1 ' 8		Genotype Commonality # 8: 9			Locus 16: 1		
B S # 4-6: 0 ' 0 ' 5		Authority System 13-14: 0 ' 1			No. of Occurr. 17-19: 0 ' 0 ' 8		
Genotype Date 7: 3		Class of Authority Systems 15: 4			Survey # 20: 5		

Occupancy Time of Town Subgroups				Max. Penetration of Subgroups		ACTION PATTERN RATINGS	
Group	No. P	Hours	OT Code	Group			
Inf	3	24	21-22: 0 ' 4	Inf	21: 1	Aes:	53: 0
Presch	12	54	23-24: 0 ' 5	Presch	22: 2	Bus	54: 1
Y S	10	87	25-26: 0 ' 6	Y S	23: 2	Prof	55: 1
O S	18	258	27-28: 0 ' 9	O S	24: 4	Educ	56: 1
Town Child	43	423	29-30: 1 ' 1			Govt	57: 1
Adol	63	1720	31-32: 1 ' 7	Adol	25: 4	Nutr	58: 1
Adult	72	1676	33-34: 1 ' 7	Adult	26: 5		
Aged	7	81	35-36: 0 ' 6	Aged	27: 2	PersAp	60: 2
Town Total	185	3900	37-38: 2 ' 3	Grand Max	28: 5		
Males	97	2264	39-40: 1 ' 9	Males	29: 5	PhysH	62: 2
Female	88	1636	41-42: 1 ' 7	Females	30: 4	Rec	63: 8
I	35	600	43-44: 1 ' 2	I	31: 4	Rel	64: 0
II	105	2236	45-46: 1 ' 9	II	32: 5	Soc	65: 6
III	42	1014	47-48: 1 ' 4	III	33: 4	MECHANISM RATINGS AffB	66: 9
N-G	3	50	49-50: 0 ' 5	N-G	34: 4	GroMot	67: 7

POPULATION (number)		PERFORMERS (number)		Manip	68: 7
Town Child	51-53: 0 ' 4 ' 3	Town Child 35-36:	0 ' 1	Talk	69: 9
Out Child	54-56: 1 ' 8 ' 7	Out Child 37-38:	0 ' 0	Think	70: 4
Total Child	57-59: 2 ' 3 ' 0	Tot Child 39-40:	0 ' 1	GEN RICH 71-72: 23	
Town Total	60-62: 1 ' 8 ' 5	Town Total 41-42:	5 ' 3		
Out Total	63-65: 9 ' 3 ' 7	Out Total 43-45:	2 ' 4 ' 9	PRESSURE RATING Children 73: 4	
Grand Total	66-69: 1 ' 1 ' 2 ' 2	Grand Tot 46-48:	3 ' 0 ' 2	Adolesc 74: 2	
Grand O.T. (code)	70: blank 71-73: 0 ' 3 ' 1	Perf/Pop 49-50:	2 ' 7	WELFARE RATING Children 75: 0	
Total Duration	74-77: 0 ' 0 ' 2 ' 4	Aver. No. 51-52:	8 ' 4	Adolesc 76: 3	
Average Attendance	78-80: 3 ' 6 ' 3			AUTONOMY RATING wtd 79: 7	

Fig. 5.1. Data sheet of behavior setting 18.5, High School Boys Basketball Game.

Auction Sale

A few behavior settings of the genotype Auction Sales, Household Furnishings and General Merchandise, occur in Midwest every year. Five glimpses of them are presented: (*a*) essential elements of the program of the genotype, (*b*) photograph of an auction in Midwest, (*c*) public notice of an auction sale, (*d*) précis of the behavior setting genotype Auction Sales in Midwest, (*e*) copy of the data sheet of one auction, as prepared for the research. (See picture facing p. 103.)

(*a*) *Program of Genotype 10 Auction Sales.* Samuel Baker, founder in 1744 of the London auction house of Messrs. Sotheby and Company, drew up a set of five conditions of sale,* four of which constitute the essential elements of auction sale programs in Midwest. They are as follows (Baker started as a bookseller; hence the reference to books):

(1) That he who Bids most is the Buyer, but if any Dispute arises, the Book or Books to be put to Sale again.

(2) That no Person advances less than Sixpence each bidding, and after the Book arises to One Pound, no less than One Shilling. [The principle that the advance in bidding is in proportion to the amount bid applies in Midwest.]

(3) The Books are in most elegant Condition, and supposed to be Perfect, but if any appear otherwise before taken away, the Buyer is at his Choice to take or leave them. [The buyer in Midwest has two minutes to examine an article; if it is not as represented by the auctioneer it may be returned.]

(4) The Books must be taken away at the Buyer's Expence, and the Money paid at the Place of Sale, within Three Days after each Sale is ended. [Articles must be paid for on the day of the sale in Midwest.]

(*b*) *Photograph of Auction Sale.* The photograph is a record of the Midwest behavior setting Household Auction Sale. It exhibits most of the behavior setting characteristics exhibited in the photograph of High School Boys Basketball Game. Differences between these behavior settings as revealed by the photographs are:

(1) The boundary of the Auction Sale is less definite than the boundary of the Basketball Game; it is not marked by a physical structure as it is in the latter setting. However, a definite boundary

* James Brough, *Auction!* (New York: Bobbs-Merrill, 1963), pp. 26–27.

Name:	*Household Auction Sales*				
Genotype # 1-3: 0·1·0	Genotype Commonality # 8: 0			Locus 16: 1	
B S # 4-6: 0·0·1	Authority System 13-14: 9·9			No. of Occurr. 17-19: 0·0·2	
Genotype Date 7: 3	Class of Authority Systems 15: 1			Survey # 20: 5	

Occupancy Time of Town Subgroups				Max. Penetration of Subgroups		ACTION PATTERN RATINGS	
Group	No. P	Hours	OT Code	Group			
Inf	2	4	21-22: 0·2	Inf	21: 1	Aes: 53: 3	
Presch	6	12	23-24: 0·3	Presch	22: 2	Bus 54: 7	
Y S	4	8	25-26: 0·3	Y S	23: 2	Prof 55: 6	
O S	5	8	27-28: 0·3	O S	24: 4	Educ 56: 0	
Town Child	17	32	29-30: 0·5			Govt 57: 0	
Adol	3	9	31-32: 0·3	Adol	25: 4	Nutr 58: 2	
Adult	47	178	33-34: 0·8	Adult	26: 5		
Aged	22	66	35-36: 0·6	Aged	27: 4	PersAp 60: 1	
Town Total	89	285	37-38: 0·9	Grand Max	28: 5		
Males	45	146	39-40: 0·8	Males	29: 5	PhysH 62: 0	
Female	44	139	41-42: 0·7	Females	30: 4	Rec 63: 3	
I	6	20	43-44: 0·4	I	31: 5	Rel 64: 0	
II	61	210	45-46: 0·9	II	32: 5	Soc 65: 5	
III	20	45	47-48: 0·5	III	33: 4	MECHANISM RATINGS AffB 66: 4	
N-G	2	10	49-50: 0·3	N-G	34: 3	GroMot 67: 6	

POPULATION (number)		PERFORMERS (number)			
				Manip 68: 3	
Town Child	51-53: 0·1·7	Town Child 35-36: 0·2		Talk 69: 7	
Out Child	54-56: 0·1·5	Out Child 37-38: 0·0		Think 70: 6	
Total Child	57-59: 0·3·2	Tot Child 39-40: 0·2		GEN RICH 71-72: 10	
Town Total	60-62: 0·8·9	Town Total 41-42: 0·7			
Out Total	63-65: 1·4·1	Out Total 43-45: 0·0·5		PRESSURE RATING Children 73: 4	
Grand Total	66-69: 0·2·3·0	Grand Tot 46-48: 0·1·2		Adolesc 74: 4	
Grand O.T. (code)	70: blank 71-73: 0·1·3	Perf/Pop 49-50: 0·5		WELFARE RATING Children 75: 0	
Total Duration	74-77: 0·0·0·8	Aver. No. 51-52: 0·7		Adolesc 76: 0	
Average Attendance	78-80: 0·9·8			AUTONOMY RATING wtd 79: 9	

Fig. 5.2. Data sheet of behavior setting 10.1, Household Auction Sale.

zone can be seen within which the standing pattern of the Auction Sale changes to the different patterns of the adjacent genotype Trafficways, and the nonpublic, family behavior settings.

(2) The shape of the standing pattern of the Auction Sale is very different from that of the Basketball Game; it resembles the pattern of iron filings in a magnetic field, whereas the pattern of the Game reminds one of a cell with partitioned, internal subparts.

(3) The synomorphy of the milieu and behavior is evident in both pictures; but the synomorphy of the Auction is in the nature of behaving inhabitants infiltrating the milieu, whereas that of the Game appears to involve tensions between salient milieu parts (e.g., the playing court) and inhabitants (e.g., spectators) that separate but position inhabitants vis-à-vis the milieu.

(4) According to the pictures, the pattern of the Auction Sale is more uniform and repetitive than that of the Basketball Game; less variety is evident in the behavior of the Auction inhabitants than in the behavior of the Game inhabitants.

PUBLIC SALE

At the John English home on north corner of Warren and Cherokee St. One block north and one block west of the Baptist Church in Midwest, Kansas.

SATURDAY, JUNE 25

STARTING AT 2:00 O'CLOCK P.M.

Electric Cook Stove	2—Stand Tables
Refrigerator	Bookcase
	Small stand
China closet	2—Dressers
Buffet	Chest of drawers
Round dining table	3—Iron beds, springs & mattresses
2—Gas heating stoves	
Ironing board	Floor Lamp
Divan	Maytag Washing Machine
2—Rocking Chairs	Few dishes and misc. items.

JOHN ENGLISH

Terms: Cash
Jack Mund, Auctioneer

Not responsible for accidents
Darlene Romney, Clerk

Household Auction Sale

High School Boys Basketball Game

(5) Some action patterns and behavior mechanisms recorded in the Auction picture differ from those appearing in the Game picture: Personal Appearance, Gross Motor Activity, and Manipulation are less in evidence in the Auction, and Verbalization is more in evidence.

(c) *Public Notice of Auction Sale.* (See announcement.)

(d) *Précis of Genotype 10, Auction Sales, Household Furnishings and General Merchandise, Midwest, 1963–64.*

Milieu: located in either residential or business area in buildings and surrounding yard areas; behavior objects are furniture, household items, tools, etc., clerk's book, cash box.

Standing pattern: consists of one synomorph, auctioning, bidding, and buying.

Program (and penetration) of performers: sellers (5) determine what is to be sold, arrange for display of articles to be sold; auctioneer (5) determines order of sale, calls for bids, sells to highest bidder; clerks (4) record bidder and accept payment. Program of other inhabitants: customers (3) bid, pay clerk, remove purchased articles, converse; onlookers (2) watch, converse.

Extent of molar environment devoted to Genotype 10: two behavior settings, three occurrences, 14 hours of duration; proportion of Midwest's total public environment, ERI (see p. 107), 0.08 per cent.

Extent of behavior product of Genotype 10: 485 person-hours of occupancy by Midwest inhabitants, which is 0.04 per cent of the occupancy of all the town's settings by Midwest residents; 1,645 person-hours of occupancy by all persons, which is 0.09 per cent of the occupancy of all Midwest settings by all persons.

Behavior settings:

10.1   Household Auction Sale
10.2   Midwest Implement Company Auction Sale

(e) *Data Sheet of Auction Sale.* See Fig. 5.2.

EXTENT OF THE MOLAR ENVIRONMENT OF MIDWEST

Behavior settings have attributes that inhere in them as whole entities, i.e., attributes that are not the sum of the attributes of their separate parts. This is clear from the defining characteristics of behavior settings and from the operations for identifying settings. We have studied a number of inherent attributes of behavior settings, namely, occurrence, duration, population makeup, penetration, action patterns, behavior mechanisms, pressure, welfare, and local autonomy. These attributes are defined in Chapter 4. They are stable; they persist even when the component parts of behavior settings, including the number and personal characteristics of the inhabitants, change within wide ranges. Because of this, these attributes of a community's behavior settings define its environmental resources for molar behavior. Public singing, teaching, worshiping, and presiding, for example, occur within a town only if behavior settings are present that have these behavior mechanisms, action patterns, and penetration zones as parts of their standing patterns; and, if such settings do exist, singing, teaching, worshiping, and presiding occur, i.e., they are produced or generated.

The nature of the whole-entity attributes of behavior settings, the sources of their stability, and theories to account for them are discussed in Chapter 6. Here we shall describe and measure the environmental resources of Midwest, in terms of the relatively permanent attributes of its behavior settings. The primary, whole-entity attribute of a behavior setting is, of course, occurring, i.e., being in existence; and this is measured for a town by enumerating its behavior settings. The first attribute to be considered is, therefore, number of behavior settings.

Number of Behavior Settings

On Thursday, April 16, 1964, at 5:00 A.M., early-rising Midwest inhabitants had immediate access to these behavior settings: Streets and Sidewalks, High School Parking Lot, Telephone Booths, Coin-operated Laundry, Park, Lake, Open Golf Play, Elementary Upper and Lower School Playgrounds, and Cemetery. These ten settings identify the public environment of the town at this time. Behavior in the town's public areas, therefore, was limited to walking, cycling, driving and parking automobiles, laundering clothes, telephoning, playing a variety of games, fishing, picnicking, inhabiting the cemetery, and to social interactions in these settings, e.g., conversing, in the case of pairs or groups of inhabitants. Four other settings were immediately accessible upon taking appropriate action at their boundaries, Hotel, Fire Station, County Jail and Sheriff's Residence, and Sherwin Funeral Home.

Between 6:00 and 6:59 A.M. five more behavior settings were added to Midwest's environment: two paper delivery routes, Pearl Cafe, Gwyne Cafe, and School Garage. And between 7:00 and 7:59 Midwest's environment was expanded by 40 behavior settings of the following genotypes: Animal Feed Mills, 1; Barbershops, 2; Beauty Shops,

1; Building, Construction and Repair Services, 3; Cleaners, Dry Cleaning Plants, 1; Clothiers and Dry Goods Stores, 1; Day Care and Home Nurseries, 1; Drugstores, 1; Factory Assembly Shops, 1; Farm Implement Agencies, 2; Fire Stations, 1; Furniture Stores, 1; Garages, 2; Grocery Stores, 2; Hallways, 2; Hardware Stores, 2; Kennels, 2; Laundry Services, 1; Lumberyards, 1; Nursing Homes, 1; Restaurants, 1; School Administration Offices, 2; School Offices, 1; Service Stations, 4; Staff Lounges, 1; Variety Stores, 1; Water Supply Plants, 1.

Midwest's environment was increased further between 8:00 and 8:59 by the addition of 75 behavior settings; these included most professional and government offices, the remaining businesses, and school classes. Seven settings became operative at 9:00 A.M.; and 43 settings became functional at various times throughout the day, for example: High School and Elementary School Visual Tests (10:00 A.M.), High School and Elementary Upper School Lunchroom (11:30 A.M.), High School Latin Class (2:00 P.M.), Boy Scout Cub Den I Meeting (4:00 P.M.), Rotary Club Meeting (6:30 P.M.), Investors Club Meeting (8:00 P.M.), Women's Late League Bowling Game (9:00 P.M.). Three settings were accessible briefly at a number of times during the day: Oil Tank Truck, Telephone Building, Kayes Rooming House.

On April 16, 1964, Midwest provided its inhabitants with 193 behavior settings. The number occurring simultaneously varied from 10 at 5:00 A.M. to 132 at 11:00 A.M. From this time until 3:00 P.M. the number fluctuated within narrow limits. At 3:00 P.M. the systematic daily closing of the environment began: the Bank closed its doors to customers at 3:00 P.M., all school class settings ceased at 4:00, most professional and government offices stopped operating at 5:00, and most businesses by 6:00 P.M. By 8:00 P.M. 20 settings were functioning, by 9:00 P.M. 17 were open, by 10:00 P.M. 13 were operating, and after midnight the 10 settings that were open at 5:00 A.M. were in operation.

On the following day approximately 175 of Thursday's behavior settings recurred, and to them were added about 20 other behavior settings. On Saturday the environment of Midwest was greatly constricted; the town lost all school-connected behavior settings and most settings under the authority of federal, state, and county governments. This reduced the town's environment to little more than one-half of its extent on Thursday and Friday. The environmental constriction was still greater on Sunday, to about one-third of the normal number of weekday settings, including 40 settings unique to Sunday.

Over the year 1963–64, to the core of 175 recurring, weekday behavior settings, others were added every day; some of these recurred at regular intervals, some recurred irregularly, others occurred only once. Together they summed to 884 behavior settings. One measure of the extent of Midwest's public environment in 1963–64 is, therefore, 884 behavior settings.

Occurrence of Behavior Settings

Another measure of the extent of Midwest's public environment is the number of occurrences of its behavior settings. This ranges for individual settings from a single occurrence to daily occurrence, i.e., to 366 occurrences in 1963–64, a leap year. For the year, the sum of the occurrences of the 884 settings is 53,376. The frequency distribution of the occurrence attribute of Midwest's 884 behavior settings is reported in Table 5.1, where the total range of the attributes is divided into seven intervals, each of which spans a common schedule of occurrence.

About one-third of all Midwest behavior settings occur only once a year; this is the most common behavior setting occurrence; examples are Elementary School District 29 Annual Electors Meeting, American Legion Memorial Day Service, Farm Bureau Board Picnic. Less than 3 per cent of Midwest's settings occur daily during most of the year (313–66 occurrences). The mean occurrence of behavior settings in 1963–64 is 60, and the median is six.

Duration of Behavior Settings

Still another measure of the extent of Midwest's environment is the duration of its behavior settings. The duration of individual behavior settings ranges from one hour to 8,784 hours; the sum of all behavior

TABLE 5.1. *Number and Per Cent of Behavior Settings within Common Occurrence Intervals, Midwest, 1963–64*

Occurrence Interval (days)	Number of Settings	Per Cent of 884	Common Schedule of Occurrence
1	310	35.1	Annual occurrence
2–12	227	25.7	Monthly for part or all of year
13–53	142	16.1	Weekly for part or all of year
54–180	89	10.1	Five days a week for school year
181–250	48	5.4	Five days a week for most of year
251–312	43	4.9	Six days a week for most of year
313–366	25	2.8	Daily for most of year

TABLE 5.2. *Number and Per Cent of Behavior Settings within Common Duration Intervals, Midwest, 1963–64*

Duration Interval (*hours*)	Number of Settings	Per Cent of 884	Common Schedule of Duration
1	66	7.5	One hour during year
2–4	225	25.4	Half of one working day during year
5–8	100	11.3	Greater part of working day during year
9–24	147	16.6	Half-days for a week
25–53	102	11.5	One hour weekly for most or all of year
54–262	89	10.1	One hour a day, five days a week for part or all of year
263–2,096	112	12.7	Eight hours a day, five days a week for part or all of year
2,097–5,124	40	4.5	14 Hours daily for part or all of year
8,784	3	0.3	Continuous for year

setting durations is 286,481 hours. The frequency distribution of the duration attribute of Midwest's behavior settings is reported in Table 5.2 by nine intervals, each of which is a commonly occurring duration. According to these data, one-third of Midwest's behavior settings occur for four hours or less in a year, and one-quarter of the settings occur for 54 hours or more. The most frequent duration of Midwest settings is 2 to 4 hours, the mean duration is 324 hours, and the median duration is 12 hours.

Ecological Resource Index (ERI)

Occurrence and duration of behavior settings are correlated; settings of greatest occurrence cannot have shortest durations, and vice versa. The Kendall tau correlation is .71 ($p < .0001$) between the occurrence and duration attributes of Midwest behavior settings. Across sets of behavior settings, number, occurrence, and duration of settings are intercorrelated. These correlations have been determined for 17 sets of behavior settings; each set includes all behavior settings receiving a high rating on an action pattern (11 sets), on a behavior mechanism (five sets), and on local autonomy (one set). The correlations (Kendall tau) within this sample of 17 sets of behavior settings are:

Number vs. occurrence
of behavior settings   .54 $(p < .003)$
Number vs. duration
of behavior settings   .41 $(p < .02)$
Occurrence vs. duration
of behavior settings   .78 $(p < .001)$

Kendall's coefficient of concordance, W, of the three measures of environmental extent is calculated by (a) converting the number, frequency, and duration of the settings in each set into per cents of the total number, frequency, and duration of behavior settings in Midwest, and (b) changing the per cents into rank orders across sets; $W = .81$ $(p < .01)$. According to Kendall, for this value of W the average of the three per cents is the best single estimate of the relative extents of parts of Midwest's environment, as indicated by number, occurrence, and duration of behavior settings in the parts. We have called this the *ecological resource index* (ERI).

There are psychological as well as statistical grounds for the ecological resource index. Molar behavior occurs in units that extend over temporal periods of various lengths. "Going to the store to shop" may endure for an hour, "Serving on the election board" may last a day, and "Getting married in the spring" may continue for months. Throughout these periods, molar activity is goal-directed within environmental circumstances that are commonly unstable. When the environment changes, compensatory alterations usually occur in the attributes, modes, and mechanisms of molar behavior so that goal-direction remains constant. Behavior setting durations and schedules of occurrence are among the unstable environmental circumstances: the store closes at 5:30 (instead of the usual 6:00), the election board remains in session till 10:30 P.M. (instead of 8:00 P.M., as announced), the County Judge's Office is, surprisingly, closed on June 6, so the marriage license cannot be obtained. Common behavior consequences of such environmental instabilities are changes in the temporal durations of behavior units: "Going to the store to shop" is carried out in short order, or it is continued to tomorrow; "Serving on the election board" is prolonged; "Getting married" is cut short or it is lengthened.

A town's molar environment consists of the behavior settings that are available for its inhabitants to enter for the pursuit of their own personal goals. The wide range and flexibility of the temporal durations of goal-directed actions means that behavior setting occurrence and duration are to a considerable degree equivalent measures of their availability.

Tomorrow's new occurrence of the store is, for many molar actions, an adequate substitute for today's half-hour curtailment of its duration; and in the case of sets of behavior settings, number, occurrence, and duration are to a great degree interchangeable. The adjustable length of molar units in response to variations in the number, occurrence, and duration of behavior settings erodes the behavioral significance of differences in these attributes of settings. Because of this, an average of the three measures of behavior setting extent is a more adequate measure than any of the measures separately.

Number (N), occurrence (O), duration (D), and ecological resource index (ERI) of behavior settings are all used to measure the extent of various environmental characteristics of Midwest. However, not all of them are presented in the case of every environmental characteristic studied; the measures used are stated in each case. When ERI is used, it will be understood that the sum of ERI for all behavior settings of Midwest is 100. The ecological resource indexes of individual behavior settings range from .04 for a one-hour, single-occurrence setting, e.g., Elementary School District 29 Annual Electors Meeting, to 1.3 for a setting occurring daily and continuously, such as Streets and Sidewalks. The largest individual behavior setting resource is greater than the smallest by a factor of 32.

VARIETY OF THE MOLAR ENVIRONMENT OF MIDWEST

The number of behavior settings in Midwest is one measure of the extent of its molar environment; it is analogous to the number of acres of land in Midwest County. The number of genotypes in Midwest is a measure of the variety of its molar environment; it is analogous to the number of types of soil in the county. A land survey of Midwest County identifies, describes, and measures the extent of each type of soil; we present analogous data for Midwest's molar environment in Table 5.3 and Appendix 2. Each genotype is identified by number and name in Table 5.3; and its extent is indicated by four measures: number (N), number of occurrences (O), hours of duration (D), and ecological resource index (ERI) of its behavior settings. (Occupancy times, which are also reported in Table 5.3, are discussed on p. 128ff.) A précis of the program of each genotype is presented in Appendix 2. The data of Table 5.3 and Appendix 2 provide a qualitative and quantitative summary of Midwest's molar environment, of the town's molar behavior resources.

Table 5.3. *Behavior Setting Genotypes of Midwest, 1963–64. Number (N),
Occurrence (O), Duration (D), Ecological Resource Index (ERI),
Occupancy Time of Town Residents (Town OT), and Occupancy
Time of All Inhabitants (Total OT) of Behavior Settings
in Each Genotype**

No.	Genotype	N	Resource Measures			Output Measures	
			O	D	ERI	Town OT	Total OT
1.	Abstract and Title Company Offices	1	305	2,500	0.52	4,054	4,606
2.	Agricultural Advisors Offices	1	250	2,040	0.43	5,206	6,559
4.	Agronomy Classes	2	4	13	0.08	72	341
5.	Animal Feed Mills	1	310	3,344	0.62	8,998	16,881
6.	Animal Feed Stores	1	307	2,736	0.55	5,857	8,127
7.	Animal Husbandry Classes	4	6	20	0.16	23	394
8.	Athletic Equipment Rooms	2	265	180	0.26	284	412
9.	Attorneys Offices	4	1,155	7,250	1.72	20,584	23,347
10.	Auction Sales	2	3	14	0.08	485	1,645
11.	Auditing and Investigating Co. Offices	1	250	2,000	0.47	2,320	2,380
12.	Automobile Washing Services	2	3	18	0.08	113	143
13.	Award Ceremonies	3	3	5	0.12	176	283
14.	Bakery Services, to Order	1	50	200	0.09	242	242
15.	Banks	1	305	1,750	0.43	26,499	36,860
16.	Barbershops	2	450	3,600	0.78	2,760	7,601
17.	Baseball Games	16	71	167	0.67	6,781	13,691
18.	Basketball Games	14	124	272	0.64	14,164	36,058
19.	Beauty Shops	1	305	3,329	0.62	13,099	15,549
20.	Billiard Parlors and Taverns	1	308	4,300	0.73	21,330	39,212
22.	Bowling Games, Ten Pins	25	725	3,204	1.77	23,862	41,214
24.	Building, Construction, Repair Services	6	1,135	9,160	2.00	14,155	19,564

* The complete, alphabetized, and numbered genotype list covers two survey years,
1954–55 and 1963–64. Genotypes that were present in the former year and absent
in the latter year are omitted from the 1963–64 list; hence the genotype numbers
are not consecutive. The occupancy times reported are from the coded values (see
Appendix 1).

Table 5.3 (*continued*)

No.	Genotype	N	O	D	ERI	Town OT	Total OT
25.	Bus Stops	2	546	42	0.42	50	1,984
26.	Card Parties	8	64	238	0.37	1,985	2,543
27.	Carnivals	1	1	3	0.04	443	575
28.	Cemeteries	1	366	1,594	0.45	1,364	1,636
29.	Charivaris	1	5	3	0.04	114	242
30.	Chiropractors Offices	1	170	864	0.24	114	914
32.	Civil Engineers Offices	1	250	2,040	0.43	3,548	6,559
33.	Classrooms, Free Time	15	2,700	1,462	2.42	8,382	18,557
34.	Cleaners, Dry Cleaning Plants	1	305	2,500	0.52	6,559	6,770
35.	Clothiers and Dry Goods Stores	1	307	3,059	0.59	14,289	21,330
36.	Club Officers Training Classes	1	1	2	0.04	21	114
37.	Commercial Classes	1	180	990	0.27	7,315	13,099
38.	Commercial Company Offices	1	250	2,040	0.43	7,000	7,200
39.	Cooking Classes	3	6	14	0.12	39	104
40.	Court Sessions, County	1	240	500	0.25	731	914
41.	Court Sessions, District	1	30	140	0.07	333	1,364
44.	Custodial Work Groups	4	64	196	0.21	346	1,459
46.	Dances	4	10	12	0.16	658	1,330
47.	Day Care Homes and Nurseries	5	409	2,527	0.74	6,771	21,825
48.	Delivery and Collection Routes	6	1,297	2,572	1.34	5,955	7,436
49.	Dentists Offices and Services	2	221	1,509	0.39	1,385	4,678
50.	Dinners and Banquets	13	29	57	0.52	927	1,939
51.	Dinners with Business Meetings	17	38	98	0.68	1,829	4,146
52.	Dinners with Dances	1	1	4	0.04	333	575
53.	Dinners with Recreational Progams	16	18	46	0.62	2,381	5,786
54.	Drugstores	1	307	3,339	0.62	30,371	39,212
55.	Educational Methods Classes	3	5	12	0.12	188	943
56.	Elections, Polling Places	4	4	40	0.16	268	427
57.	Elections, Public Posting of Returns	1	1	4	0.04	72	114
58.	Elementary School Basic Classes	13	2,250	8,945	2.94	98,251	222,119

Table 5.3 (*continued*)

No.	Genotype	N	O	D	ERI	Town OT	Total OT
			Resource Measures			Output Measures	
59.	English Classes	2	181	669	0.27	9,019	16,923
60.	Examinations, Boy Scout.	1	3	1	0.04	9	9
61.	Examinations, Standardized	5	6	16	0.19	184	361
62.	Excavating Contracting Services	3	340	1,380	0.49	1,905	2,298
63.	Excursions and Sightseeing Trips 15		18	124	0.59	2,033	3,957
64.	Factory Assembly Shops .	1	270	2,643	0.51	6,559	18,288
65.	Farm Implement Agencies	2	620	3,500	0.87	5,730	13,051
67.	Fashion Shows	2	2	7	0.08	62	113
68.	Fire Alarms and Fire Fighting	2	22	9	0.09	284	314
69.	Fire Drills	2	18	2	0.09	185	412
70.	Fire Stations	2	309	1,009	0.39	1,195	1,195
71.	Fireworks Sales Stands ..	2	18	150	0.10	155	228
72.	Floor-laying Services	1	60	400	0.12	575	914
73.	Food and Rummage Sales	7	9	42	0.27	106	198
74.	Football Games (American Football) ..	5	52	114	0.23	6,911	15,144
75.	Funeral Directors Services	1	180	46	0.16	443	731
76.	Funeral Services, Church.	3	16	17	0.13	817	1,602
77.	Furniture Stores	1	305	2,763	0.55	10,920	11,976
78.	Garages	2	620	6,600	1.23	19,856	28,578
79.	Gift Showers	3	13	28	0.12	421	511
80.	Golf Games	3	243	888	0.37	2,496	3,005
81.	Government Offices: Business, Records	9	1,997	15,124	3.35	27,386	75,140
82.	Graduation and Promotion Ceremonies	4	4	6	0.15	495	1,131
83.	Grocery Stores	3	654	7,118	1.35	66,396	83,187
84.	Hallways	4	950	8,100	1.69	26,275	71,356
85.	Hardware Stores	2	610	5,060	1.05	10,106	12,181
86.	Hayrack Rides	1	1	3	0.04	72	81
87.	Hikes and Camps	4	21	309	0.20	2,988	3,991
88.	Home Economics Classes.	5	189	521	0.37	2,526	4,115
89.	Home Economics Competitions	2	2	4	0.08	44	446
90.	Horseshoe Pitching Contests	1	1	1	0.04	9	21

Table 5.3 (*continued*)

No.	Genotype	N	Resource Measures			Output Measures	
			O	D	ERI	Town OT	Total OT
92.	Hotels	3	766	2,975	0.94	3,312	4,293
93.	Ice Cream Socials	2	2	4	0.08	113	143
96.	Installation and Induction Ceremonies	3	3	6	0.12	114	283
97.	Insurance Offices and Sales Routes	2	500	3,400	0.78	4,671	5,418
98.	Ironing Services	5	350	2,400	0.69	2,460	2,460
99.	Jails	1	366	8,784	1.29	9,037	9,237
100.	Jewelry Stores	1	300	2,200	0.48	4,054	4,606
101.	Judges Chambers	2	300	2,380	0.54	3,199	3,816
102.	Kennels	2	720	1,090	0.65	1,170	1,186
103.	Kindergarten Classes	1	97	242	0.13	2,285	3,548
104.	Knitting Classes and Services	2	45	186	0.13	412	503
105.	Land Condemnation Hearings	1	2	12	0.04	21	114
106.	Landscaping and Floriculture Classes	1	1	4	0.04	72	242
107.	Latin Classes	2	181	341	0.23	3,199	5,449
108.	Laundries, Self-Service	1	366	8,784	1.29	10,920	22,970
109.	Laundry Services	1	300	2,400	0.50	5,206	5,467
110.	Libraries	3	338	1,653	0.52	15,425	29,625
111.	Locker and Shower Rooms	2	360	70	0.31	2,368	4,722
112.	Lodge Meetings	7	137	325	0.39	2,464	6,425
114.	Lumberyards	2	600	4,700	1.00	8,141	10,412
115.	Machinery Repair Shops	4	701	2,622	0.89	6,662	11,224
116.	Mathematics Classes	1	180	660	0.23	5,857	9,929
117.	Meetings, Business	103	684	1,544	4.49	5,054	15,562
118.	Meetings, Cultural	20	136	266	0.87	4,822	7,144
119.	Meetings, Discussion	12	23	56	0.47	629	1,550
120.	Meetings, Social	3	16	31	0.13	383	578
121.	Memorial Services	1	1	1	0.04	21	30
122.	Motor Vehicle Operators Classes, Exams	2	102	178	0.16	1,708	3,240
123.	Moving Picture Shows	2	13	35	0.09	817	1,356
124.	Music Classes, Instrumental	7	800	987	0.88	5,168	8,325
125.	Music Classes, Vocal	10	875	970	1.04	13,512	29,798
126.	Music Competitions	2	3	11	0.08	179	356
127.	Newspaper Reporters Beats	1	50	100	0.08	114	170

Table 5.3 (*continued*)

No.	Genotype	N	O	D	ERI	Town OT	Total OT
128.	Newspaper and Printing Plants	1	300	2,500	0.52	9,928	10,920
129.	Nursing Homes	1	366	3,650	0.69	6,605	6,805
130.	Optometrists Services ..	1	1	5	0.04	72	242
131.	Painting Classes	1	33	100	0.07	443	914
132.	Parades	7	16	37	0.28	1,543	2,766
133.	Parking Lots	1	366	2,800	0.59	1,943	4,054
134.	Parks and Playgrounds .	4	1,464	1,808	1.28	16,514	29,670
135.	Parties	16	195	78	0.73	1,225	2,637
136.	Parties, Stag	1	1	7	0.04	170	333
137.	Pastors Studies	1	260	1,100	0.33	1,148	1,198
138.	Photographic Studios ..	5	5	36	0.20	169	387
139.	Physical and Biol. Science Classes	2	276	726	0.33	5,520	10,634
140.	Physical Education Classes	11	1,836	1,209	1.70	17,143	37,685
142.	Piano Recitals	2	2	2	0.08	50	93
143.	Picnics	8	9	31	0.31	386	982
144.	Plays and Programs	28	86	196	1.13	6,291	15,458
145.	Plumbing, Heating, and Electrical Companies ..	2	600	3,000	0.80	6,170	7,691
146.	Post Offices	1	366	3,024	0.62	13,099	19,770
147.	Programs of Band Music.	5	29	71	0.22	1,044	1,810
148.	Programs of Choral Music	6	7	16	0.23	758	3,513
149.	Psychological Research Offices	1	250	2,040	0.43	8,998	10,920
150.	Psychological Service Offices	1	250	1,008	0.31	1,124	1,364
151.	Public Speaking and Drama Competitions ..	2	2	8	0.08	123	356
153.	Real Estate Agents Offices	3	325	1,200	0.46	1,699	1,809
154.	Receptions	2	5	20	0.08	191	404
155.	Refreshment Stands	1	3	26	0.04	114	242
156.	Refuse Hauling Services .	2	210	1,020	0.33	1,018	1,018
157.	Religion Classes	42	1,707	1,573	2.83	7,657	14,329
158.	Religion Study Groups ..	25	372	431	1.23	2,602	5,382
159.	Religious Fellowship Meetings	10	95	146	0.45	731	1,565
160.	Religious Prayer, Meditation Services	6	125	146	0.32	696	2,293

Table 5.3 (*continued*)

No.	Genotype	N	Resource Measures			Output Measures	
			O	D	ERI	Town OT	Total OT
161.	Religious Worship Services	24	535	440	1.29	12,648	26,435
162.	Restaurants and Dinners for the Public	15	1,352	12,821	2.90	91,037	118,860
163.	Retarded Childrens Classes	1	42	84	0.07	443	914
164.	Roller Skating Parties	3	13	44	0.13	292	979
166.	Sales Promotion Openings	9	10	87	0.36	800	1,775
167.	Sales Promotion Parties	1	4	7	0.04	72	90
168.	Sales Routes	7	259	1,142	0.56	1,439	1,633
169.	Savings Stamp Sales Stands	1	20	5	0.05	72	114
170.	School Administrators Offices	3	650	4,060	0.99	3,549	7,975
172.	School Enrollment Periods	3	3	14	0.12	194	433
173.	School Offices	2	380	2,380	0.59	1,969	4,497
174.	School Rallies	5	47	50	0.22	598	1,066
175.	Scout Meetings	7	186	222	0.41	1,599	1,858
177.	Service Stations	4	1,408	15,780	2.87	28,408	39,281
178.	Sewing and Dressmaking Classes	3	14	30	0.13	155	227
179.	Sewing Club Meetings	2	49	286	0.14	2,399	2,479
180.	Sewing Services	2	400	2,400	0.60	2,518	2,674
181.	Sheriffs Offices	1	250	2,040	0.43	4,920	5,206
183.	Sign Painting Services	1	75	500	0.14	515	515
184.	Social Science Classes	2	270	578	0.31	6,330	12,213
185.	Soil Conservation Service Offices	1	250	2,040	0.43	1,636	2,665
186.	Solicitation of Funds	10	35	113	0.41	388	448
187.	Solicitation of Goods	1	10	70	0.05	41	170
188.	Speech Therapy Services	2	80	180	0.15	284	412
189.	Spelling Bees	1	1	2	0.04	0	242
190.	Staff Lounges	1	190	400	0.20	333	575
191.	Street Fairs	2	4	24	0.08	3,589	12,048
192.	Swimming Excursions and Classes	4	32	76	0.18	2,601	4,413
193.	Tank Truck Lines	1	300	1,000	0.34	1,124	1,124
194.	Taverns	1	308	4,450	0.75	13,099	18,288
195.	Teacher Conferences with Parents	2	2	16	0.08	113	185
196.	Telephone Automatic Exchange Buildings	1	300	600	0.30	575	914

Table 5.3   (*continued*)

No.	Genotype	N	Resource Measures			Output Measures	
			O	D	ERI	Town OT	Total OT
197.	Telephone Booths	1	366	400	0.31	333	443
199.	Timber Sales and Tree Removal Services	1	125	500	0.17	1,124	1,364
200.	Tool Sharpening Services.	1	250	650	0.27	700	710
201.	Track and Field Meets ..	7	44	130	0.31	3,511	7,739
202.	Tractor Pulling Contests .	1	1	3	0.04	575	1,636
203.	Trafficways	1	366	8,784	1.29	87,376	95,827
204.	Trips by Organizations to Visit Sick	1	8	32	0.05	170	242
205.	TV and Radio Repair Shops	1	300	2,000	0.46	2,222	2,232
208.	Variety Stores	1	305	3,060	0.58	15,549	21,330
210.	Vocational Counseling Services	1	1	6	0.04	72	170
211.	Volleyball Games	2	5	14	0.08	575	1,489
212.	Wallpapering and Painting Services	2	52	400	0.15	446	446
213.	Water Supply Plants	1	366	250	0.30	333	333
214.	Weed Inspectors Offices..	1	250	330	0.23	3	333
215.	Weddings, Church	2	5	8	0.08	284	974
216.	Weddings, Civil	1	27	7	0.06	9	21
217.	Welfare Offices	1	250	2,040	0.43	7,315	21,330
218.	Welfare Workers Classes.	1	1	6	0.04	9	114
219.	Woodworking and Machine Shop Classes.	1	180	495	0.21	2,285	4,606
220.	X-Ray Laboratories	1	1	6	0.04	41	72

These data show that there are 198 genotypes among Midwest's 884 behavior settings, i.e., 198 standing patterns of behavior and milieu with noninterchangeable programs. If the town were abandoned by its present inhabitants and resettled by people of totally alien culture, they would require 198 instruction books and/or training programs to reconstitute the behavior environment of Midwest. A person familiar with midwestern American culture is informed by the genotype list and the data on their extents of the behavior possibilities within Midwest in the same way that a soil survey tells an agronomist of the suitability of Midwest County for the production of corn, walnut trees, hay, etc.

A midwesterner would learn from the list and the appendix of four loci in Midwest for engaging in attorneys office behavior (genotype 9), i.e., in briefest outline, for giving and receiving legal advice; for initiating legal actions; for preparing legal defense in civil and criminal cases; for drawing up contracts, preparing wills, and making out federal and state income tax returns; for carrying out law-office routines. He would learn that the four behavior settings, occurring on 1,155 setting-days, for 7,250 setting-hours constitute 1.72 per cent (ERI) of Midwest's molar environment. And he would learn that there are 103 loci for engaging in business-meeting behavior (genotype 117), i.e., for participating in meetings as officer or member where organization business is transacted in accordance with Roberts Rules of Order. He would learn that the 103 behavior settings occurring on 684 setting-days for 1,544 setting-hours constitute 4.49 per cent (ERI) of Midwest's molar environment.

For students of comparative culture, the list and appendix provide data for investigating the relative diversity of towns in other cultures. For example, the town of Yoredale (population 1,300) in Yorkshire, England, had 213 behavior setting genotypes in 1963–64, and the town of Svelvik in Norway had 134 genotypes in 1960–61. Furthermore, genotype data make it possible to determine the degree of commonality of the molar environments of different communities. In the case of Midwest and Yoredale, for example, 91 fully equivalent genotypes occurred in both towns, i.e., the programs of these genotypes were interchangeable. In terms of ERI, 56.7 per cent of Midwest's environment is identical with parts of Yoredale's environment; and 58.3 per cent of Yoredale's environment is identical with parts of Midwest's environment.

The extents of Midwest's genotypes differ from 0.04 per cent (ERI) of the town's total environment (e.g., genotype 60, Boy Scout Examinations) to 4.49 per cent (ERI) of the environment (genotype 117, Business Meetings). The most extensive genotype is greater than the least extensive by a factor of 100.

The distribution of the extents of Midwest genotypes as measured by ERI is reported in Table 5.4. The dozen most extensive genotypes, with ERI, are Hallways 1.69, Physical Education Classes 1.70, Attorneys Offices 1.72, Bowling Games, Ten Pins 1.77, Building, Construction and Repair Services 2.00, Classrooms, Free Time 2.42, Religion Classes 2.83, Service Stations 2.87, Restaurants and Dinners for the Public 2.90, Elementary School Basic Classes 2.94, Government Offices: Records & Business 3.35, and Meetings, Business 4.49. These 12 genotypes (6 per cent of the total number) extend over 31 per cent of Midwest's environment.

TABLE 5.4. *Number and Per Cent of Behavior Setting Genotypes of Different Extents as Measured by Ecological Resource Index* (ERI)

ERI	Number of Genotypes	Per Cent of 198
0.04–0.49	132	66.7
0.50–0.99	41	20.7
1.00–1.49	13	6.6
1.50–1.99	4	2.0
2.00–2.49	2	1.0
2.50–2.99	4	2.0
3.00–3.49	1	0.5
3.50–3.99	0	0
4.00–4.49	1	0.5

The 20 smallest genotypes (10 per cent of the total number) extend over 0.8 per cent of the town.

Instructive equivalent and relative genotype extents are apparent in the ERI data of Table 5.3. For example, Jails, Laundries Self-Service, and Religious Worship Services are identical in extent; ERI 1.29. Music Classes, Vocal, are four times as extensive as Athletic Equipment Rooms, and twice as extensive as Dinners and Banquets; ERI 1.04, 0.26, 0.52, respectively. The relative extents of Cooking Classes, Chiropractors Offices, Sales Promotion Openings, and Jewelry Stores are 1 : 2 : 3 : 4; ERI 0.12, 0.24, 0.36, and 0.48, respectively.

ATTRIBUTES OF THE MOLAR ENVIRONMENT OF MIDWEST

The behavior settings of Midwest have overlapping attributes varying in degree of prominence. Midwest State Bank is high on the action pattern Business and low on the behavior mechanism Gross Motor Activity; High School Boys Basketball Game is low on Business and high on Gross Motor Activity. This is analogous to the situation that obtains for the soils of Midwest County. Soil of type #5 is high in silty clay loam and low in fine sandy loam; soil of type #71 is low in silty clay loam and high in fine sandy loam. The extent of fine sandy loam across all soil types is an important feature of the soil resources of Midwest County. Similarly, the extent of the action pattern Business across the behavior settings of Midwest is an important feature of the town's molar behavior resources.

Data concerning the extent of Midwest's behavior setting attributes are reported by means of graphic profiles that exhibit two degrees of prominence of the attributes: attribute *present* (rating 1+), attribute *prominent* (rating 6+). For example, the action pattern Religion is present in *some* degree in 31.2 per cent of Midwest's behavior settings, in 12.3 per cent of their daily occurrences, and in 7.1 per cent of their total hours of duration; ERI of these behavior settings is 16.9. Religion is prominent in 15.5 per cent of the town's behavior settings, in 6.1 per cent of their daily occurrences, and in 1.3 per cent of their hours of duration; ERI of these behavior settings is 7.6. These data are represented in the first section of Fig. 5.3, and data for the other action patterns are represented in successive sections of the profile. Data for other behavior setting attributes are reported in the profiles that follow; for some of these, the only data available are per cents of behavior settings with the attribute.

Measures of the extent to which an attribute is present are indications of the prevalence of the attribute *in some degree* across Midwest's environment; it is a measure of an attribute's maximal breadth of distribution. Measures of the extent to which an attribute is prominent are indications of the prevalence of the attribute as a *major resource* for the generation of behavior; we look upon them as equivalent to a soil expert's report that x per cent and y per cent of the area of Midwest County have silty clay loam and fine sandy loam as major soil components.

Action Pattern Profile

The action pattern profile is shown in Fig. 5.3; see pp. 52–66 for definitions. Action patterns are ordered in the profile by increasing ERI for action pattern present. The data show that Midwest is preeminently a social town; some interpersonal behavior occurs in all of its environment. It is a highly professional town, too; in most of the environment there are some paid leaders and functionaries (ERI, 86.1). Other action patterns that are distributed over more than half of Midwest are, with ERI in each case, Business 59.4, Recreation 59.6, Aesthetics 70.4, and Government 72.1. Religion, 16.9, is the least widely distributed action pattern, and Physical Health, 21.2, is highly restricted, too; other action patterns that occur over less than half of Midwest are Personal Appearance 28.0, Education 35.4, and Nutrition 48.5. The extent to which the most prevalent action pattern is present exceeds the extent of the least prevalent by a factor of 5.9.

The order of prevalence of action patterns when they are prominent

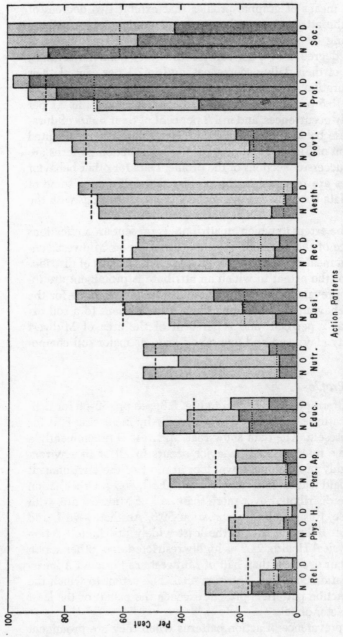

Fig. 5.3. Action pattern profile of Midwest behavior settings. Number (N), number of occurrences (O), and duration (D) of behavior settings with high ratings (dark stippling, action pattern prominent), with medium and low ratings (light stippling, action pattern present but not prominent), and with 1+ ratings (entire column, action pattern present). Ecological resource index for action pattern present (-----) and for action pattern prominent (.....). The number, occurrence, and duration of behavior settings are reported in terms of per cent of number (884), occurrence (53,376 days), and duration (286,481 hours) of behavior settings in Midwest.

is given below, with the ecological resource index and an example of a behavior setting in which the stipulated action pattern is prominent:

Physical Health, 2.6; High School and Elementary School Dental Inspection

Personal Appearance, 3.4; Home Economics Fashion Show and Tea for Mothers

Aesthetics, 4.6; District Music Festival

Nutrition, 7.0; Mrs. Lyon Home Bakery

Religion, 7.6; Presbyterian Church Worship Service

Recreation, 12.3; Girls Team Baseball (Softball) Game

Government, 15.0; County Court Session

Education, 15.3; Agricultural Extension Dairy Short Course

Business, 18.2; Household Auction Sale

Social Contact, 60.6; Halloween Dance

Professionalism, 69.4; Cabell Department Store

Midwest's action pattern resources are prominent about one-third as extensively as they are present; mean ERI for action pattern present is 54.3 and for action pattern prominent 19.6. There is a low positive correlation between the resource indexes of action pattern present and prominent, tau = .49. There are, therefore, wide differences in the extent to which particular action patterns are present and prominent; at one extreme the action pattern Aesthetics is present in some degree across most of the town (ERI 70.4), but it is prominent in a very restricted part of the town (ERI 4.6). On the other hand, Religion is not widely present across the town (ERI 16.9), but Religion is more widely prominent than Aesthetics (ERI 7.6). The action pattern Professionalism is both widely present (ERI 86.1) and prominent (ERI 69.4); this is true, too, of Social Contact, which is widely present (ERI 100) and widely prominent (ERI 60.6).

We are particularly interested in the *relative* extents of Midwest's major resources for generating five important action patterns; they are as follows, with their relative extents: Aesthetics, 1.0; Religion, 1.6; Recreation, 2.7; Education, 3.3; Business, 4.0.

The extent of the most prevalent prominent action pattern (Professionalism) is greater than the extent of the least prevalent one (Physical Health) by a factor of 26.

Behavior Mechanism Profile

The behavior mechanism profile is shown in Fig. 5.4; see pp. 66–70 for definitions. The format of the profile of behavior mechanisms is parallel to that for action patterns. The data show that Midwest is a Talking town; some talking occurs in 87.2 per cent of its environment; Thinking (ERI 76.8) and Manipulation (ERI 73.9) are also widespread; and Gross Motor Activity is only a little less prevalent (ERI 62.0). Overt Affective Behavior occurs in some degree in only half of Midwest (ERI 50.1). The extent to which the most prevalent behavior mechanism is present is greater than the extent of the least prevalent one by a factor of 1.7. The extents of the different behavior mechanisms in Midwest are more uniform than the extents of the different action patterns.

The order of prevalence of behavior mechanisms when they are prominent is given below, with ERI and an example of a setting with the stipulated prominent mechanism:

Talking, 11.2; Golden Wedding Anniversary Reception
Affective Behavior, 12.6; Methodist Church Youth Fellowship
  Halloween Party
Thinking, 22.8; District Court Judges Chambers
Gross Motor Activity, 28.6; High School Football Practice
Manipulation, 30.9; City Summer Band Practice

Midwest's behavior mechanism resources are prominent 30 per cent as extensively as they are present; mean ERI for behavior mechanism present is 70.1, and for behavior mechanisms prominent is 21.2. There is no correlation between ecological resource indexes of behavior mechanisms present and prominent. Manipulative behavior is a prominent component of almost one-third of Midwest's behavior setting programs, and some degree of manipulation extends over almost three-quarters of the town; Midwest is, above all, a manual town. At the other extreme, Affective Behavior in both degrees is relatively low in extent, being present in half of the town and prominent in one-eighth of it. Midwest is a less emotionally expressive town than it is a talking, thinking, manipulative, or muscular town. Talking, which almost covers the town, has very restricted prominence; Midwest does not make a big thing of its widespread oral behavior. Gross Motor Activity and Thinking are roughly equivalent in extent, occupying a middle place among the behavior mechanisms; both extend over about a quarter of the town in a prominent degree, and over two-thirds of the town in some degree.

The *relative* extents of Midwest's major resources for generating behavior mechanisms occur in these proportions: Talking, 1.0; Affective Behavior, 1.1; Thinking, 2.0; Gross Motor Activity, 2.5; Manipulation, 2.8.

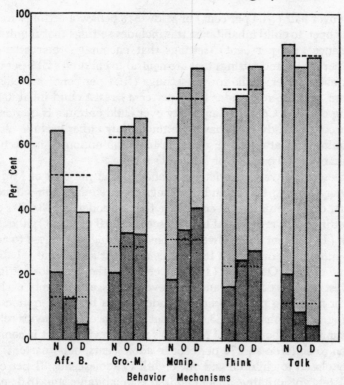

Fig. 5.4. Behavior mechanism profile of Midwest behavior settings. Number (*N*), number of occurrences (*O*), and duration (*D*) of behavior settings with high ratings (dark stippling, behavior mechanism prominent), with medium and low ratings (light stippling, behavior mechanism present but not prominent), and with 1+ ratings (entire column, behavior mechanism present). Ecological resource index for behavior mechanism present (- - - - -) and for mechanism prominent (. . . . .). The number, occurrence, and duration of behavior settings are reported in terms of per cent of number (884), occurrence (53,376 days), and duration (286,481 hours) of behavior settings in Midwest.

Pressure Profile: Children and Adolescents

The pressure profile is shown in Fig. 5.5; see pp. 70–75 for definitions. In the profile, pressure rating categories 2 (urged) and 3 (invited) are combined into the category *attendance encouraged*; and rating categories 5 (tolerated) and 6 (resisted) are combined into the category *attendance discouraged*. The per cents of Midwest's behavior settings falling in each pressure category are reported.

Just over half (54.4 per cent) of Midwest's behavior settings are completely open to child inhabitants; this includes settings that require their attendance (6.6 per cent), settings that encourage their attendance (17.9 per cent), and settings that are neutral to children (29.9 per cent); about one-quarter of the town's settings (24.4 per cent) are closed to children, and the remainder (21.3 per cent) resist child inhabitants in varying degrees. Complete authority over child entrants is exercised by 31 per cent of Midwest behavior settings: they either exclude children or require their attendance; children have the option of inhabiting or not inhabiting 69 per cent of Midwest's settings.

Adolescents have unrestricted entrance to 69.1 per cent of Midwest's behavior settings; this includes settings that require their attendance (4.6 per cent), settings that encourage their attendance (33.6 per cent), and settings that are neutral to adolescents (30.9 per cent); about one-eighth (12 per cent) of Midwest's behavior settings are closed to adolescents and almost one-fifth (18.9 per cent) resist adolescent inhabitants to some degree. One-sixth (16.6 per cent) of the behavior settings of Midwest exercise complete authority over adolescent entrants, excluding them or requiring their attendance; adolescents have the option of inhabiting or not inhabiting 83.4 per cent of Midwest's behavior settings.

In summary, about half of Midwest's molar environment is completely open to children and 70 per cent to adolescents, one-quarter is completely closed to children and one-eighth to adolescents, 31 per cent is completely authoritative about children as inhabitants, and 16.6 per cent is authoritative about adolescents.

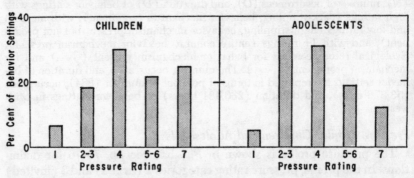

Fig. 5.5. Pressure profile of Midwest behavior settings. Per cent of behavior settings (884), with indicated strengths of pressure upon children and adolescents to enter and participate. Rating of degree of pressure: 1, entrance required; 2–3, entrance encouraged; 4, behavior setting neutral; 5–6, entrance discouraged; 7, entrance prohibited.

Welfare Profile: Children and Adolescents

·The welfare profile is shown in Fig. 5.6; see pp. 75–76 for definitions. The data and format of this profile are parallel to those for Pressure. The data indicate that the function of about one-fifth (19 per cent) of Midwest's behavior settings is the welfare of their child inhabitants (rating 1), and 4.2 per cent serve the welfare of children who are inhabitants of other settings (rating 2). Almost one-quarter (24.7 per cent) of the town's settings serve their adolescent inhabitants, and 4.5 per cent serve the welfare of adolescents in other settings. In all, 23.2 per cent of Midwest behavior settings function for the welfare of the town's children, who constitute 19.2 per cent of its population; and 29.2 per cent of the settings function for the welfare of its adolescents, who constitute 10.1 per cent of the population. Midwest's public behavior-generating resources operate for the welfare of children in almost the same proportion as there are children in the population; but the proportion of Midwest's resources devoted to its adolescents is almost three times their proportion in the population.

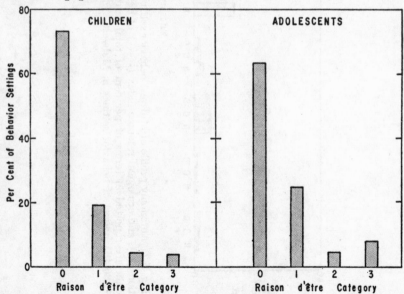

Fig. 5.6. Welfare profile of Midwest behavior settings. Per cent of behavior settings (884), with stated *raison d'être* with respect to children and adolescents: 0, unconcerned; 1, serves child (adolescent) inhabitants; 2, serves child (adolescent) inhabitants of other settings; 3, children (adolescents) serve other inhabitants.

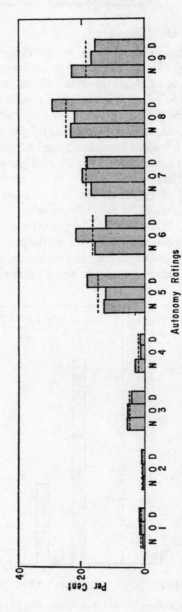

Fig. 5.7. Autonomy profile of Midwest behavior settings. Number (N), number of occurrences (O), duration (D), and ecological resource index (----) of behavior settings with specified autonomy ratings. The data are reported in terms of per cent of total number (884), frequency (53,376 days), and duration (286,481 hours) of behavior settings in Midwest.

Child performers operate 3.7 per cent and adolescents operate 7.7 per cent of Midwest settings for the benefit of other age groups (rating 3).

Local Autonomy Profile

The local autonomy profile is shown in Fig. 5.7; see pp. 76–80 for definitions. This profile provides data on the number, occurrence, duration, and ecological resource index of behavior settings with stipulated degrees of local autonomy. The data show that the loci of power for selecting performers and members, for fixing fees and prices, and for establishing policies of Midwest's behavior settings are predominantly local. Local autonomy rating and ERI are positively correlated; tau $= .83$ ($p < .001$). For autonomy rating 9 (locus within boundary of Midwest), ERI is 18.4; for ratings 7+ (locus within rural district, including town), ERI is 61.5; for ratings 5+ (locus within county, including rural district and town), ERI is 92.1; for ratings 3+ (locus within state, including county, rural district, and town), ERI is 98.5. Decisions regarding the programs of almost two-thirds of Midwest's behavior-generating resources are made within the town or immediately surrounding rural district; over nine-tenths of the decisions are made within the county.

Zones of Maximal Penetration

See Fig. 5.8 and pp. 49–52 for definitions. The per cent of Midwest's behavior settings with the specified zones of maximal penetration are reported in this profile. There is a single leader with authority over the whole setting (zone 6) in just over half (54.3 per cent) of Midwest's behavior settings; leadership is shared (zone 5) in the case of 43.2 per cent of the town's settings. Less than 3 per cent of Midwest's behavior settings are without designated leadership (zones 3 and 4).

Midwest's behavior settings are almost equally divided between those with a single authority and those with shared or no authority.

Profile of Classes of Authority Systems

The profile of classes of authority systems is shown in Fig. 5.9; see pp. 89–90 for definitions. The number, occurrence, duration, and ecological resource index of behavior settings in the different classes of authority systems are reported; the classes are ordered by increasing ecological resource index. The data show that business settings have wider authority over Midwest's environment than any other class of settings

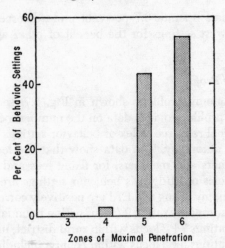

Fig. 5.8. Penetration profile of Midwest behavior settings. Per cent of behavior settings (884), with specified zones of maximal penetration.

(ERI, 40.5) and that voluntary associations and churches have least authority (ERI, 10, in each case). The authority of schools is about half as extensive, the authority of government settings (other than school settings) about two-fifths as extensive, and the authority of churches and voluntary associations about one-quarter as extensive as that of business.

BEHAVIOR OUTPUT OF MIDWEST'S MOLAR ENVIRONMENT

A behavior setting has one changeable attribute that results from the interaction of its stable, whole-entity attributes and variable properties of its actual and potential inhabitants. This is its occupancy time. Whether a Sunday school class meeting has large or small occupancy is the cumulative resultant of independent actions by separate persons. The sum of individual decisions "to go" or "not to go" and, when there, "to stay" or "not to stay" is the occupancy time. (See pp. 48–49.)

We shall see in Chapter 6 that behavior settings exert pressure, which is sometimes very strong, upon persons to enter and occupy them; and that most settings have lower and upper limits of permissible occupancy. Furthermore, the degree of occupancy of a setting has consequences for some of the more stable attributes of settings, such as their frequency of occurrence. Nevertheless, within a wide middle range of values, the

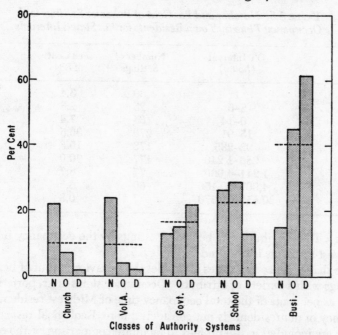

Fig. 5.9. Authority system profile of Midwest. Number (N), number of occurrences (O), duration (D), and ecological resource index (-----) of behavior settings in stipulated classes of authority systems. Data reported as per cents of number (884), occurrence (53,376 days), and duration (286,481 hours) of behavior settings in Midwest.

occupancy of a behavior setting is not an inherent, whole-entity attribute, but one that is a summation of independently occurring actions. The occupancy time of a behavior setting is not a community behavior resource; it is, rather, a behavioral product of the interaction of a behavior-generating facility of a community and its more or less compliant inhabitants.

The inhabitants of a behavior setting act in accordance with its standing pattern as long as they occupy it, i.e., as long as they are inhabitants. Person-hours of occupancy is, therefore, a measure of behavior output, i.e., of amount of behavior that is produced by a behavior setting.

The 830 Midwest inhabitants spent 1,125,134 hours in the town's behavior settings during the survey year. The time spent in particular settings ranged from 1 hour in the behavior setting Saddle Club Organizing Meeting to 87,376 hours in the setting Trafficways (streets and side-

TABLE 5.5. *Number and Per Cent of Behavior Settings with Occupancy Time by Town Residents within Stated Intervals*

OT Interval (*hours*)	Number of Settings	Per Cent of 884
1	30	3.4
2–5	25	2.8
6–14	65	7.4
15–91	270	30.5
92–285	173	19.6
286–1,240	177	20.0
1,241–4,900	77	8.7
4,901–20,150	60	6.8
20,151–87,376	7	0.8

walks). The distribution of behavior settings by the occupancy times of Midwest residents is reported in Table 5.5.

We shall analyze in a series of profiles the behavior output of behavior settings with a variety of attributes. Occupancy times are reported in all cases as per cents of the total occupancy time of Midwest residents. Occupancy of nonresidents is not considered here. Ecological resource indexes are included in the profiles to facilitate comparison of the extents of Midwest's molar behavior resources and their behavior products.

Occupancy of Behavior Settings with Different Action Patterns

The profile of action pattern occupancy time is shown in Fig. 5.10; it may be explicated by an example (see Religion, first column). Behavior settings where the action pattern Religion is prominent account for 2.4 per cent of the town's total occupancy time, and settings where Religion is present account for 11.2 per cent of the occupancy time. In each of these cases the occupancy of the town's settings with the action pattern Religion is less than would be predicted on the basis of the town's behavior setting resources for Religion. Midwest's resources for Religion in a prominent degree are, according to ERI, 7.6 per cent of the town's total behavior-generating resources; but these resources produce 2.4 per cent of Midwest's total behavior. Midwest's molar behavior resources for Religion are relatively underproductive.

The order by occupancy time and the order by ERI of behavior settings where the different action patterns are present are highly correlated; tau = .93 ($p < .0001$); furthermore, ERI and per cent occupancy do not differ greatly in absolute amount; mean ERI is 54.3 and mean per cent occupancy 59.4. It is clear that on the average the behavior settings where action patterns are present generate behavior in close relationship to the extent of their resources. The greatest deviations are found in the case of resources for Religion, which undergenerate behavior (ERI, 16.9, occupancy 11.2), for Nutrition, which overproduces behavior (ERI, 48.5, occupancy 63.4), and for Government, which overgenerates behavior (ERI, 72.1, occupancy 88.6).

Measures of the amount of behavior produced by settings where different action patterns are *prominent* are given below in terms of per cent of total occupany time; the action patterns are listed in order of occupancy time.

Physical Health	1.8	Nutrition	15.7
Religion	2.4	Education	18.8
Personal Appearance	3.2	Business	26.5
Aesthetics	3.5	Social	62.8
Government	10.9	Professionalism	86.0
Recreation	12.3		

From this list interesting relations are clear, e.g., more of the limited time of Midwest residents is allocated to behavior setting programs where Education is prominent than to settings where Recreation is prominent, more to primary Business settings than to primary Government settings, more to behavior settings where action patterns concerned with Personal Appearance are prominent than to those where Religion is primary.

The order by occupancy time and the order by ERI of behavior settings where the different action patterns are prominent are positively correlated; tau = .78 ($p < .001$); the mean ERI is 19.6 and the mean per cent occupancy is 22.2. Behavior settings where five action patterns are prominent undergenerate behavior, relative to their resources, namely, Religion (ERI 7.6, occupancy 2.4), Personal Appearance (ERI 3.4, occupancy 3.2), Physical Health (ERI 2.9, occupancy 1.8), Aesthetics (ERI 4.6, occupancy 3.5), Government (ERI 15.0, occupancy 10.9). Settings where other action patterns are prominent overgenerate behavior, namely, Education (ERI 15.3, occupancy 18.8), Business (ERI 18.2, occupancy 26.5), Nutrition (ERI 7.0, occupancy 15.7), Professionalism (ERI 69.4, occupancy 86.0), Social Contact (ERI 60.6, occupancy 62.8). The behavior settings where Recreation is prominent generate behavior in exact proportion to their resources (ERI 12.3, occupancy 12.3). The least productive action pattern relative to its resources is Religion; behavior settings where Religion is prominent generate 32

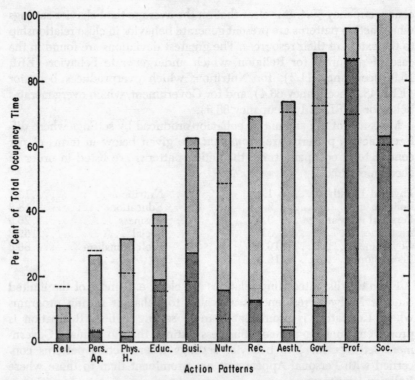

Fig. 5.10. Occupancy time of behavior settings with different action patterns. Per cent of occupancy time of Midwest residents (1,125,134 hours), which occurs in behavior with high ratings (dark stippling, action pattern prominent), with medium and low ratings (light stippling, action pattern present but not prominent), and with 1+ rating (entire column, action pattern present). Ecological resource index for action pattern present (-----) and for action pattern prominent (......).

per cent of the occupancy expected on the basis of its resources. The most productive action pattern is Nutrition; behavior settings where Nutrition is prominent generate 224 per cent of the occupancy expected on the basis of its resources.

Occupancy of Behavior Settings with Different Behavior Mechanisms

The profile of behavior mechanism occupancy time is shown in Fig. 5.11. The format of this profile is parallel to that of action patterns. Inspection of the profile shows that extent of resources for behavior mechanisms and occupany of behavior settings are closely related; this is true for behavior settings where mechanisms are present and where they are prominent. Mean ERI for behavior settings where behavior mechanisms are present is 70.1 and mean per cent occupancy is 80; mean ERI for behavior settings where mechanisms are prominent is 21.2 and mean per cent occupancy is 23.6.

Measures of the amount of behavior produced by behavior settings where different behavior mechanisms are prominent, with the per cent of total occupancy time, are given below in order of occupancy time:

> Affective Behavior 10.7
> Talking 11.4
> Thinking 28.0
> Gross Motor Activity ... 29.4
> Manipulation 38.6

The greatest proportion of the time of Midwest residents is allotted to behavior settings where Manipulation is prominent and the least to settings where Affective Behavior is prominent. Settings where Thinking is essential generate almost the same amount of behavior as those where a strong back (Gross Motor Activity) is essential.

Resources where Affective Behavior is prominent are the only ones that generate less than the amount of behavior expected, on the basis of ERI (ERI 12.6, occupancy 10.7). Resources where Manipulation is prominent generate more behavior than expected (ERI 30.9, occupancy 38.6); this is true, too, of Thinking (ERI 22.8, occupancy 28.0). Behavior settings where Talking and Gross Motor Activity are prominent generate behavior at the level expected on the basis of their resources.

Manipulation is the most extensive resource of prominent behavior mechanism in Midwest (Fig. 5.4); we see, here, that it is also the most productive resource.

Occupancy of Behavior Settings with Different Degrees of Local Autonomy

The profile of local autonomy occupancy time is shown in Fig. 5.12; it provides data on the occupancy and the ecological resource indexes of behavior settings with stipulated degrees of local autonomy.

The inhabitants of Midwest allocate 9.7 per cent of the total person-hours of occupancy of the town's behavior settings to settings that have complete local autonomy (rating 9); this is 53 per cent of the occupancy expected on the basis of the ecological resource index of these settings. The completely local settings of Midwest generate less than the expected occupancy. Almost two-thirds (62.2 per cent) of the total occupancy

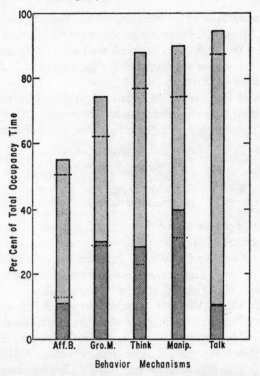

Fig. 5.11. Occupancy time of behavior settings with different behavior mechanisms. Per cent of occupancy time of Midwest residents (1,125,134 hours), which occurs in behavior settings with high ratings (dark stippling, action pattern prominent), with medium and low ratings (light stippling, action pattern present but not prominent), and with 1+ rating (entire column, action pattern present). Ecological resource index for behavior mechanism present (-----) and for behavior mechanism prominent (. . . . .).

time of Midwest's behavior settings occur in settings controlled within the town and the surrounding district (ratings 7 to 9); this corresponds almost exactly with the resource index (61.5) of these behavior settings. Settings controlled outside the district but within the county (ratings 5 and 6) produce 33.5 per cent of the town's occupany time; this, too, is in close accord with the ERI of these behavior settings (30.6). Behavior settings controlled outside the county, at state and federal levels, constitute 8 per cent of the behavior setting resources of Midwest, and they generate 4.5 per cent of the town's person-hours of occupancy.

The rank order correlation between the degree of local autonomy and the occupancy time of behavior settings is .58 ($p < .04$).

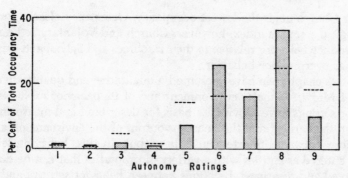

Fig. 5.12. Occupancy time of behavior settings with different autonomy ratings. Per cent of the total occupancy time of Midwest residents (1,125,134 hours) that occurs within settings with specified autonomy ratings. Ecological resource index (-----).

Occupancy of Classes of Authority Systems

The profile of authority systems is shown in Fig. 5.13. This profile reports the per cents of the total person-hours of occupancy of Midwest behavior settings by Midwest residents that occur in the different classes of authority systems. The data show that behavior settings under the authority of Business settings have the highest occupancy and those

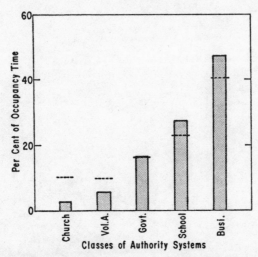

Fig. 5.13. Occupancy time of behavior settings in different classes of authority systems. Per cent of total occupancy time of Midwest residents (1,125,-134 hours) that occurs in specified classes of behavior settings. Ecological resource index (-----).

under Church aegis the lowest occupancy. Occupancy closely parallels ecological resource index; however, Church and Voluntary settings underproduce behavior relative to their resources and School and Business settings overproduce behavior.

In this chapter we have presented a qualitative and quantitative survey of Midwest's molar environment and of its behavior products. Behavior settings have provided a basis for describing and measuring the extent, the variety, and the behavior output of the environment, and of relations between its extent and its output. In this, behavior settings have entered as entities with a variety of properties that can be directly observed and measured. Relations between behavior settings and their inhabitants remain to be considered. This is a dynamic and theoretical problem; it will be treated in Chapters 6 and 7.

6

A Theory of Behavior Settings

PSYCHOLOGY IS A COMPLEX of overlapping, interdependent sciences encompassing widely disparate phenomena, methods, and theories. An explication of any part of psychology requires that the position of the part on the main dimensions of the total complex be set forth. We shall do this, briefly, for the phenomena and for the methods of ecological psychology, and in some detail for its theory. In doing this, we shall reconsider in wider contexts some of the topics already covered.

PHENOMENA OF ECOLOGICAL PSYCHOLOGY

The range of phenomena with which psychologists have dealt is encompassed by the round of events, which extends from distal objects in the ecological environment (e.g., a fly ball in a baseball game), to proximal events at receptor surfaces (e.g., the image of the moving ball on a player's retinas), to afferent, central, and efferent processes within the silent intrapersonal sector of the circuit (e.g., perceiving the ball), to molecular acts (e.g., raising the hands), and finally to molar actions that alter the ecological environment (e.g., catching the ball). The three major sectors of this unit are marked on the diagram of Fig. 6.1, namely, the ecological sector of objects and physical events that become stimuli; the organism or intrapersonal sector of receptive, central, and effector processes; and the behavioral sector of actones and achievements that occur, again, in the ecological environment. Brunswik (1955) convincingly demonstrated the value of this environment-organism-environment continuum (E-O-E arc, psychological unit, behavior unit) for identifying and appraising many facets of psychological science, and he placed representative schools and problems of psychology upon this basic unit, as shown in the figure. From this it appears that psychologists have ranged in their prospecting along the length of this mother lode of psychological ore, usually staking out claims in limited sectors; a few

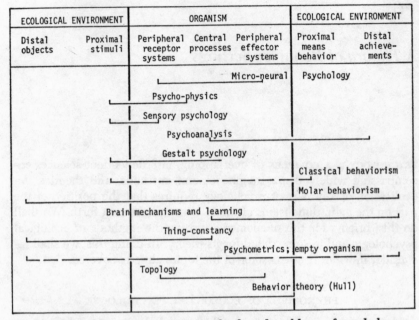

Fig. 6.1. The place of representative schools and problems of psychology on the basic psychological unit defined by Brunswik. All phenomena considered (———); only initial and terminal phenomena considered (— — —), e.g. stimulus and response.

have gone so far as to claim the whole arc from its origin to its termination as the province of psychology (e.g., Brunswik, 1955; Murray, 1959; Miller *et al.*, 1960; Zener and Gaffron, 1962).

Ecological psychology encompasses the whole E-O-E arc, and, in addition, certain phenomena within the ecological environment which transmit and shape influences that extend from the termination of one arc to the origins of others. For example, ecological psychology deals not only with events involved in a player's catching a ball in a ball game, but also with the playing field (its size and shape), the other players (their number and skill), the rules of the game, and other ecological phenomena that affect the consequences for subsequent behavior of catching or not catching the ball. The subject matter of ecological psychology cannot be represented by an arc joining, via receptor, central and effector systems, ecological objects and events on the afferent and efferent sides of persons; it must be represented by circuits that incorporate the behavior of persons with objects and events of the ecological

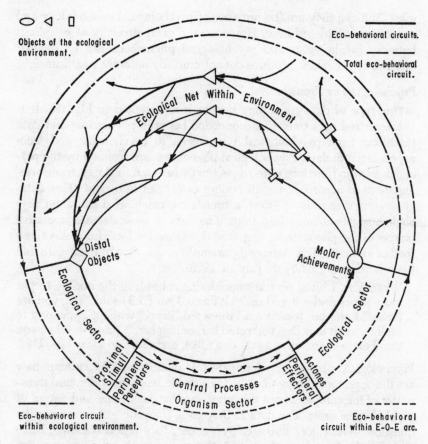

Fig. 6.2. Eco-behavioral circuits. The solid, directed lines represent the circuits; the broken lines are labeling guides.

environment to form interdependent units (Fig. 6.2). Ecological psychology is more than a behavior science; it is an eco-behavioral science.

METHODS OF ECOLOGICAL PSYCHOLOGY

The phenomena of a science occur without benefit of scientists, but the data of a science are the joint product of scientists and phenomena coupled within specially contrived data-generating systems. The characteristics of the data-generating systems of psychology, including the details of the couplings between psychologists and phenomena, are almost limitless; they are the province of psychological methodology and cannot be considered here. However, the great diversity of couplings between psychologists and psychological phenomena can be divided into two types, which produce data of crucially different significance.

Psychologists as Transducers: T Data

One type of data-generating system is represented in Fig. 6.3. It is characterized by a transitive connection between phenomena and data extending from psychological phenomena to psychologist and from psychologist to data. Psychological phenomena are scanned by the psychologist who functions with respect to them as a transducer, transforming them in accordance with coding categories into data. This data-generating system is, in effect, a translating machine; it translates psychological phenomena into data. The data it generates are operative images of the phenomena, prepared in retrievable form for storage and further analysis. Here is an early example of this type of data, gathered by Susan Isaacs (1950) on July 19, 1926:

> When Mrs. I lifted up the smouldering rubbish in the bonfire to put more paper under it and make it flame, Dan (5:2) said, "Oh, you *are* brave!" Later on, Jessica used the word "brave" without appearing to understand it and Dan corrected her, telling her, " 'Brave' is when you stand close to something you don't like, and don't go away" [p. 112].

Psychological phenomena dominate this data-generating system: they are the operators; the psychologist is a docile receiver, coder, and transmitter of information about the input, interior conditions, and output of psychological units. The data as they issue from the system answer the question, "What goes on here?"; en masse, they report the abundance and distribution of psychological phenomena with varying input, interior, and output attributes.

T data can be translated back into psychological phenomena, and the agreement between the original phenomena and the reconstituted phenomena is the ultimate test of the adequacy of T data. In actual fact, psychological phenomena are infrequently completely reconstituted in psychological science, but often intermediate steps of the first translation are reconstituted in the course of data analysis. This is the case when ratings of the content or quality of the original phenomena are made from T data. In court proceedings, behavior phenomena are sometimes reenacted from data supplied by witnesses; and most of the so-called performing arts are based upon the possibility of reconstituting behavior from coded records. See Wiener (1963) and Ashby (1956).

Here are examples of analyses of transducer data:

(*a*) (1) Two-thirds of the behavior units of the children of Midwest receive some input from persons or animals, i.e., they are social units; in three-fifths of these social units the person providing the input is an adult, and in two-thirds of the units, a female; animals are the source of 3 per cent of the social input; (2) adults dominate children in about one-third of the units to which they supply input; children dominate children in one-sixth of the units to which they provide input; (3) the input to two-thirds of the social units is compatible with the child's behavior in the unit (Barker and Wright, 1955; Wright, 1967).

(*b*) Disturbances, i.e., unpleasant disruptions in a child's experience as indicated by his expressive behavior, occur at a median rate of 5.4 disturbances per hour; half of these disturbances are evoked by adults, and 5 per cent of them are occasioned by the loss of something the child values (Fawl, 1963).

(*c*) The units of Midwest children are of shorter duration, on the average, than those of comparable Yoredale children (Schoggen, Barker, and Barker, 1963).

(*d*) Yoredale adults provide children with devaluative social inputs four times as frequently as Midwest adults (Barker and Barker, 1963b).

This data-generating system provides information about psychological phenomena in terms of transformations made by a psychologist; the transformations constitute the psychologist's *only* contribution to the data of the system. By using the psychologist as a transducer only, and not as operator, this system produces data that denote a world the psychologist did not make in any respect; they signal behavior and its conditions, *in situ*.

Data-generating systems of this type have no commonly accepted name, so we have called them, after the psychologist's role, *transducer data systems*, and, for short, T systems. We shall also use the terms transducer methods, or T methods, and transducer data, or T data.

Psychologists as Operators: O Data

The other type of data-generating system is represented in Fig. 6.4. In it there are two kinds of couplings between psychological phenomena and psychologist: in addition to functioning as transducer, as in the first type, the psychologist is coupled into the psychological unit as an operative part of it, regulating input, and/or influencing interior conditions, and/or constraining output. The psychologist dominates this system; as operator, he sends messages via the unit to himself as receiver and transducer. The data answer the question, "What goes on here, under the conditions of input, interior conditions, and output that I impose?" Here is an example of this type of data from the Stanford-Binet test, 1937 revision (11-year level—Terman and Merrill, 1937, p. 269):

Psychologist as Operator: What do we mean by *courage*?

Subject: Do something you don't want to do 'cause you're afraid of getting hurt.

The crucial feature of this data-generating system is that by becoming involved as an operator in the units he is investigating, the psychologist

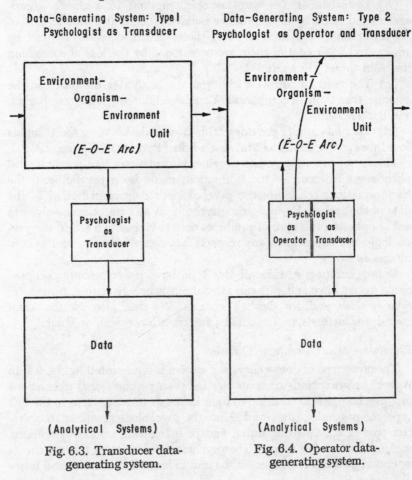

Data-Generating System: Type I
Psychologist as Transducer

Data-Generating System: Type 2
Psychologist as Operator and Transducer

Fig. 6.3. Transducer data-
generating system.

Fig. 6.4. Operator data-
generating system.

achieves control that allows him to focus upon segments and processes of particular concern to him, via data that refer to events that he, in part, contrives.

Data-generating systems of this type may be appropriately called, after the psychologist's role, *operator data systems*; we shall also use the terms O method and O data. These are, in essence, experimental methods. We have not used the term, however, because of its common restriction in psychology to operations carried out in laboratories, and hence its exclusion of clinical methods, a restriction and an exclusion that do not apply in any degree to O methods.

Ecological Methods

We are now in a position to locate ecological psychology with respect to this methodological dichotomy as follows: *ecological psychology is a transducer science; in it, research psychologists function as sensors and transducers; its data record behavior and its conditions* in situ.

One may well ask: Why should ecological psychology be satisfied with less than the most rigorously defined and controlled data-generating arrangements? Why bother with the role of transducer? Similar questions have been asked in connection with a motley class of methods variously called field methods, naturalistic approaches, observational techniques. These methods have not infrequently been judged and found wanting. It is commonly said of them that almost anything they can do, experiments can do better. Their advantage is said to lie in their relative simplicity, which makes them useful as rough-and-ready methods for reconnoitering new problems. It is not easy to evaluate these judgments about the untidy class of methods to which they refer, but it is clear that they do not apply to transducer and operator methods.

The models show that T data refer to psychological phenomena that are explicitly excluded when the psychologist functions as operator. Indeed, the primary task of the psychologist as transducer is carefully to preserve phenomena that the psychologist as operator carefully alters, namely, psychologist-free units. We have to say, therefore, that what T methods do, O methods cannot do at all: O methods cannot signal behavior and its conditions unaltered by the system that generates the data.

The models show, too, that O data refer to phenomena that psychologists as transducers explicitly exclude, namely, psychological units arranged in accordance with the curiosities of the psychologist. The primary task of the operator is to alter, in ways that are crucial to his interests, phenomena that the psychologist as transducer leaves intact. It should be noted, however, that an investigator can sometimes select T data that refer to psychological units with the particular attributes in which he is interested. We have to say, therefore, that what O methods do, T methods usually cannot do at all, or can do less efficiently: T methods cannot focus so clearly upon the particular events within psychological units that interest the investigator.

That the data which psychologists produce as operators and as transducers differ in ways that are of fundamental significance for the science is obvious in concrete cases. Take intelligence, for example. Millions of reliable and valid intelligence tests have been administered, scored, and reported, thus providing a vast store of O data, for psychologists are strong operators in test situations, supplying input ("What do we mean by courage?"), regulating interior conditions ("Work carefully; speed is not important"), and constraining output ("Underline the correct response"). These data provide basic information about intellectual functioning within test-score generating systems, and about intellectual processes and their constants: about IQ, about general factors, about verbal factors, etc. But this great and successful scientific assault upon the problem of intelligence has provided almost no information about the intellectual demands the environments of life make upon people, and how people respond to the "test items" with which they are confronted in the course of living. The science of psychology provides virtually no information about the intelligence of people outside of data-generating systems operated by psychologists.

Or take frustration as another example. Experiments have provided basic information about the consequences for children of frustration, as defined and contrived in the experiments, e.g., Barker *et al.* (1941). But Fawl, who did *not* contrive frustration for his subjects, but studied it in transducer records of children's everyday behavior, reported (Fawl, 1963, p. 99):

> The results ... were surprising in two respects. First, even with a liberal interpretation of frustration fewer incidents were detected than we expected.... Second ... meaningful relationships could not be found between frustration ... and consequent behavior such as ... regression ... and other theoretically meaningful behavioral manifestation.

In other words, frustration was rare in children's days, and when it did occur it did not have the behavioral consequences observed in the laboratory. It appears that the earlier experiments simulated frustration very well as defined and prescribed in theories, but the experiments did not simulate frustration as life prescribes it for children.

The conclusion is inescapable that psychologists as operators and as transducers are not analogous, and that the data they produce have fundamentally different uses within the science. One may contend that the phenomena denoted by T data are unimportant, or that they are not psychology. One may argue that O data refer, potentially at least, to more fundamental, universal, invariant psychological processes than T data. But, however the phenomena denoted by T data are classified and evaluated, they comprise a realm of phenomena forever inaccessible via O data. The data that psychologists produce as transducers are not horse-and-buggy versions of the data they produce as operators. If one wishes to know, for example, such information as the duration of behavior units, the sources of social input, or the frequency of disturbances, only T data will provide the answers.

This state of affairs is most surprising in view of the situation in the old, prestigeful sciences that psychology so admires and emulates in other respects. In these sciences, the quest for the phenomena of science as they occur unaltered by the techniques of search and discovery is a central, continuing task; and the development of techniques for identifying entities and signaling processes without altering them (within organisms, within cells, within physical systems, and within machines) is among the sciences' most valued achievements. Handbooks and encyclopedias attest to the success of these efforts. We read, for example, that potassium (K) ranks seventh in order of abundance of elements, and constitutes about 2.59 per cent of the igneous rocks of the earth's crust; that its compounds are widely distributed in the primary rocks, the oceans, the soil, plants, and animals; and that soluble potassium salts are present in all fertile soils (*Encyclopædia Britannica*, 1962). The fact that there is no equivalent information in the literature of scientific psychology (about playing, about laughing, about talking, about being valued and devalued, about conflict, about failure) confronts psychologists with a monumental incompleted task. This is the task of ecological psychology, and for it T methods are essential.

DISCOVERY OF BEHAVIOR SETTINGS

At the Midwest Field Station we were confronted with the practical problem of what to record, as transducers, and what to count as analysts of T data. What *is* a unit of a person's unbroken behavior stream? This question is ordinarily settled very shortly: a unit is an answer to a questionnaire item (the investigator's item); it is a trial on a maze (the investigator's maze); it is the completion of a sentence (the investigator's sentence). But when an investigator does not impose *his* units on the stream of behavior, what are *its* units?

Molar Units of Individual Behavior

When observers approach subjects' behavior streams as sensors and transducers, signaling in literary language what they see, structural-dynamic units are always found. Here is an example of transducer data denoting two such units; these data refer to five-year-old Maud Pintner in Clifford's Drugstore in Midwest on December 5, 1950. The two units occurred successively and they occupied, together, less than one-half minute.

> Maud sat at the fountain waiting to order the treat her mother had promised her. On the stool next to Maud was her two-year-old brother, Fred; her mother sat beside Fred.

> 2:48 p.m. From her jeans pocket Maud now took an orange crayon. She brushed it across her lips as if it were a lipstick.

> Maud then leaned over, sliding her arms along the counter, as she watched a man serve a strawberry soda to his blond, curly-headed, three-year-old girl.
> Maud seemed fascinated by the procedure; she took in every detail of the situation.

The analyst titled these units *Pretending to Use Lipstick* and *Watching Girl Eat Soda* (Barker and Wright, 1951a, p. 248).

Herbert Wright and others have studied these units, called behavior episodes, in great detail and have discovered some of their attributes (Barker and Wright, 1955; Barker, 1963b; Dickman, 1963; Wright, 1967), namely, constancy of direction, equal potency throughout their parts, and limited size-range. Like crystals and cells that also have distinguishing attributes and limited size-ranges, behavior episodes have as clear a position in the hierarchy of behavior units as the former have in the hierarchies of physical and organic units. It is impressive that empirically identified behavior episodes should agree so well with Brunswik's independent, theoretical formulation of the E-O-E unit of psychological phenomena.

The discovery of behavior episodes, and the accumulation of evidence that they are fundamental molar units of the behavior stream, solved the problem of what to record as transducers, and what to count as analysts of T data; but we were then confronted with the questions: What is the environment of behavior episodes? How are episodes and their environments related? The search for answers to these questions led to the discovery of behavior settings. And during the search we learned some things about naturally occurring behavior and its environment that must be reported.

Environment of Molar Behavior Units

On the basis of Brunswik's model of the E-O-E arc and of operator data-generating systems, we expected congruence between environmental inputs and behavior episodes. We expected behavior episodes to march along single file preceded by inputs from the environment and terminating in outputs to the environment, as they do when psychologists are operators in psychophysics experiments (stimulus with response), in intelligence tests (problem with attempted solution), and in polling interviews (question with answer). We expected to be able to predict with some accuracy from ecological inputs to behavioral outputs. But we were wrong.

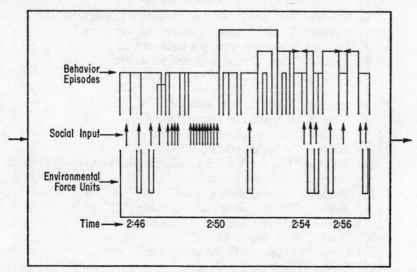

Fig. 6.5. Behavior setting: Cliffords Drugstore. Maud Is Treated to Ice Cream Cone.

According to T data, behavior episodes do not move along Indian file, but, rather, one, two, or three abreast quite irregularly. In the upper row of Fig. 6.5, the structure of Maud's behavior in the corner drugstore is represented in terms of episodes. During this 11-minute period Maud engaged in 25 episodes of behavior, including *Pretending to Use Lipstick* and *Watching Girl Eat Soda*. Ten of these episodes occurred singly, but 15 of them occurred simultaneously with other episodes, and in one case there was a triple overlap, namely, *Eating Ice Cream Cone, Watching Girl Eat Soda* (on another occasion), and *Trying to Get Her Mother's Attention*. This segment of behavior is by no means atypical; in over 200 hours of children's specimen records, including 18 day-long records, 73 per cent (median) of Midwest children's episodes overlap simultaneously with one or more other episodes (Barker and Wright, 1955).

Furthermore, according to T data, units of environmental input and units of behavior are not regularly coupled and congruent, and prediction of behavior episodes from ecological inputs is poor. The 26 social inputs Maud received in the drugstore, as they occurred in temporal order, are listed below (the source of the input is given first in each case).

(1) Mother: "We'll all go to the drugstore."
(2) Mother: "Not now; you're not having a comic now."
(3) Mother: "Leave things [Christmas cards] alone."
(4) Mother: "Come on now, get your coat off."
(5) Mother: "Maud, come back and sit down."
(6) Mother: Pushes Maud toward the stool.
(7) Mother: "Now you sit here."
(8) Mother: "What do you want, Maud?"
(9) Mother: "*Oh*, you don't want a *soda!*"
(10) Mother: "No, you don't get a soda."
(11) Mother: "What do you want?"
(12) Mother: "You don't want a soda. Besides you wouldn't drink it if you had it."
(13) Mother: "Do you want a coke?"
(14) Mother: "Do you want an ice cream cone?"
(15) Mother: "*Do* you want an ice cream cone?"
(16) Clerk: "What flavor, Maud?"
(17) Clerk: "Vanilla, that's the white one."
(18) Clerk: "Don't eat Fred's cone."
(19) Mother: "Come on. Get your coat on, Maud."
(20) Mother: Refuses Maud's whispered request.
(21) Fred: Snatches Maud's coat.
(22) Clerk: "Hi, Maud," as she ruffles Maud's hair.

(23) Mother: "Come on."
(24) Mother: Pushes Maud toward her coat.
(25) Fred: Asks Maud for gum (from gum machine).
(26) Mother: Urges children from store with words and motions.

Like the stem of an incomplete sentence that might be given Maud in a test, each social input could serve as the origin of a congruent behavior episode, or of a limited range of episodes, in Maud's behavior stream. For example, there is only one action by Maud that is congruent with the mother's first input, "We'll all go to the drugstore," namely, the episode *Entering Drugstore*. But there are a number of congruent completions for the eighth input "What do you want, Maud?," e.g., *Asking for Ice Cream Cone, Asking for Coke, Asking for Soda,* etc. A social input has a requiredness, or direction, with respect to the behavior of the receiver, and the person who provides an input selects the one from those available to him that he presumes, on the basis of experience or primitive theory, is most likely to be effective, i.e., to initiate an episode he desires for the recipient. The ensuing behavior of the recipient provides an immediate test of the correctness of the presumption. Here are some of the social inputs to Maud in the drugstore, the episodes that are congruent with them, and the actual, ensuing episodes.

Social Input	Congruent Episode	Ensuing Episode
(1) We'll all go to the drug-store.	Entering Drugstore	Entering Drugstore
(2) Not now; you're not having a comic now.	Returning Comic to Shelf	Looking at Comic (continuation of ongoing episode)
(6) Pushes Maud toward stool.	Moving Toward Stool	Moving Toward Stool
(8) What do you want, Maud?	Choosing Treat	Choosing Treat (soda)
(9) *Oh,* you don't want a *soda!*	Choosing Different Treat	Choosing Treat (continuation of ongoing episode)
(21) Fred snatches Maud's coat	Retrieving Coat	Ignoring Fred

Three of these inputs were the origin of congruent behavior in Maud's behavior stream and three were not. In all, about one-third of the social inputs to Maud in the drugstore elicited congruent behavior episodes from her, namely, inputs 1, 6, 7, 8, 15, 17, 20, 25, 26. In large samples of children's behavior about one-half of all social inputs elicit congruent behavior episodes (Barker and Wright, 1955; Hall, 1965).

This finding was discouraging to us; it seemed to foreclose the possibility of discovering lawfulness between ecological inputs and behavior episodes within the undisturbed stream of behavior. Although it is true according to Brunswik that the prediction of behavior from input can only be made "probabilistically," predictions with only 50 per cent accuracy are not impressive. And although it is true, too, that the associates of children are not scientists with explicitly formulated theories to guide them, they are nonetheless experts in the art of providing effective inputs, and it does not appear likely that their record can be greatly improved.

Despite this evidence, we were loath to abandon the precision of exactly identified, reliably described, and correctly enumerated inputs and episodes; they satisfied the first requirement of good research, replicable data. They seemed to provide firm ground in an unfirm region. So we persisted in the effort to find lawfulness between inputs and behavior episodes. We were encouraged in this by the theories and traditions of psychology which affirmed that lawfulness, if it existed, would be discovered between points of the E-O-E arc. These traditions and theories strongly indicated that ecological phenomena more remote than the distal objects at the origins and terminations of the arcs were not lawfully related to behavior.

For one thing, it is generally agreed that the nonsocial, ecological environment does not demand behavior, that it enters psychology only as permissive, supportive, or resistive circumstances, and that the intrapersonal sector of the E-O-E arc is the arbiter of what will be received as stimuli and how it will be coded and programmed before it emerges as output (Lawrence, 1963; Ratliff, 1962; Schoenfeld and Cumming, 1963). It is true that a language is often used that implies at least a triggering function for the ecological environment: events in the environment are said to stimulate, to evoke, to instigate behavior. And the fact that data are usually provided by data-generating systems that are designed by the investigator to stimulate gives support to the language used. The simple fact is, however, that to function as a stimulus, an environmental variable must be received by the organism. So in most psychological thinking, nonsocial ecological occurrences at the afferent end of the E-O-E arc are assumed (a) to be indifferent to their ends via the arc, and (b) to be endowed with directedness and purpose only within the intrapersonal sector. This view was supported by our findings: if predictions of children's behavior episodes from *social* inputs, which can at least demand that they be received, are only 50 per cent accurate, predictions from nonsocial inputs will surely be much lower.

Another reason for limiting ecological phenomena to those at the origins and terminations of E-O-E arcs is the fact that beyond these points the regress within the environment is without limit. Where does one draw the line? Where does the environment of the episode "Maud ... watched a man serve a strawberry soda ... to his girl" end? With the man, the soda, and the girl? With the stools on which they sit and the counter from which they eat? With the whole fountain area? The whole drugstore? The town of Midwest? Or beyond?

Yet another reason for not venturing beyond the limits of the E-O-E arc is found in the fact that psychologists who have considered the problem have found the ecological environment on the afferent side of the person to be unstable, and to exhibit at best only statistical regularities. This has confronted students of the total E-O-E arc with the difficult problem of making precise derivations and predictions on the basis of unstable, disordered independent variables. In consequence, the selective and organizing powers of the intrapersonal segment of the arc—which to quote Leeper (1963, pp. 387–88), "yield relatively stable effects out of the kaleidoscopically changing stimulation they receive"—have claimed the greatest efforts of psychologists. It is here that the problems of perception and learning fall. This is one reason for the predominance of operator data-generating systems in psychological science: in this way the investigator is able to impose order upon the ecological input and so bypass the problem.

Finally, the concepts that are adequate for ecological phenomena are inadequate for, i.e., incommensurate with, psychological phenomena. The theories and concepts of psychology are not today reducible to those of biology, physics, and sociology, and for this reason only probabilistic, empirical relations can be discovered between variables of psychology and those of other sciences.

Here were four barriers to including within psychological science more of the ecological environment than that which lies along the E-O-E arc. These barriers rested upon certain conceptions of the ecological environment, namely, that it is without direction with respect to behavior, that it is infinite, that it is disordered, and that it is conceptually incommensurate with the intrapersonal sector of the E-O-E arc.

Texture of the Environment

Despite these barriers, however, we continually made field observations, *pari passu* with our systematic effort to record the stream of behavior and its immediate ecological inputs, which called attention to the significance for behavior of the more remote environment. We were overwhelmed with individual behavior. The 119 children of Midwest with whom we were most concerned engaged in about 100,000 episodes of behavior each day, over 36,000,000 in a year. We had to sample this universe, and we found that our sample was improved if, in addition to using the usual stratification guides (age, sex, social class, race, education), we sampled behavior in such divergent places as drugstores, Sunday school classes, 4-H Club meetings, and football games. When we recorded behavior episodes in a representative sample of such Midwest locales, the variability of the episodes was greater than when we recorded in restricted locales. Variety of behavior episodes was positively related to variety of ecological sampling areas.

Related to this were three observations made during the making of day-long records of children's behavior and situation. (*a*) The characteristics of the behavior of a child often changed dramatically when he moved from one region to another, e.g., from classroom, to hall, to playground; from drugstore to street; from baseball game to shower room. (*b*) The behavior of different children within the same region was often more similar than the behavior of any of them in different regions. The behavior of John and Joe was frequently more similar in a Boy Scout meeting than the behavior of John (or Joe) in a Scout meeting and in a Sunday school class. (*c*) There was often more congruence between the whole course of a child's behavior and the particular locale in which it occurred than between parts of his behavior and particular inputs from the locale. This is shown in Maud's case. Although, as we have seen, Maud did not conform to most of the social inputs she received in the drugstore, the whole course of her drugstore behavior was actually harmonious with and appropriate to the drugstore setting: Maud had her treat and enjoyed it, she did not read the comics or handle the Christmas cards to an appreciable extent, she *did* sit on the stool, she did *not* have a soda, she *was* uncoated, recoated, and shepherded from the store in a generally agreeable way. Maud's relation to her environment was quite different in the large and in the small. If we look upon this as a test of Maud's drugstore behavior, we see that Maud failed most of the items, but she passed the test.

All of this was evidence to us that the ecological environment beyond distal objects of the E-O-E arc is in some way causally implicated in behavior. When we finally looked beyond immediate, discrete ecological inputs to the behavior streams of individual persons, it was not difficult to identify larger environmental units. Schoggen identified such a unit, which he called an environmental force unit (EFU), i.e., an action by an environmental agent toward a recognizable end state for a person (Schoggen, 1963). The unity of an EFU comes from its constancy of direction with respect to the person upon whom it bears. EFU's often involve series, or programs of discrete inputs. The EFU's acting upon Maud in the drugstore are represented in the third row of Fig. 6.5. Her 25 behavior episodes and the 26 social inputs she received in the drugstore are encompassed by the eight EFU's. Each EFU includes at least one social input, and the large, inclusive EFU (Maud to Have Treat at Drugstore) has 18 social inputs. Schoggen discovered many interesting facts about EFU, but for us the most interesting finding is that a person's behavior is more frequently responsive and conforming to intact EFU than to separate components of EFU. Simmons and Schoggen (1963) and Hall (1965) found that half of the EFU's whose initial inputs elicited unresponsive or unconforming behavior elicited responsive and conforming behavior at the terminal EFU input. Here was documentation of what we observed in general, namely, that conformity between the environment and behavior is more frequent over long than over short segments of the behavior stream.

Some basis for this is found in Schoggen's data, which showed that EFU's usually endure longer than episodes. This means that if behavior episodes are used to mark off parts of the environment, the resulting segments are usually not unitary parts of the environment, or multiples thereof, but random fragments. To use such fragments in an investigation of the relation between environmental input and behavioral output is, therefore, analogous to studying the relation between the slope of four-foot sectors of a roadway (the circumference of a wheel) and the speed of vehicles over them. According to these findings, the environmental component of a psychological unit, that is, the originating object or event within the E-O-E arc, is often not the environment of the unit.

These observations and fieldwork experiences led us to look again at the environment as it exists before being received within the E-O-E arc. Egon Brunswik wrote (1957, p. 5) in this connection:

> Both organism and environment will have to be seen as systems, each with properties of its own, yet both hewn from basically the same block. Each has surface and depth, or overt and covert regions . . . the interrelationship between the two systems has the essential characteristic of a "coming-to-terms." And this coming-to-terms is not merely a matter of the mutual boundary or surface areas. It concerns equally as much, or perhaps even more, the rapport between the cen-

tral, covert layers of the two systems. It follows that, much as psychology must be concerned with the texture of the organism or of its nervous processes and must investigate them in depth, it also must be concerned with the texture of the environment as it extends in depth away from the common boundary.

We raised the question: What is the texture of the environment?

The physical and biological sciences have amassed almost limitless information about the environment, and some of it bears directly and univocally upon the issues before us. The three environmental attributes we shall mention have been independently affirmed and reaffirmed by many observing techniques and instruments. They are far removed from the human observer; most of them are properties of the environment as revealed directly by photographic plates and recording instruments. They are elementary facts.

(a) *Order in the Preperceptual Environment.* The environment as described by chemists, physicists, botanists, and astronomers is not a chaotic jumble of independent odds and ends, and it has more than statistical regularity. It consists of bounded and internally patterned units that are frequently arranged in precisely ordered arrays and sequences. The problem of identifying and classifying the parts of the environment, i.e., the taxonomic problem, is very great, but the problem is not, primarily, to bring order out of disorder. On the contrary, its first task is to describe and explain the surprising structures and orders that appear in nature: within carbon atoms, within DNA molecules, within developing embryos, within oak trees, within baseball games, within nations, within solar systems; and to account for the occasional absence of order and organization, in atomic explosions, in cancerous growths, and in social disorder.

It must be noted, however, that order and lawfulness are by no means spread uniformly across the nonpsychological world; not every entity is lawfully related to every other entity. The preperceptual world is not one system but many, and their boundaries and interconnections have to be discovered.

A frequent arrangement of ecological units is in nesting assemblies. Examples are everywhere: in a chick embryo, for example, with its organs, with the cells of one of the organs, the nucleus of one of the cells, the molecular aggregates of the nucleus, the molecules of an aggregate, the atoms of one of the molecules, and the subatomic particles of an atom. A unit in the middle ranges of a nesting structure such as this is simultaneously both circumjacent and interjacent, both whole and part, both entity and environment. An organ—the liver, for example—is whole in relation to its own component pattern of cells, and is a part in relation to the circumjacent organism that it, with other organs, composes; it forms the environment of its cells, and is, itself, environed by the organism.

(*b*) *Direction and Purpose in the Preperceptual Environment.* Most units of the ecological environment are not directionless in relation to their parts. They are, rather, self-regulated entities (or the products of such entities) with control circuits that guide their components to characteristic states and that maintain these states within limited ranges of values in the face of disturbances. Some of the strongest forces in nature and some of the most ubiquitous patterns of events are found within ecological units: in atomic forces and in developmental sequences of organisms, for example. The new understanding of cybernetic processes makes it no longer necessary to be skeptical of the reality of target-directed systems within the ecological environment.

There are mutual causal relations up and down the nesting series in which many environmental entities occur; the preperceptual environment is made up of systems within systems. An entity in such a series both constrains and is constrained by the outside unit that surrounds it and by the inside units it surrounds. This means that entities in nesting structures are parts of their own contexts; they influence themselves through the circumjacent entities that they, in part, compose. A beam determines its own strength by its contribution to the structure into which it is built; a word defines itself by its contribution to the meaning of the sentence of which it is a part.

(*c*) *Incommensurability in the Preperceptual Environment.* The conceptual incommensurability of phenomena which is such an obstacle to the unification of the sciences does not appear to trouble nature's units. The topologically larger units of nesting structures have, in general, greater variety among their included parts than smaller units: an organism encompasses a greater variety of structures and processes than a cell; a river is internally more varied than a tributary brook. Within the larger units, things and events from conceptually more and more alien sciences are incorporated and regulated. In an established pond, a great variety of physical and biological entities and processes are integrated into a stable, self-regulated unit; the component, interrelated entities range from oxygen molecules to predacious diving beetles. This suggests that within certain levels of nesting structures conceptual incommensurability of phenomena does not prevent integration and regulation. In fact, self-regulated units with widely varied component entities are, in general, more stable than units with lesser variety (Ashby, 1956).

In summary, the sciences that deal with the entities and events of the nonpsychological environment directly, and not propaedeutically as in psychology, do not find them to be chaotic or only probabilistic in their occurrences. It is within the physical and biological sciences that the greatest order and lawfulness have been discovered, an order and lawfulness much admired by psychologists. These sciences do not find environmental entities to be without direction with respect to their component parts, and conceptual incommensurability does not prevent the integration and lawful regulation of ecological entities.

At this point we began to take seriously the discoveries of the biophysical sciences with respect to the preperceptual environment, and we sought to identify and examine the environment of behavior as they identify and examine the environments of physical or biological entities: of animals, of cells, of satellites. This was neither more nor less difficult than it is to identify and examine the habitat of an animal, the organ in which a lesion occurs, or the planetary system within which a satellite orbits. The investigator first identifies the animal, the lesion, the satellite, or, in this case, the behavior unit with which he is concerned, and he then explores the surrounding area until he identifies and then examines the circumjacent unit. It was by this process that we discovered behavior settings.

Boundary between Entity and Environment

Within any included-inclusive series the question arises where, precisely, each entity in the series ends and its environment begins. The answer to this question has been implied in the discussion above. The operations for identifying the boundary of an entity will now be given. If one moves from a position within any phenomenon and reaches a point at which the concepts and theories that account for the phenomenon cease to apply, but beyond which there are, nevertheless, linked (interdependent) phenomena, this point marks the boundary of an entity; phenomena beyond this point which co-vary with the entity are parts of its environment.

By way of example, the movements of an automobile and towed trailer are highly interdependent, and the interdependence can be explained in terms of the concepts and theories of strength and direction of physical force. At no point in the continuum between automobile and trailer do the laws governing the movements change; automobile and trailer are, therefore, a single entity; the automobile is not a part of the trailer's environment, and vice versa. On the other hand, the movements of two unattached automobiles driven on the highway as a caravan are also interdependent; but the interdependence is mediated by psychological laws, i.e., the laws of the perceptual-cognitive-motor systems of the drivers, rather than by the physical laws that govern the interdependences within each automobile. The cars in the caravan are, therefore, separate entities; each is a part of the other's environment. It should be noted that a towed vehicle may correspond less closely to the movements of the towing vehicle than does the following car in a caravan; the distinction between entity and environment has nothing to do with closeness of coupling.

Similarly, the movements of cattle trucks on the roads of Kansas and the price of beef on the Chicago market co-vary in spite of the fact that as one goes from the trucks to the cattle market the relevant concepts and theories change utterly, e.g., from miles per hour to market demand, from pressure on pistons to pressure on prices. These paired explanatory concepts are irrelated, discongruous, incommensurable; it is impossible to derive miles per hour from market demand. Yet the cattle trucks move in response to market demand, so the market constitutes a part of the environment of the cattle trucks.

Still another example may be helpful. The tenth ring of a 50-year-old tree does not form the environment of the ninth ring; the outer ring is governed by the same laws as the inner ring; they are parts of the same entity. On the other hand, some parts of a tree do form the environment of other parts; the branches and foliage on the windward side of a tree protect and are therefore coupled with those on the sheltered side, but the coupling is not by direct biological connections; it is, rather, via the meteorology of the region and the dynamics of air movement around obstacles. Men form the environment of men in this way, too; they have no direct psychological links. William James (1950) referred to this when he remarked that no gulf is more complete in nature than that which separates man from man. Such gulfs occur between all entities that are coupled by phenomena on disparate conceptual levels.

The relationships that define entity and environment within ecological psychology are: inside-outside (the environment is outside the entity), independent-interdependent (the environment and the entity are interdependent), and commensurate-incommensurate (the linkage between environment and entity is via incommensurate laws). The last defining relation means that the identification of an entity and its environment, and the locus of the boundary between them, is relative to the concepts in terms of which the phenomena are comprehended; what is entity and what is environment change as understanding of the governing laws changes.

Entity and Component Parts

It is unfortunate that there is no name for the inside of an entity that is equivalent to the name of its outside, i.e., *environment*; for within an entity there are, also, interdependent phenomena on incommensurable conceptual levels. The links between an entity and its interior are in some ways more mysterious and impressive than the links with its environment. A substance, we say, is composed of its molecules, and its molecules of its atoms; the cells "make up" the organism. Yet the laws of atoms, molecules, and cells are not the laws of molecules, compounds, and organs. Nevertheless, these interior, incommensurate phenomena often seem to be more closely coupled with the state of an entity than the external phenomena that comprise its environment. The latter influence the entity, but are not often seen as required for its continuance. Phenomena within an entity, on the other hand, appear not only to be coupled with the entity, but to be essential for its occurrence. So the problem of how the essences of an entity can differ from the entity with respect to their laws has arisen as a crucial issue, as a paradox, even. Yet this is so clearly true that we have an axiom for it, namely, that an entity (a whole) is different from the totality of its interior elements (its parts). It is an interesting question why the reverse relationship, namely, that the component parts are different from the whole entity which they comprise, is not also considered worthy of an axiom. Interrelations between attributes of entities and attributes of their interiors, e.g., between a person's energy and his endocrines, between an animal's learning and his brain chemistry, between motor achievements and musculature, have been extensively explored; but the nature of the connections are as empirical and probabilistic as those with the environment.

Within the framework of these definitions of entity, environment, and interior elements, the problem of ecological psychology is clear. In terms of the eco-behavioral circuit (Fig. 6.2), the organism sector (the person) constitutes the entity; the receptor, central, and effector systems are its interior parts, and the remainder of the circuit within the circumjacent behavior setting constitutes the ecological environment. A task of ecological psychology is to discover how the properties of the person and the properties of the ecological environment are related, *in situ*.

THEORY OF BEHAVIOR SETTINGS

Until someone is able to present an overarching system of concepts within which such presently alien phenomena as those of perception and economics, of motivation and technology are subsumed, it has been generally believed that we have to be content with probabilistic predictions across the person-environment boundary on the basis of empirical correlations. But the question will not down: is it not possible that variables of the person may enter *upon their own terms* yet in a systematic and derivable way, into the structure and processes of the environment, and vice versa? Are there not theories that can account for some of the consequences of the interaction of conceptually irrelated phenomena, while these phenomena continue to operate according to their own disparate laws?

Thing and Medium

We believe we can find some help here in a remarkable paper by Heider (1959) written over thirty-five years ago. In this paper, entitled "Thing and Medium," Heider anticipates some of the concepts of cybernetics and information theory, and applies them to certain psychological problems in ways that are still ahead of the time. We cannot do justice to this important contribution here; we can only present our interpretation of the points we consider relevant to the present discussion.

Heider considered the problem of perception at a distance within the afferent, ecological sector of Brunswik's unit (Fig. 6.1). He attempted to distinguish the attributes of objects of perception from the attributes of the phenomena that mediate between them and the perceiving organism. Heider pointed out, as is still largely true, that only processes at the receptor surface and within the organism had previously been considered. He noted that distal objects in the ecological environment at the origin of the perceptual unit have different physical properties from the particles that intervene between these objects and the receptor surface. He called the former objects *things* and the latter entities *media*. There are two essential differences between things and media. First, things are intrinsically constrained; they are relatively independent of extrinsic events for their forms and for the distribution of energy within them. A stone is an example of an object with strong thing-characteristics; its firm, strong unity seems to issue from its own intrinsic nature. Media, on the other hand, are to a high degree extrinsically constrained; they are relatively dependent upon extrinsic events for the form and energy characteristics they exhibit; media are docile. The pattern of light reflected from a stone is an example of a manifold of entities with high medium-character; the pattern of the light is determined in some way by the extrinsic, alien stone.

The second differentiating feature of thing and medium is this: things are unitary; their parts are *interdependent*. A change in one part of a thing causes a change in the next part, and is in turn caused by a change in a previous part. The variety they can exhibit is limited by intrinsic arrangements. A medium manifold is a composite; there is no inherent internal arrangement of its elements; its parts are independent; changes in every part of a medium manifold are caused separately from the outside. The variety a perfect medium can exhibit is not limited; it is versatile.

With these characteristics, things become centers of the causal texture of the world, and their influence is carried in the form of *spurious thing-units* (to use Heider's term) by media whose forms and processes are molded by things. It is the stable, but imposed, spurious thing-units that make it possible for a medium to represent a thing at a distance.

It is important to note, however, that each *single* element of even the most docile medium has its own structure and dynamics; thus light has its own unique reflection characteristics with respect to a stone. A single quantum of light represents itself rather than the stone from which it is reflected. However, a *manifold* of light rays, each reflected independently of the next ray, but with the same index with reference to the surface of the stone, does *as a pattern* represent the stone. Other things being constant, the number of parts of a set of entities, its differentiation, is directly related to the medium-quality of the set. A single building block has poor medium-qualities, a set of 50 blocks is a better medium, and a set of 500 building blocks is much better yet: it is a medium by means of which many different structures can be built.

We begin here to get a glimpse of a lawful relationship between phenomena on different conceptual levels that is more than an empirical probability. The laws governing the behavior of stones and light cannot now be subsumed within the same system. But the consequences of their interaction are univocally lawful, and beyond this some of the conditions determining this lawfulness begin to appear. Perception of objects is possible because the same spurious thing-unit is imposed upon the light manifold by the object every time they meet, and this spurious unit, in turn, has a univocal impact upon the medium of the receptor system at the periphery of the organism, which is governed by still other laws. To function in this way, light and receptor systems must have the properties of media.

The physical sciences are replete with instances in which small particles on one level provide the medium for quite different phenomena on other levels, while continuing to function according to their own laws. A jet of gas issuing under pressure from a puncture in a container has its own characteristics of velocity and diameter, yet the gas molecules within the stream continue to behave according to their own laws, of thermal agitation, for example.

Every entity, as we shall use the term, stands between phenomena on its outside and on its inside which belong to different orders of events from the entity itself and from each other. An entity forms the environment of the coupled, alien phenomena within it; and it, along with other entities, forms the inside manifold of a superordinate alien, environing unit.

In summary, we may say with respect to coupled phenomena that have a thing-medium relationship: (*a*) The medium complies with the forces of the thing; if it is a perfect medium it does not resist, counter, or enhance them; it is docile; it is receiver and transducer so far as the pattern of forces from the thing is concerned. (*b*) The thing imposes its pattern upon the medium via its own driving forces; if it is a perfect thing, it is unaltered by the medium; it is operator and effector so far as the pattern within the medium is concerned. (*c*) Although we may be unable to discover the mechanism by which thing-forces are changed into medium-patterns, e.g., how an idea is transformed into words, still, if the docility of the medium can be measured *on its level,* and if the driving forces of the thing can be measured *upon its level,* it may be possible to account in *some* degree for the consequences that occur across unbreachable boundaries. We have tried this in connection with a particular medium-thing, entity-environment relation, namely, persons and behavior settings.

Thing-Characteristics of Behavior Settings

An essential property of a thing is a firm, strong unity and stability relative to the medium manifold with which it is coupled. One source of the stability of behavior settings is a balance between many independent forces that bear upon them. Some of the forces issue from the larger community, some are intrinsic to the setting itself, and some originate

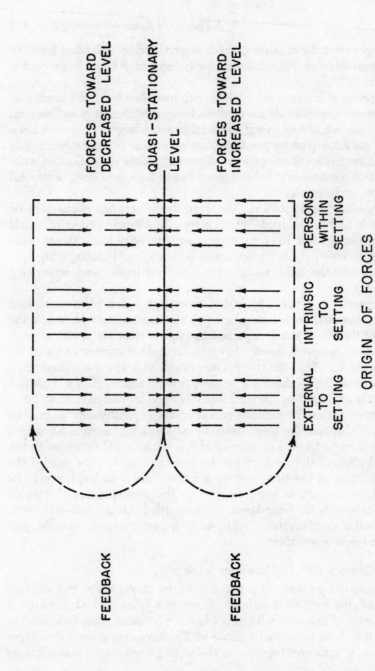

Fig. 6.6. Pattern of forces maintaining stable level of behavior settings.

within the individuals who populate the setting. Here, for example, are influences pressing a school class toward an increase and toward a decrease in functional level, i.e., toward larger and toward smaller enrollment; toward a "better" and toward a "poorer" curriculum.

Influences from the larger community:
Toward an increase in functional level
There is a waiting list of applicants for enrollment.
Parents urge a richer curriculum.
Toward a decrease in functional level
It is the policy of the school board to limit the number of students per class.
A richer curriculum is expensive, and there is great resistance to higher taxes.
Influences intrinsic to the behavior setting:
Toward an increase in functional level
With a few more pupils, three suitable reading groups arranged on the basis of ability would be possible; with the enrollment as it is, the two groups have ranges of reading ability that are too great.
The classroom is equipped for showing moving pictures.
Toward a decrease in functional level
The room is overcrowded as it is.
The course of study is so full there is no time to use moving pictures.
Influences from individuals within settings:
Toward an increase in functional level
The teacher wants to extend her influence to as many children as possible.
The girls of the class want to have a costume party.
Toward a decrease in functional level
The teacher is dead tired at night as it is, without any more pupils.
The boys of the class refuse to cooperate upon a costume party.

Such forces as these operate on every setting. The situation can be represented as in Fig. 6.6. The multiple, balanced forces assure that the functional level of a behavior setting is more stable than most of its parts or conditions singly, that its standing pattern of extra-individual behavior-and-milieu is firmer than the behavior tendencies of the persons who inhabit it.

Essential to the strong unity and intrinsic integrity of behavior settings are their homeostatic regulatory systems; these are described below. Altogether it is understandable that behavior settings can have the requisite stability and permanence to operate as things relative to the people who inhabit them.

Medium-Properties of People

People conform in a high degree to the standing patterns of the behavior settings they inhabit. Schoggen (1963) and Hall (1965) found that children comply with about 75 per cent of the social inputs from environmental force units, and conformity to the total patterns of behavior setting forces is much greater than this. While it is possible to smoke at a Worship Service, to dance during a Court Session, and to recite a Latin lesson in a Machine Shop, such matchings of behavior and behavior settings almost never occur in Midwest, although they would not be infrequent if these kinds of behavior were distributed among behavior settings by chance. When an individual's behavior deviates from the pattern of a setting, it is usually symptomatic of mental or physical illness, or of the normal incapacities of extreme youth and age. People, en masse, are remarkably compliant to the forces of behavior settings; in this respect the relation between people and settings is like that between medium and thing in Heider's sense.

Of all behavior setting components, the inhabitants exhibit the most varied patterns and perform the most varied functions. Rooms do not readily expand, tables do not hurry, typewriters do not make speeches. But people quickly spread out or crowd together, speed up or slow down, write or talk. People are versatile. In Midwest, for example, they produce such varied spatial-temporal structures as those involved in a Band Concert, a Prayer Service, a Football Game, a Spelling Bee, a Dance, an X-Ray Laboratory, a Horse Show, a Piano Recital, a Telephone Booth, a Wedding. It is not unusual for a particular person to participate in this whole range of standing patterns. Do atoms, cells, and bricks exhibit a greater variety of patterns within molecules, organs, and buildings? The versatility of people within behavior settings is striking; in this respect, too, people and behavior settings are related as media to things.

However, no medium manifold is perfect. Two sources of inadequacy have been mentioned. First, the separate parts (components or elements) of every medium have their own structure and dynamics and there are interdependencies between the elements of most media (p. 160). For these reasons, different media resist thing-forces to different degrees, and therefore differ in their adequacy as media. A region of sand dunes represents the pattern of wind currents much better than a field of lava; each component of the dunes (each grain of sand) is less resistant to the force of the wind and less closely tied to its neighbors than each component of a lava field (each lava cinder). Second, a source of the adequacy of a medium resides in the number of its parts, a medium-attribute that is irrelevant to the parts separately. There is an optimal number of elements in the medium manifolds of most thing-medium systems below which the adequacy of the medium declines. The inadequacy of a medium due to too few elements may be absolute; three lines will not form a hexagon no matter what the pressure (but they will easily form a triangle). The inadequacy may not be absolute, but it may be so great that a distorted pattern of the thing occurs whatever the thing-force may be; a 900-word vocabulary will produce a distorted version of *Hamlet* even with the utmost effort and care on the part of the translator. The inadequacy may not distort the pattern of the thing, but it may require unusual effort to impose the pattern upon the medium; a patient, energetic, skillful two-finger typist may be able to transcribe in ten hours a recorded interview that a skillful, ten-finger typist can transcribe in 45 minutes.

We have considered behavior settings (as things) and their inhabitants (as media) in the light of the second source of medium-inadequacy: too few elements. This provides one basis for making derivations from behavior settings to their inhabitants, and vice versa. We have made use of this source of variation in medium-quality because the optimal number of inhabitants of a setting, and the deviations from it, are able to be determined with more precision than variation in medium-quality owing to differences in the personal attributes of the inhabitants.

Thing-medium relations between phenomena are frequently modified via feedback loops from media to things. The feedback may strengthen the forces of the thing: when my pen (medium) fails to write, feedback from the pen where it impinges upon the paper via my perceptual system instigates me (thing) to press harder, and the pen writes. Or the feedback may change the pattern of the thing-forces: when my vocabulary (medium) is inadequate to express an idea (thing), feedback from my tongue-tied state modifies the idea so that I am able to express it, in less precise form perhaps. Both kinds of feedback may occur simultaneously, e.g., feedback may modify the thing in ways that strengthen its forces vis-à-vis the medium. This simultaneous occurrence takes place in the case of behavior settings and their inhabitants.

Undermanned Behavior Settings

It has been pointed out that one of the attributes of a behavior setting is its firm, strong unity and stability relative to the medium manifold with which it is coupled (p. 161). Because of this stability, a decrease in the number of inhabitants of a behavior setting below the number required for optimal medium-quality does not, within limits, change the program or the standing pattern of the setting. This has inevitable consequences for the inhabitants. Behavior setting constancy under these circumstances necessarily changes the environment of the inhabitants. We shall call behavior settings with fewer than optimal inhabitants *undermanned* settings. We can make the following derivations with respect to them, in comparison with optimally manned behavior settings:

(*a*) the number of forces acting upon each inhabitant of undermanned settings is greater because the same forces are distributed among fewer inhabitants;

(*b*) the range of directions of the forces upon each inhabitant is greater because fewer inhabitants mediate the same field of forces.

From this it follows that the inhabitants of undermanned behavior settings, in comparison with those of optimally manned settings,

(*a*) are more active within the settings,

(*b*) in a greater variety of actions.

These consequences are exemplified in a baseball game played by eight-man teams on a regulation nine-man field according to the official rules. If the center fielders of the teams are missing, the left fielders are the recipients of forces normally terminating in center field in addition to the usual left-field forces; the right fielders receive some center-field forces, too; and a few marginal center-field inputs will be added to the usual quota of the second basemen. In fact, in the distribution of the center fielder's environmental "load" among the remaining team members, something will be added to each player's usual share. So, with the regular nine-man number and constellation of forces distributed among fewer players,

(*a*) the number of forces-per-player will be greater, and each member will play "harder"; and

(*b*) each player will be pressed in more directions; he will engage in a greater variety of plays.

This is a paradigm of all behavior settings with fewer than the optimal number of inhabitants.

It is important to note that this paradigm holds only within a limited range of population decrement, for at some point in the course of population decrement a behavior setting is transformed into a different setting. Baseball may be transformed into "work-up."

CONNECTIONS BETWEEN BEHAVIOR SETTINGS AS THINGS AND THEIR INHABITANTS AS MEDIA

The word *force* is used to indicate any kind of directed connection between thing (T) and medium (M), between behavior settings and inhabitants. In addition to force, some other terms are used to convey the same idea, e.g., M is *determined by* T, T *provides input to* M, T is *the source of the causal texture of* M, M is *dependent upon* T, T *influences* M, M is *controlled by* T, T *imposes upon* M, T *transmits to* M, there is *feedback from* M to T, T *expends effort upon* M, M *communicates with* T, T *induces* pattern in M. Directed connections may convey energy, information, order of events, and they may involve many kinds of phenomena: mechanical, physiological, electrical, perceptual, thermal, and social, for example. We use a number of terms, too, to designate particular connections between behavior settings and inhabitants, e.g., circuit, route, channel, action, mechanism.

There are many phenotypic expressions of the primary behavior derivations, and secondary resultants arise from the nature of the particular circuitry that connects behavior settings as things with their inhabitants as media. Some of this circuitry is open to inspection.

Circuits That Join Behavior Settings and
Inhabitants via the E-O-E Arc

Goal Circuits. Within a behavior setting there are routes to goals that are satisfying to the inhabitants. A setting exists only so long as it provides its inhabitants with traversable routes to the goals their own unique natures require. In a behavior setting of the genotype Baseball Games, for example, the pitcher may achieve satisfactions by striking out batters, the umpire by earning $25, the concessionaire by selling many hot dogs, and the hometown fans by cheering the team to victory. Unless a sufficient number of the inhabitants of a baseball game are at least minimally satisfied, they will leave the setting, or will not return on another occasion, and the setting will cease.

Action along a goal route is reported in the italicized parts of the following record of the behavior of Mary Chaco, age one year, ten months, within the Midwest behavior setting Chaco Home, Mealtime (Barker and Wright, 1953). The Chaco family was seated around the kitchen table eating the noonday meal. Mary had been eating heartily.

12:10 p.m. *Mary indicated that she wanted something else to eat by a string of words apparently unintelligible to her parents.*

She pointed toward the table, raising her voice slightly as she spoke. Her father started to give her some meat.

She became more upset than before. The meat definitely was not what Mary had in mind.

Her voice changed to a whine. She kicked her feet against the foot rest on the high chair. She was demanding and impatient.

By lifting each dish in turn, Mr. and Mrs. Chaco found it was jello salad that Mary wanted.

Her father immediately gave her a helping of salad.

Mary seemed pleased, but took this as a matter of course.

The essential features of this connection between inhabitants and behavior settings are (*a*) perception by inhabitants of goals within settings and of paths to them, (*b*) achievement of goals, and (*c*) satisfaction of needs via consumatory behavior.

Program Circuits. The program of a behavior setting has been defined and discussed previously (see p. 80); it is the schedule of eco-behavioral occurrences that comprise a particular behavior setting. The complete program of a setting is usually stored within the inhabitants of penetration zone 5/6; parts of it are stored within the inhabitants of more peripheral zones. The program is sometimes written out, as in the lesson schedule of a teacher or the agenda and operational guides (e.g., Roberts' Rules of Order) of a business meeting.

Actions along a program circuit are reported in the italicized parts of the following record of Steven Peake, seven years, nine months, within the Yoredale behavior setting Upper Infants Music Class (Barker *et al.*, 1961). The class was assembled for rhythm band in the Cooking and Woodworking room of the school; it was taught by Miss Rutherford. The workbenches were pushed against the wall and the piano brought to the center of the room. The children stood in a semicircle around the piano.

1:52. *Miss Rutherford said, "All find your places."*

Steven stood next to Herbert.

Steven exchanged a playful remark with Oran.

Miss Rutherford started to give out the instruments, castanets, triangles, tambourines, drums, and cymbals.

Cymbals were suspended from straps by which they were held.

1:53. Miss Rutherford handed a cymbal to Steven.

When all the instruments had been distributed, Miss Rutherford asked that, first of all, they all stop talking.

Steven struck his cymbal lightly with his fist.

The essential features of this circuit are knowledge of the program by one or more inhabitants of the setting and actions by them that control the order of the occurrences that characterize the program.

Deviation-countering Circuits. This is one of two types of circuits by which a behavior setting is maintained with its routes and goals intact. Deviation-countering circuits are involved within a behavior setting of the genotype Grocery Stores, for example, when the proprietor corrects a clerk's errors in pricing articles, when an employee repairs a broken shelf, when the refrigerators operate and keep their contents cool. Inaccurate employees, broken shelving, and warm refrigerators are grocery store components that destroy and/or block routes to goals (profits, wages, groceries) that various inhabitants achieve; they are deviancies, or inadequacies, that must be dealt with if the program of a grocery store is to be carried out and the inhabitants are to achieve the satisfactions they seek. One way of dealing with inadequacies or deviancies of this kind is to correct or counter them. Actions on deviation-countering circuits are reported in the section of the record of Steven Peake immediately following that reported above:

> *Miss Rutherford went to the corner of the room and came back with a number of long red pencils and said, "We are short some parts of the instruments so we have to make do with these, to improvise." Each child who had a cymbal was given a pencil to tap it with.*

> Steven took his pencil matter-of-factly.

A few minutes later another deviation-countering action occurred.

> *1:54. Miss Rutherford said to the class, "You never saw a real band playing all slumped over, leaning on things; now let's stand up straight."*

This circuit is characterized by (*a*) the sensing by inhabitants, or other components of a behavior setting, of conditions that prevent carrying out the program of the setting (achieving goals, in the case of inhabitants), and (*b*) actions to *counteract* the interfering (deviant, inadequate) conditions.

Vetoing Circuits. These circuits are identical with deviation-countering circuits except that the behavior setting deviancy is not countered;

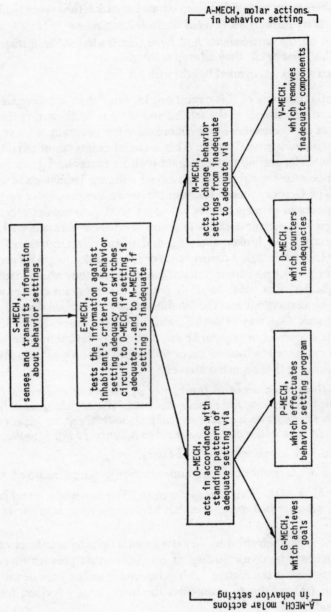

Fig. 6.7. Parts of the control unit of an E-O-E circuit.

rather, the deviant component is eliminated. Vetoing circuits are involved when an inaccurate employee is not corrected, but fired; and when a broken shelf is not repaired, but discarded. Action along this circuit is exhibited in the behavior toward Oran of Miss Rutherford at a later point in the record of Steven Peake; the vetoing action is italicized.

2:10. Miss Rutherford commanded, "Pick up your instruments."
Oran was acting silly.
Miss Rutherford said, "Evidently you do not wish to play in our band, Oran." She took his cymbal away from him and gave it to Selna Bradley. The string holding her triangle had broken and she was without an instrument. *Miss Rutherford put Oran on the far side of the piano away from the class.*

Vetoing circuits have as essential features (*a*) the sensing by inhabitants, or other components of a behavior setting, of conditions that prevent carrying out of the program of the setting (achieving goals in the case of inhabitants); and (*b*) actions by inhabitants to *eliminate* the interfering (deviant, inadequate) conditions.

Regulation of Circuits That Join Behavior Settings and Inhabitants via the E-O-E Arc

Within each of the circuits there is a control unit consisting of a behavior setting sensing mechanism (S-MECH), which senses and transmits information about behavior settings; an executive mechanism (E-MECH), which tests information about settings against inhabitants' criteria of behavior setting adequacy and switches the circuit to the appropriate goal program, deviation-countering, or vetoing channel. The control unit is located within the organism sector of the E-O-E arc; it is, in fact, the mechanism of the TOTE unit identified by Miller, Galanter, and Pribram (1960) as the fundamental unit of behavior. The parts of the control unit, their functions, order of functioning, and the alternative circuits they provide within the E-O-E arc are shown in Fig. 6.7; and examples of control units in operation, as described or implied in the illustrative records (pp. 168–71) of the circuits, are presented in Table 6.1.

Details of the location and connections of the parts of the control unit within the eco-behavioral circuit (Fig. 6.2) are diagrammed in Fig. 6.8. The distal objects of Fig. 6.2 are the behavior setting components of Fig. 6.8. Their state is sensed by S-MECH and transmitted to E-MECH where it is compared with the inhabitant's criteria of an adequate set-

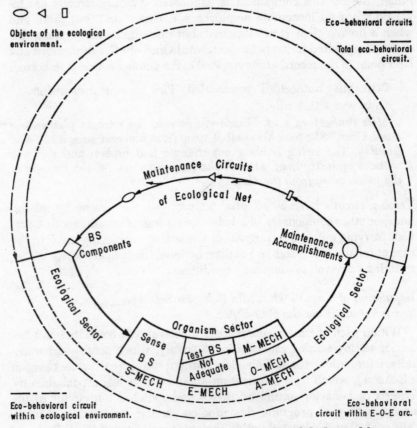

Fig. 6.8a. Eco-behavioral maintenance circuits. The solid, directed lines represent the circuits; the broken lines are labeling guides.

ting in view of his goal aspirations and program plans. If the state of the setting does *not* pass the inhabitant's test for these actions, i.e., if there is a discrepancy between the state of the setting as sensed by S-MECH and the inhabitant's standard of an adequate state for his goals and plans, the eco-behavioral circuit is routed via M-MECH into maintenance channels (Fig. 6.8a). The strength of the influence along the circuit from E-MECH to M-MECH is proportional to the discrepancy between the sensed state of the setting and the inhabitant's standard. The consequences of these changes within the setting recur as input to S-MECH, and if there is still discrepancy the circuit is again channeled to M-MECH, and further alterations occur in the setting. But if the behavior setting

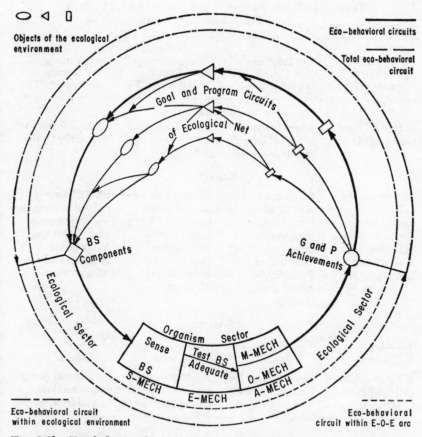

Fig. 6.8b. Eco-behavioral operating circuits. The solid, directed lines represent the circuits; the broken lines are labeling guides.

components pass the inhabitant's test within E-MECH, the circuit is routed via O-MECH into operating channels, becoming goal or program circuits.

The control units of the eco-behavioral circuits function in connection with particular behavior settings; however, they need not refer to total settings. The mechanism governing the temperature within the refrigerator of the Grocery Store tests and maintains no other components of this setting; similarly, in a setting of the genotype Business Office the testing and maintenance mechanisms of the janitor may operate with respect to a part of the setting only (the order and cleanliness of the office); the janitor may be insensitive to other components of the set-

TABLE 6.1. *Examples of the Operation of Control Units in Four Eco-behavioral Circuits*

Goal Circuit via Mary (M)	Program Circuit via teacher (T)	Deviation Countering Circuit via teacher (T)	Vetoing Circuit via teacher (T)
S-MECH			
M sees BS component (salad)	T sees BS components (children and instruments)	T sees BS component (slumping children)	T sees BS component (silly Oran)
E-MECH			
BS component judged adequate for M's need; circuit switched to G-MECH via A-MECH and O-MECH	BS components judged adequate for intention of carrying out BS program; circuit switched to P-MECH via A-MECH and O-MECH	BS components judged inadequate for BS program; circuit switched to D-MECH via A-MECH and M-MECH	BS component judged inadequate for BS program; circuit switched to V-MECH via A-MECH and M-MECH

A-MECH			
O-MECH		M-MECH	
G-MECH	P-MECH	D-MECH	V-MECH
M's goal achieved and consumed; M satisfied	Lesson plan effectuated; intention carried out	Inadequacy of components (slump) corrected	Inadequate component (Oran) removed from setting

ting. This points to the important fact that behavior settings do not necessarily exist *qua* behavior settings for their inhabitants; an inhabitant need only apprehend that a particular goal is inaccessible, or that a part of a behavior setting program cannot be carried out, unless certain alterations are made in particular components of the setting. The reality and the nature of behavior settings as eco-behavioral entities do not reside in psychological processes of the inhabitants, but in the circuitry that interconnects behavior settings, inhabitants, and other behavior setting components. The components of behavior settings are richly joined (Ashby, 1956) by a complex net, which produces a self-governing entity with attributes quite different from the psychological and mechanical processes that govern its interior connections. The varied joinings that have been described suggest some of the sources of behavior setting complexity. But there are other sources.

The control unit of a maintenance circuit may be located within a single inhabitant, or its parts may be distributed among different inhabitants. When Miss Rutherford apprehended Oran's deviancy and removed its source (Oran) from the setting, all the mechanisms were within Miss Rutherford. On another occasion, Miss Rutherford noted a pupil's deviancy (a misspelled word on the blackboard in this case); she asked another pupil what was wrong and, upon receiving a correct answer, requested him to correct the error. In this maintenance circuit the S-MECH and E-MECH of Miss Rutherford were involved, and also the S-MECH, E-MECH, and M-MECH of the second pupil. The circuit originated in Miss Rutherford, and it occurred by induction in the pupil. Induction of maintenance forces is an important behavior setting process. It augments the maintenance forces of multi-inhabitant settings. Here is an example. The director of a play notes (S-MECH) that the behavior setting Play Practice is not going well, that it is inadequate for the program of the setting and for his goals within it (E-MECH): the sets are not ready, the lines are not learned. One deviation-countering course he could take (E-MECH) would be to construct the sets and drill the cast himself (M-MECH). Another would be to bring the state of the setting as he sees it to the attention of some deviant members of the cast, e.g., provide input about the state of the setting to member A and member B. If A and B were to agree with the director's observations (S-MECH) and with his evaluation (E-MECH), actions (M-MECH) along maintenance circuits would increase, and three members would exhibit increased activity via M-MECH, rather than one. If A and B were to act, in addition, upon two other setting members, seven would engage in greater activity on the maintenance circuits; and if each of these in turn was to act via his own M-MECH upon two other members of the cast, 15 would become more active. Such arborization of maintenance actions occurs by induction in all multi-inhabitant settings.

Another complication of behavior settings comes from the fact that not only the milieu and the other inhabitants of behavior settings are recipients of a person's maintenance efforts, but he is, himself, a recipient. If a person observes that his own attributes (physique, appearance, behavior) are below the minimal level of adequacy for a setting he inhabits, thus endangering the opportunities for satisfaction that it provides, maintenance circuits terminating in himself as a behavior setting component will be instigated. An aging member of a tennis club who observes that his play is slowing down and his skill declining, thus reducing the functional level of the tennis settings in which he participates and reducing his own and others' satisfactions, may take maintenance

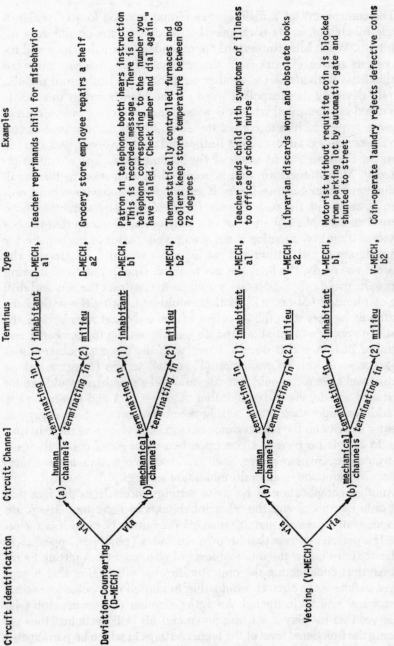

Fig. 6.9. Types of behavior setting maintenance circuits.

Circuit Identification	Circuit Channel	Terminus	Type	Examples
Deviation-Countering (D-MECH)	(a) human channels	(1) inhabitant	D-MECH a1	Teacher reprimands child for misbehavior
		(2) milieu	D-MECH a2	Grocery store employee repairs a shelf
	(b) mechanical channels	(1) inhabitant	D-MECH b1	Patron in telephone booth hears instruction "This is a recorded message. There is no telephone corresponding to the number you have dialed. Check number and dial again."
		(2) milieu	D-MECH b2	Thermostatically controlled furnaces and coolers keep store temperature between 68 72 degrees
Vetoing (V-MECH)	(a) human channels	(1) inhabitant	V-MECH a1	Teacher sends child with symptoms of illness to office of school nurse
		(2) milieu	V-MECH a2	Librarian discards worn and obsolete books
	(b) mechanical channels	(1) inhabitant	V-MECH b1	Motorist without requisite coin is blocked from parking lot by automatic gate and shunted to street
		(2) milieu	V-MECH b2	Coin-operate laundry rejects defective coins

actions against himself by vetoing himself out of the club or by trying to improve his play.

We are particularly concerned with the maintenance mechanisms and circuits, for they are most relevant to behavior setting theory. We shall consider some special characteristics of these circuits.

Behavior Setting Maintenance Circuits

When the test of behavior setting adequacy within E-MECH finds the behavior setting to be inadequate and the circuit is switched to M-MECH, there occurs within E-MECH another decision, namely, between V-MECH and D-MECH. The behavior setting is again tested via the adequacy criterion. This time the test is of the relative adequacy of the setting if the defective component is eliminated vs. its adequacy if the defective component is corrected. In some cases the result is clear: the only way to deal with such deviant behavior setting components as flies in a restaurant is to eliminate them; there is no effective way to correct or counter flies. But in the case of a silly pupil, a judgment must be made of the relative adequacy of the setting if he is vetoed from the setting or if his behavior is corrected.

Two facts are relevant to this judgment: first, it often requires less effort to veto a deviant behavior setting component than to counter its deviancy (Ashby, 1956); second, within wide ranges, reducing the number of behavior setting components reduces the medium-quality of its interior manifold and increases the effort required to maintain the setting at an adequate level. It is often easier to discard broken shelves than to repair them (but limited shelving makes it difficult to operate a store); it is often easier to fire an inaccurate employee than to supervise him and correct his errors (but an understaffed store presents problems). The task of E-MECH is to balance the effort-cost of countering a deviant component against the effort-cost of maintaining the adequacy of the setting with its reduced components. Many behavior setting attributes influence this balance.

Both deviation-countering and vetoing circuits may terminate in a behavior setting inhabitant or in a milieu component; and both circuits may operate via mechanical or human channels. There are, therefore, eight types of maintenance circuits, as shown, with examples, in Fig. 6.9.

The behavior setting maintenance circuits that operate via human channels (D-MECH, a1 and a2; V-MECH, a1 and a2) have the following psychological processes within their control units:

S-MECH

(a) Perception by inhabitants of behavior setting attributes.

E-MECH

(b) Sensitivity of inhabitants to own needs and/or intentions.

(c) Identification of goals and goal-routes within behavior setting; and/or knowledge of program of setting.

(d) Judgment of minimally adequate state of setting (in view of needs and intentions, and of goals, routes, and programs).

(e) Discrimination between present state of setting (process a) and minimally adequate state (process d); judgment that setting is inadequate in view of needs and intentions; switch circuit to M-MECH in proportion to degree of inadequacy.

M-MECH

(f) Perception of maintenance routes.

(g) Molar actions along maintenance routes.

Interior Circuitry of Undermanned Behavior Settings

According to the general theory of behavior settings, there are more forces *per inhabitant* in more directions in undermanned behavior settings than in settings with an optimal number of inhabitants, because the same field of forces is distributed among fewer inhabitants (p. 166). This is accompanied by differences in the interior circuitry of undermanned and optimally manned settings, which provide a basis for more precise predictions.

Program Circuits in Undermanned Behavior Settings. Undermanned and optimally manned settings have, by definition, the same standing patterns and the same programs. This means that the same lists of programmed actions are implemented by fewer inhabitants in the former case, and that there are, in consequence, more program actions and a greater variety of program actions per inhabitant. The program of a behavior setting is a time-ordered list of changes in the components of the setting. In the case of the human components, the program describes changes in behavior without directions for the implementation of the changes. In fact, behavior settings carry out their programs via multiple channels, including such automata as the timed signal systems in schools, which terminate, for example, reading behavior and initiate arithmetic behavior. Behavior setting programs when in operation within settings are not merely permissive action guides; they are lists of orders that are enforced by input from other inhabitants and from the milieu of the setting, e.g., from a teacher, from objects on an assembly line moving at fixed speed. If a programmed connection between behavior setting and inhabitant is not strong enough to instigate the programmed action, there is, in consequence, an inadequacy in the setting, and supporting maintenance forces are generated. We turn to these next.

Maintenance Circuits in Undermanned Behavior Settings. There are a greater number of stronger, and more varied maintenance circuits in undermanned than in optimally manned behavior settings. The medium manifolds of undermanned behavior settings are, by definition, less adequate than those of optimally manned settings, and in the normal course of variation of behavior setting attributes, they are actually inadequate more frequently; their maintenance circuits are, therefore, more often activated via E-MECH. How this occurs in one case can be seen in a setting of the genotype Baseball Games, when it is played by eight-man rather than by regulation nine-man teams. Three phases are discernible:

(*a*) Certain plays that are routine for nine-man teams are not completed by eight-man teams, because their members must cover a greater spatial area in the same time.

(*b*) The game notices these plays (e.g., dropped balls) via the S-MECH of its players, coaches, and rooters.

(*c*) The game evaluates them as deviancies and inadequacies via the inhabitants' E-MECH, causing the circuits to be switched to M-MECH and to hum with maintenance actions (advice, encouragement, demands for greater alertness, speed, and control, and/or for the sacking of especially inadequate players). In this connection, see Fig. 6.10. This occurs more often in undermanned behavior settings because inadequacies are more frequent.

The greater number of maintenance circuits in undermanned behavior settings are multiplied and increased in strength by induction. Consider the net of maintenance circuits in the baseball game at the moment when a player has a precisely defined task, namely, to catch a critical fly ball when the game is in an uncertain state. The crucial ball is in the sky; the ball's image is on the player's retinas; the ball approaches, the player moves to be under the ball (if he does not move correctly, he receives deviation-countering input from other players and from spectators), the player raises his arms, his catching hand encounters the ball, and feedback #1, via proprioceptive S-MECH, reports that the ball is not caught; feedback #2 via visual S-MECH reports that the ball is not

© United Feature Syndicate, Inc., 1967

Fig. 6.10. Vetoing circuits.

caught, that it is rolling on the ground; feedback #3, via auditory S-MECH from the umpire, reports that the ball is not caught and the batter is safe; feedback #3a (simultaneously with #3), via auditory S-MECH from the other players and the spectators, reports that the ball is not caught, the batter is safe, and the game is in jeopardy. Feedback #3a conveys not only information, but counter-deviancy and/or vetoing influences as well; both of these are delivered directly and also via the team manager and other powerful persons, where the strength of the influence is increased. All of these circuits instigate maintenance actions by the inadequate player: retrieving the ball and returning it to the game as quickly as possible. If channels #1 to #3a fail to deliver the message of what happened and to instigate counter-deviancy, there is delayed feedback #4, via the coach's memory storage, his verbal mechanism, and the player's auditory channels: the coach reports ten minutes later that the ball was not caught, the batter was safe, the game lost, and all because the player was too slow. A ball game takes no chances in delivering to the player the report of and corrections for his behavior deviancy.

Objectively equivalent inadequacies are actually more injurious to undermanned than to optimally manned behavior settings. A behavior setting is a unit; a weakness in any part weakens all parts. The more frequent and more serious inadequacies of undermanned behavior settings mean that they require more frequent shoring up in more different parts than optimally manned settings. The more varied deficiencies require, via E-MECH, more varied maintenance circuits.

Deviation-countering and Vetoing Circuits in Undermanned Behavior Settings. The interior circuitry of behavior settings produces more deviation-countering and fewer vetoing maintenance circuits within undermanned than within optimally manned settings. This occurs because the cost in effort and time of countering deviant behavior in undermanned behavior settings is usually less than the combined cost of vetoing the deviant inhabitants and of maintaining the settings in a state of adequacy with their reduced numbers of inhabitants. The reverse holds in optimally manned behavior settings: the cost of vetoing deviant inhabitants is usually less than the cost of countering their deviant behavior. Some details of deviation-countering and vetoing circuits follow.

A major source of the inadequacy of behavior settings with optimal numbers of inhabitants is the low medium-qualities of inhabitants with defective physiques, low intelligence, poor motor skills, little interest, "difficult" personalities, uncooperative attitudes, etc. These behavior settings lose little or nothing when they discard such inhabitants, for they usually have replacements available, and they are saved the strong and persisting deviation-countering efforts that are usually required to obtain conformity to the patterns of the settings from such inhabitants. If there are 30 candidates for players in the baseball game, a better game will result with less fuss and bother (less energy devoted to maintenance) if all four-year-olds, mothers, and others who are likely to produce deviant behavior are vetoed out. The situation is different for behavior settings with fewer than the optimal number of inhabitants. These settings must make great use of deviation-countering control mechanisms because their inhabitants are functionally too important to be casually eliminated by veto. When E-MECH within the maintenance circuits of an undermanned behavior setting balances the inadequacy of a particular inhabitant against the reduction in medium-quality of the total manifold of inhabitants if the inhabitant is eliminated, the balance often favors retaining the inhabitant and correcting his deviancies. So one sees a four-man ball game of nine-year-olds tolerate and nurse along via deviation-countering controls a four-year-old participant, or even a mother. In this case an outfielder, even an inefficient, inept one who requires frequent help, instruction, and correction, is likely to produce a better game than no outfielder. There are exceptions. Some inhabitants of undermanned settings are so resistant to deviation-countering controls that vetoing controls must be used.

There are, in addition to undermanned behavior settings, some other special settings whose programs can usually be effectuated only, or more efficiently, via deviation-countering controls. This is true of most settings that are programmed to educate their inhabitants. When this is the case, even amply inhabited settings must use deviation-countering controls such as helping, encouraging, disciplining, however "inefficient" they may be. In a study of third grade classes, Gump (1967b) found that teachers engaged in from 103 to 229 deviation-countering acts during a five-hour day, but that there were very few vetoing acts. There are other types of behavior settings with special programs that are not affected by the undermanned state; Wicker (1967) has identified a number of them. But the exceptions and special programs do not destroy the generalization that deviation-countering maintenance circuits are relatively more frequent in undermanned behavior settings and that vetoing circuits are relatively more frequent in optimally manned settings.

Internal Interdependence, Unity, and Centripetal Forces of Undermanned Behavior Settings

One consequence of the differential occurrence of deviation-countering and vetoing circuits in undermanned and optimally manned settings is a difference in the prevailing direction of forces within them. The prevailing forces in undermanned behavior settings are inward; they press behavior, materials, and processes into more appropriate formats within the setting; they are centripetal, setting-unifying, and strengthening forces. Deviation-countering circuits are discriminating; they are "against" the deviant *attributes* of behavior setting components, they are "for" the deviant *components*. The direction of forces within optimally manned behavior settings is more often centrifugal; they shunt some components, both inhabitants and milieu components, out of the setting; although the final effect is to strengthen the setting, these forces are, in their immediate consequences, divisive and weakening. Vetoing forces are not discriminating; they are against the deviant attributes of behavior setting components and they are against the component, too.

Deviation-countering regulatory systems are one of the bases of an essential attribute of behavior settings, namely, interdependence of parts. The index of interdependence, K (see p. 40), was established on an empirical basis, with only general ideas about how the observed interdependence might be effected. The theories of thing and medium, of the relation of the number of parts of a manifold of elements to its medium-quality, and of the feedback loop between the adequacy of a behavior setting and the actions of inhabitants along maintenance routes, elucidate the inner working of this observable behavior setting attribute.

It should be noted, too, that the deviation-countering and vetoing maintenance circuits are evidence that a behavior setting is not only structurally bounded but dynamically bounded as well. The dynamic limits of behavior settings are usually not as definite as their structural boundaries. Deviation-countering circuits, in particular, frequently extend beyond the structural boundaries of behavior settings to bring appropriate inhabitants and potential inhabitants into the temporal-physical bounds of the settings. Printed and broadcast announcements of behavior setting occurrences are parts of deviation-countering circuits that extend beyond the temporal-physical bounds of behavior settings.

We arrive at the general conclusion that behavior settings are entities that are able to compensate, within limits, for lack of components by the increased application of force. Involved in this process is a higher rate of communication via maintenance forces between undermanned behavior settings and their components; and among their components there are more deviation-countering forces, more induced forces, and more centripetal forces. Undermanned settings are, therefore, more interdependent internally than optimally manned settings; they have stronger unity and intrinsic integrity; they have stronger thing-characteristics vs. their human medium manifolds.

Other Connections between Behavior Settings and Inhabitants

The receptor, central, and effector systems of the E-O-E arc (Fig. 6.2) and the goal, program, operating, and maintenance circuits they implement (Fig. 6.8) are not the only channels that join behavior settings and their inhabitants. When a motorist skids into a highway guard rail and is deflected back onto the roadway, when a policeman subdues, handcuffs, and takes a rioter to prison, or when a locked vault prevents a theft, the deviant behavior setting components (the motorist, the rioter, the thief) are not dealt with via their E-O-E circuits but by the direct application of physical force in no way different from the way

Undermanned behavior settings <u>relative to optimally manned settings</u> have:

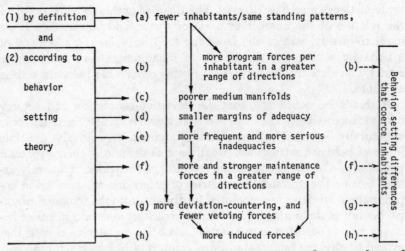

Fig. 6.11. Attributes of undermanned behavior settings relative to those of optimally manned settings.

water is guided down a river channel, or wind-blown laundry on a line is subjugated by the laundress, or noise is kept from a room by acoustical insulation. There are direct connections, too, between behavior settings and inhabitants by way of the physiological processes of the inhabitants and, for example, the composition and temperature of the air, and radiation. These connections between behavior settings and inhabitants enter behavior setting circuitry as techniques by means of which human or milieu components of behavior settings carry out program, deviation-countering, or vetoing actions with respect to inhabitants by interventions outside of their E-O-E arcs.

RECAPITULATION OF BEHAVIOR SETTING THEORY

The theory of behavior settings has pointed to some ways that undermanned settings differ from optimally manned settings. By way of summary, these differences and their sources in terms of the theory are charted in Fig. 6.11. The chart may be narrated as follows:

Undermanned behavior settings *in comparison with optimally manned settings* have, by definition, (*a*) fewer inhabitants and the same standing patterns; according to the theory these produce (*b*) more program forces per inhabitant in a greater range of directions, (*c*) poorer medium manifolds, which have (*d*) smaller margins of adequacy, that result in (*e*) more frequent and more serious inadequacies, which instigate (*f*) more, stronger, and more varied maintenance forces; because of difference (*a*), the maintenance forces are (*g*) more frequently deviation-countering and less frequently vetoing forces, and because of difference (*f*) there are (*h*) more induced maintenance forces.

In general terms, undermanned behavior settings in comparison with optimally manned behavior settings impose more and stronger forces on their inhabitants in more varied directions; the forces are, however, more prevailingly directed inward and toward other inhabitants. According to this, undermanned behavior settings have stronger internal interdependence and cohesiveness; they are stronger things vis-à-vis their inhabitants than optimally manned behavior settings.

7

Applications of Ecological Psychology

HERE WE CONFRONT the question of whether different ecological environments produce different behavior; and whether the differences, or lack of them, can be predicted from the environments. The answer of Brunswik and of Lewin was that behavior cannot be predicted from information or theories about the environment, that this must be determined by empirical investigation in each case, and that predictions from empirical evidence must be made probabilistically because the environment and the connections between it and people have only statistical stability.

The theory of behavior settings allows us to go somewhat further than Brunswik and Lewin thought possible. They and other psychologists have assumed that environmental variables occur without regard for the behavior of the inhabitants of the environment, i.e., that they are independent variables. According to behavior setting theory, the ecological environment of human molar behavior and its inhabitants are not independent; rather, the environment is a set of homeostatically governed eco-behavioral entities consisting of nonhuman components, human components, and control circuits that modify the components in predictable ways to maintain the environmental entities in their characteristic states. These states are defined by schedules, or programs, of intra-entity occurrences. If one control circuit does not produce the programmed occurrence from an inhabitant or other component, other circuits are activated in accordance with feedback from the component. This means that the ecological environment varies systematically from inhabitant to inhabitant. A behavior setting of the genotype Trafficways is a very different environment for a slow than for a fast motorist. It provides a motorist whose speed is slower than that programmed for the setting with recurring "speed up" inputs of varying modalities and force-fulness: social pressure from the succession of passing cars, from the horns of following motorists, from gesturing traffic officers, from police summons; and physical force from the forward air pressure created by the passing cars, and from rear-end collisions. All of these are slow-speed-countering, maintenance inputs; in case none of them corrects the motorist's deviation from the standing pattern of the setting Trafficways, vetoing inputs await him: a rear-end crash destroys his car or propels it out of the setting, a court order withdraws his driver's license. A motorist whose speed is faster than that programmed for the setting receives an entirely different set of "slow down" inputs; for example, social pressure from overtaken cars, from gesturing traffic officers, from prosecution for speeding; obstructions from the conforming traffic; and physical resistance from the curves engineered for the programmed speeds. All of these are fast-speed-countering, maintenance inputs; in case none of them corrects the motorist's deviation from the programmed speed, vetoing inputs await him, too; a head-on collision that destroys his car, centrifugal force that propels him out of the setting on a curve, a court order withdrawing his driver's license. On the other hand, Trafficways provide inhabitants who travel in accordance with the standing pattern of the setting with *program* inputs almost entirely, e.g., posted speed limits. In these examples, feedback from behavior that deviates from the standing pattern of the setting produces countering or vetoing actions by the environment that are roughly proportional in strength to the degree of the deviancy.

The conceptual breach between psychological and ecological phenomena is not closed by behavior settings and their homeostatic controls. Indeed, the goal of formulating a unitary eco-behavioral theory was abandoned early in our consideration of the general problem of entity and environment. There, the environment of an entity was defined as the surrounding context with which the entity is coupled by laws that are incommensurate with those that govern the entity, and the locus of the boundary between entity and environment was identified as that point at which the concepts and theories that account for the entity cease to apply, but beyond which there are phenomena with which the entity is joined and with which it co-varies. So the conceptual breach is as great as ever. However, within behavior settings the problem is restated so that, on the one hand, the sublime but millennial goal of developing a single conceptual system incorporating psychological and ecological phenomena is detoured, and, on the other hand, the discouraging prospect of mere empiricism and probabilism is avoided. The environment in terms of behavior settings opens up the more modest and hopeful possibility of discovering general principles of eco-behavioral organization and control without a comprehensive theory of the phenomena that are regulated. It does this by means of the processes involved in the thing-medium relation.

The thing-medium relation (see pp. 159–67) refers to the transmission and maintenance of pattern between thing and medium, not to the transformation of thing-phenomena into medium-phenomena. The thing-medium processes involved in perception do not, for example, transform a stone into light and light into the precept of a stone. The only aspects of the phenomena at the origin and termination of a thing-medium connection that are relevant are the degrees to which they have thing-characteristics (i.e., interdependence of parts and internally determined pattern) and medium-characteristics (i.e., independence of parts and externally determined pattern). Knowing that A and B are related as thing to medium makes it possible to predict something about B from information about A, and vice versa, but only with respect to the patterns that are transmitted; the prediction tells us nothing about the substance behind the pattern. Nevertheless, when the thing-medium connection obtains, certain consequences with respect to pattern follow with complete certainty.

We have made predictions from differences in the number of inhabitants of behavior settings (as media) to differences in the attributes of behavior settings (as things); these predictions are listed in Fig. 6.11. Some of the predicted differences in *behavior setting attributes*, in turn, *require different behavior* from the inhabitants of the settings. We have called them primary behavior differences; they are open to observation, and so provide a test of the theory of the environment that has been presented.

The situation in this respect may be clarified by an analogy. In the process of remodeling a house, (a) a number of structural components are removed, e.g., walls and foundation stones (analogous to fewer inhabitants of a behavior setting); this action (b) does not change the house in essential respects (analogous to same standing pattern); but it (c) does change the pattern of forces that maintain the house (analogous to greater range of direction of forces); this, in turn, (d) changes the pressures and strains upon the remaining components, e.g., cross beams, corner posts (analogous, for example, to differences in the induced forces); and this (e) changes the shape of the remaining components, e.g., curvature of beams (analogous, for example, to differences in effort exerted by inhabitants). In the absence of instrumented measures of the changes in the pattern of forces within the house, the changes in the shape of the remaining components provide alternative, cruder measures. Differences in the behavior of inhabitants of undermanned and optimally manned settings provide analogous data; they are one test of the theory that the ecological environment is connected with its human components and has predictable effects upon them.

The differences are not only important for the testing of behavior setting theory; they are of immediate practical significance as well. They provide information about the consequences for people of inhabiting undermanned and optimally manned behavior settings. The population explosion makes this a crucial social issue. The increase in population is usually considered in connection with economic and nutritional problems, but its more direct effects upon behavior deserve consideration, too. Undermanned behavior settings are without doubt becoming less frequent, and optimally manned (and overmanned) settings more common. This change within the United States has relevance for theories of American culture and character. The United States has been known as a *land of opportunity* and its inhabitants have been called a *people of plenty*; its environment is said to have been dominated by the *free frontier*. Involved in the complex of ideas behind these aphorisms is the idea that there has been a superabundance of goals to be achieved and an excess of tasks to be done in relation to the nation's inhabitants, and that these have been important influences on the American society and people. This is, in important respects, a theory by historians of the influence of undermanned behavior settings upon a society and the characteristics of its members. An eco-behavioral science should have something to say about this theory, and about the consequences of the change from a society of undermanned settings to one of optimally manned and overmanned settings.

DIFFERENCES IN THE BEHAVIOR OF INHABITANTS OF UNDERMANNED AND OPTIMALLY MANNED BEHAVIOR SETTINGS: PRIMARY DIFFERENCES

According to the summary of behavior setting theory, Fig. 6.11 (p. 184), the different medium manifolds of undermanned and optimally manned behavior settings produce differences in the strength, direction, origin, and termination of forces that impinge upon the inhabitants. According to the theory, too, behavior setting control systems assure that the differences produce these predictably different actions (primary behavior) via the inhabitants' S-MECH, E-MECH, and A-MECH: In comparison with the inhabitants of optimally manned behavior settings, the inhabitants of undermanned settings

(1) engage in *more program actions,* and

(2) in *more varied program actions* (from difference *b*, Fig. 6.11); they

(3) engage in *more maintenance actions,*

(4) in *more varied maintenance actions,* and

(5) in *stronger maintenance actions* (from difference *f*, Fig. 6.11); they

(6) engage in *more deviation-countering maintenance actions,* and in

(7) *fewer vetoing maintenance actions* (from difference *g*, Fig. 6.11); they

(8) engage in *more induced actions* (from difference *h*, Fig. 6.11).

These consequences for the inhabitant components of undermanned behavior settings may be summarized as follows: the inhabitants of undermanned behavior settings, in comparison with the inhabitants of optimally manned settings, engage in *more* actions (1 and 3, above), *stronger* actions (5), *more varied* actions (2 and 4), *more centripetally directed* actions (6 and 8), and in more actions that *originate and terminate in other inhabitants* (8). The picture that emerges is one in which the inhabitants of undermanned behavior settings are busier, more vigorous, more versatile, and more oriented vis-à-vis the settings they inhabit, and more interdependent.

It is important to note that these predictions are not made from empirical correlations between counts of the number of inhabitants within behavior settings and measures of their behavior; and they are not made from the psychological characteristics of the inhabitants, beyond the fact that all possess S-MECH to sense the state of the setting, E-MECH to test it against program requirements and their own needs, and A-MECH to act in accordance with the test. In making the predictions, the inhabitants have been considered as fixtures and paraphernalia of an extra-individual behavior-and-milieu entity, a behavior setting; i.e., as instruments that sense and test the state of a setting against a standard, and as machinery that makes the indicated adjustments in the setting. According to behavior setting theory, there are sources of power and there are control mechanisms within undermanned behavior settings to generate the greater number of more varied and more vigorous actions and the more frequent centripetal and interpersonal actions required of the inhabitants. This power and control are effective over a wide range of inhabitant motivation and ability; if they are not effective, the setting disintegrates and ceases to exist.

It is important to note, too, that the predictions refer to the actions of inhabitants as behavior setting processes, not as psychological phenomena. The prediction that the inhabitants of undermanned behavior settings act more often and more strongly upon other inhabitants carries no implications about the experiences accompanying the greater number of interpersonal acts. If the processes within a setting were completely mechanized, as sometimes happens, the machines would exhibit analogous differences between "underequipped" and "optimally equipped" installations.

The program of a particular behavior setting is a detailed schedule of concrete occurrences. So far as the human components are concerned, the list may refer to such simple motor movements as tapping the keys of a typewriter in a programmed order, or it may call for complicated behavior. But in every case the program includes only behavior that can be sensed and tested by the control system of the setting, i.e., by mechanical devices or by S-MECH and E-MECH of inhabitants. Within the limits of the precision of its control system, behavior within a setting can be predicted with complete accuracy from its program.

The programs of some behavior settings imply the involvement of central psychological processes such as learning (in school classes), enjoyment (in circuses), and spiritual awakening (in worship services). However, the control systems of these settings test only occurrences that are accessible to the settings' sensors, and so far as the human components are concerned, these occurrences are all objective actions (movements) emitted by A-MECH. There are continual efforts to improve methods of testing behavior setting adequacy; thermometers, photometers, hydrometers, etc. often substitute for or augment S-MECH and E-MECH in testing nonhuman components; and technically sophisticated, standardized methods are highly developed for testing human components of behavior settings. A teacher no longer has to use his own sensors and judgment to test the adequacy of a pupil in mathematics; he can read the pupil's adequacy from a standardized test report. Many of the tests are based upon psychological theories that relate actions on the tests to presumed psychological states, e.g., to intelligence, to adjustment, to secretarial adequacy. Sensing and testing the adequacy of behavior settings is, in some settings, a specialized activity of professional personnel: of inspectors, of auditors, of safety engineers, of personnel psychologists, of company police; and their aim often is to detect incipient inadequacies before they interfere with the program of a setting. However, even the most advanced testing and control techniques are unable to govern the full psychological content of the actions occurring within behavior settings. Although the program of a Worship Service may include the occurrence "Silent Prayer," the control system of the setting can only deal with deviations from silence.

DIFFERENCES IN THE BEHAVIOR OF INHABITANTS OF UNDERMANNED
AND OPTIMALLY MANNED BEHAVIOR SETTINGS:
SECONDARY DIFFERENCES

In behavior setting theory, a net of connections intervenes between inhabitants' actions via A-MECH and succeeding input from the setting via S-MECH (see text and Fig. 6.8); the net consists of shorter or longer chains of alterations in the human and nonhuman components of behavior settings. Most behavior settings are such large and richly joined systems it is impossible to trace within this net the detailed consequences of particular actions; in fact, the alterations that finally result from particular actions are indeterminate. This indeterminacy is handled within the control systems of behavior settings by sensing the state of the setting after each action via S-MECH, testing it via E-MECH, and correcting inappropriate alterations via A-MECH. But the primary behavior differences between undermanned and optimally manned behavior settings reported above do not refer to particular actions; they refer to general attributes of actions; and these lead, singly and in combination, to certain behavior differences one or more steps removed within the net from the primary actions emitted by A-MECH. We shall consider these next. They are numbered beginning with 9, to follow the eight primary behavior differences.

In comparison with the inhabitants of optimally manned behavior settings:

(9) The inhabitants of undermanned behavior settings *enter more frequently into the central zones* of behavior settings. Obstacles to entering central zones 4, 5, and 6 of behavior settings (functionary, joint leader, single leader) are greater than those to entering peripheral zones 1, 2, and 3 (visitor, audience, member). The greater number of more vigorous actions (primary differences 1, 3, and 5) and their more centripetal direction (primary differences 6, 7, and 8) impel the inhabitants of undermanned settings into central zones more frequently than the less vigorous and less inward-directed actions of inhabitants of optimally manned settings. Example: a member of a small high school class who is without special aptitude for dramatics is under greater pressure from the setting to take part in Class Play than a similar member of a large class, and he takes more vigorous action toward the setting; these

primary action differences carry him through obstacles surrounding the central zones of the setting (e.g., long hours of practice) into the central zone of cast member, a zone that a similar member of a large class does not penetrate.

(10) The inhabitants of undermanned behavior settings *engage in difficult actions more frequently*. Inhabitants of behavior settings engage in actions that vary in difficulty, where difficulty is defined in terms of abilities, the more difficult actions being nearer the top of the inhabitants' ability ranges. The greater number of more vigorous actions by the inhabitants of undermanned behavior settings (primary differences 1, 3, and 5) overcome ability difficulties more frequently. Example: the untalented member of the small class after long hours of practice engages in more actions that are difficult for him personally (e.g., speaking loudly and clearly) than a counterpart member of a large class.

(11) The inhabitants of undermanned behavior settings *engage in important actions more frequently*. The inhabitants of behavior settings engage in actions that vary in importance where importance is defined as the amount of impairment suffered by a setting when an inhabitant is inadequate or absent. The more varied program and maintenance actions of inhabitants of undermanned settings (primary differences 2 and 4) and their entrance into more central zones of settings (secondary difference 9) make their actions more important than those of inhabitants of optimally manned behavior settings. Example: consider (*a*) a member of a small high school class who because of shortage of members has two positions within zone 4 of the setting Class Play, namely, a part in the play and electrician in charge of the lighting and sound equipment; and (*b*) two members of a large class with ample membership, one of whom has a part in the play, and the other of whom is the electrician. Since the actions of the player-electrician implement the same eco-behavioral circuits as the actions of the player *and* of the electrician in the large class, his inadequacy or absence is more damaging to the setting than the inadequacy or absence of either of the large-class members; he is a more important person.

(12) The inhabitants of undermanned behavior settings *behave in response to important actions more frequently*. The greater frequency of induced actions (primary difference 8) in undermanned behavior settings has dual significance: the inhabitants induce actions in others more frequently and actions are induced in them more frequently. The greater number of inducing actions that inhabitants of undermanned settings give and receive differ from those given and received by in-

habitants of optimally manned settings on all the characteristics listed, i.e., they give and receive more, stronger, more varied, and more important actions. It is important to note not only that inhabitants of undermanned behavior settings engage in more important actions (secondary difference 11) but that they behave in response to more important actions, also.

NATURE OF PREDICTIONS FROM BEHAVIOR SETTINGS
TO BEHAVIOR

The 12 predictions of primary and secondary behavior differences can be made univocally within the limits prescribed by behavior setting theory. These limits will now be reviewed.

First, only attributes of overt actions can be predicted from the programs and medium manifolds of behavior settings; motives and experiences of inhabitants cannot be predicted. This is the case because the control systems of behavior settings sense only ecological events (objective, spatial-temporal movements) pertaining to behavior setting functioning.

Second, only total medium manifolds are regulated by the control systems of behavior settings; individual inhabitants as unique entities are not regulated. As components of the medium manifolds of behavior settings, only those limited attributes of inhabitants are discriminated that implement or interfere with behavior setting programs; and persons who possess the same implementing or interfering attributes are equivalent, i.e., are interchangeable within behavior settings.

Third, behavior settings impose their standing patterns upon inhabitants in two ways: by coercing inhabitants to behave appropriately via deviation-countering influences and by eliminating deviant inhabitants. Behavior settings are self-validating entities, and statements of the following kind are true: If individual X *inhabits* behavior setting A, then his behavior is congruent with some part of the behavior pattern of A. But statements of the following kind are not true: If individual X *enters* behavior setting A, then his behavior is congruent with some part of the behavior pattern of A. The latter is not true because after entering behavior setting A, the behavior of X may prove to be so incompatible with every part of the behavior pattern of A that he is eliminated.

Fourth, the dual control system of behavior settings ensures that the behavior of all inhabitants of a behavior setting is within the limits set by the program that defines its standing pattern. Since the standing pattern of most behavior settings is not homogeneous, inhabitants can act appropriately while engaging in different actions. Nevertheless, the behavior of individual inhabitants can be predicted within the bounds of the standing pattern of a setting. All inhabitants of a setting of the genotype Drugstore behave drugstore, and all inhabitants of a Tavern behave tavern. Despite the heterogeneity of the standing patterns of drugstores and taverns, there are clear, meaningful differences between them, well recognized by people who know their programs. Behavior settings require conformity of their inhabitants, but they do not require uniformity.

Fifth, the control systems of behavior settings are unprecise in varying degrees; there is noise in the systems. This allows for some behavior deviancy that is not corrected.

The kind of prediction that can be made from behavior setting theory is not the kind Lewin considered to be adequate for a scientific psychology; only univocal derivations of individual behavior from the contemporaneous situation of the subject were acceptable to him. To accomplish this he created the concept of the life space, a psychological concept. While it is true that predictions of the sort he demanded cannot be made on the basis of behavior setting theory, the theory does advance beyond the empiricism and probabilism that Lewin thought were the only possibility for an eco-behavioral science, and that Brunswik accepted as the basic model for the science of psychology.

PSYCHOLOGICAL DIFFERENCES BETWEEN UNDERMANNED AND OPTIMALLY MANNED BEHAVIOR SETTINGS

The motives and experiences of inhabitants of behavior settings issue from interactions between the motivational and cognitive processes that inhabitants bring to settings and the input that settings provide inhabitants. Since the resulting motives and experiences are not sensed, tested, and selected by behavior setting control systems, they cannot be univocally predicted from behavior settings as actions can.

However, some probabilistic predictions can be made. Some motivational and cognitive processes have basic similarity across most people, and some input from a behavior setting is similar across all of its inhabitants. To the degree that these conditions hold, the motives and experiences of the inhabitants of a setting are similar; and they are different from the motives and experiences of the inhabitants of other settings with different input. Here is a simple example: most inhabitants of a behavior setting illuminated with light of wave length 512 mu (an attribute of the radiant input of the setting) see the setting as emerald green, and they see behavior settings that are illuminated with light of all other wave lengths differently. There are exceptions to this generalization; about 8 per cent of male inhabitants and 0.5 per cent of female inhabitants do not have a green experience from wave length 512 mu. If one knows (a) the per cent of the inhabitants of a setting who have common motivational and cognitive processes, (b) the per cent who receive common input from the setting, and (c) the motivational and cognitive resultants of the interaction of the common processes and inputs, one can make a probabilistic prediction of the motives and experiences of the inhabitants. To the degree that different behavior settings have different inputs to all of their inhabitants, and to the degree that the inhabitants of all settings have common motivational and cognition processes, the motives and experiences of the inhabitants of different behavior settings differ in predictable ways. This basic mechanism tends to homogenize the motives and experiences of inhabitants of a behavior setting. Two other processes have the same tendency. First, behavior settings that veto inhabitants and potential inhabitants because of their inadequate actions reduce some of the diversity of motives that would otherwise obtain within them. This occurs because there are positive correlations between some actions and some motives. When the behavior setting Football Practice vetoes inhabitants who do not engage in the fast and strong physical actions that the program of the setting requires, it also eliminates negative motivation for football because one source of slow speed and low vigor in football is low motivation. Second, people select behavior settings that satisfy their motives and harmonize with their cognitive styles; they inhabit behavior settings (except those they are required to inhabit, such as school and court settings) only so long as they gain some personal satisfactions. But behavior settings are limited in the goals and cognitive possibilities they provide; hence the inhabitants of most settings are self-selected for a limited range of motives and experiences.

For these reasons, the inhabitants of settings of the genotype Parties are, in general, psychologically happy: these settings provide "happy" inputs (inputs that are known on the basis of long experience to generate happiness in most inhabitants), potential grumblers are not invited (they are vetoed in anticipation), and the despondent and depressed eliminate themselves. The happy behavior of Parties is for most inhabitants more than a behavior emission of A-MECH triggered by E-MECH. The inhabitants of behavior settings of the genotype Attorneys Offices are usually serious, psychologically: the inputs are "serious," inhabitants who regularly engage in frivolous actions are eliminated, and blithe spirits seeking gaiety pass by Attorneys Offices.

On the basis of empirical associations between psychological states and a number of the ecological conditions that differentiate under-manned and optimally manned behavior settings, differences in the motives and experiences of their inhabitants can be predicted. Probabilistic predictions of these kinds, in addition to the univocal derivations of actions, were made prior to a series of investigations of undermanned and optimally manned behavior settings (Barker, 1960a). These investigations were carried out in voluntary, nonacademic behavior settings of small high schools, where the settings were predominantly under-manned, and similar, optimally manned settings in large high schools (Barker and Gump, 1964). The predicted differences are numbered, beginning with 13, to follow the list of primary and secondary behavior differences.

In comparison with the students of large high schools with optimally manned behavior settings:

(13) The students of small high schools have *less sensitivity to and are less evaluative of individual differences in behavior*; they are more tolerant of their associates. This is a consequence of the greater variety in the direction of forces within the small school settings; under their influence inhabitants and their associates engage in a variety of activities, for some of which they are not well fitted. Nevertheless, an inhabitant must accept himself and others as suitable for a number of roles despite wide differences among occupants of the same roles. It is a consequence, too, of the greater strength of maintenance forces; recalcitrant media (the self and others) are relatively docile and an inhabitant accepts as right the diverse behavior in which he and others are coerced to engage. And it is a consequence of the greater number of deviation-countering forces; when essential personnel are in short supply, it is necessary to "accept" those persons who are available and can do the job.

(14) The students of small high schools see themselves as having *greater functional importance* within the schools' settings; the relative scarcity of inhabitants makes them more important people. It sometimes happens that everyone in a setting of a small school is a key person, and knows it.

(15) The students of small high schools have *more responsibility*. In striving to maintain a setting for his own personal reasons, the individual in a setting where he is a key inhabitant inevitably contributes some-

thing essential to the other inhabitants. Responsibility is experienced by a person when a behavior setting and what others gain from it depend upon his actions. A setting that is optimally populated does not burden itself with indispensable personnel; people are too unreliable; so substitutes, vice-presidents, a second team are regular features of optimally manned settings.

(16) The students of small high schools have *greater functional identity*. When the population of a behavior setting is below the optimum for the setting, the questions "What has to be done?" and "Who can do this job?" are crucial, and the inhabitants are seen in terms of the varied and important functions they can perform. A person with an essential function is seen as more than a person, as a person-in-context. There is less possibility of judging a person-in-context with respect to the kind of person he is; the concern is, rather, "Is the job coming off?" If it is an important job, and it is being done, the person takes on some of the value of this achievement no matter what "kind of person" he is. When a behavior setting has an optimal number of inhabitants so that the operations are fully manned by functionally adequate persons, the question "What kind of a person am I? (is he?)" and the interpersonal relations of being liked or not liked are important, individual differences are salient, and personality analysis (by self and others) regularly occurs.

(17) The students of small high schools *experience greater insecurity*. Under the pressure of engaging in more difficult and more varied actions, a person in an underpopulated setting is in greater jeopardy of failing to carry through his tasks. To his personal uncertainty is added that which arises from lack of reserves in the behavior setting as a whole. The latter amounts to increased dependence upon every other person carrying through his assignments.

We have made eight derivations of differences in primary behavior (A-MECH emissions), four derivations of difference in the secondary behavior consequences of A-MECH emissions, and five probabilistic predictions of psychological differences of undermanned and optimally manned behavior settings. We turn, finally, to data bearing upon the correctness of the derivations and predictions.

DIFFERENCES IN THE BEHAVIOR OF INHABITANTS OF UNDERMANNED AND OPTIMALLY MANNED BEHAVIOR SETTINGS: EVIDENCE

Studies of undermanned and optimally manned behavior settings carried out at the Midwest Psychological Field Station in high schools (Barker and Hall, 1964; Gump and Friesen, 1964; Wicker, 1967; Willems, 1963, 1964, 1965) yielded the following findings about students in small schools with relatively few associates within behavior settings, in comparison with students of large schools with relatively many associates: *

(1) They report twice as many pressures upon them to take part in the programs of the settings. In their own words, small school students report more frequently "I had to march in the band"; "My family urged me to take part"; "Everyone else was going." These pressures are neither uniformly nor randomly distributed among the students; they occur selectively, and the basis of the selection differs in the two types of schools. In the small schools, marginal students (students without the abilities and backgrounds that facilitate school success) report almost as many pressures to participate as do regular students (students with the abilities and backgrounds for school achievement). But within large schools, the marginal students report about one-fourth as many pressures to participate as do the regular students. Not even one of the marginal students in the small schools reports no pressures to participate in school settings, whereas about one-third of the marginal students in large schools report no pressures. The small behavior settings with modest activity programs generate more forces toward participation than the large settings with ambitious programs.

(2) They perform in 2.5 times as many responsible positions, on the average; and for crucial, central positions, such as team members or chairmen of meetings, they perform in six times as many positions. Two per cent of the small school students fill no important and responsible positions, whereas 29 per cent of their counterparts in the large school are nonperformers. Furthermore, the students in the small school fill important and responsible positions in twice as many behavior setting genotypes as their counterparts. The schools with the smaller and less varied settings are, for their students, functionally larger and more varied than the schools with the more populous and more varied settings.

(3) They report having *more* satisfactions related (*a*) to the development of competence, (*b*) to being challenged, (*c*) to engaging in important actions, (*d*) to being involved in group activities, (*e*) to being valued, and (*f*) to gaining moral and cultural values. In their own words, students report having more experiences of these kinds in the small schools: "It gave me confidence"; "It gave me a chance to see how good I am"; "I got the speakers for all of these meetings"; "The class

* A relevant study has recently come to our attention, "Big School, Small School, A Critical Examination of the Hypothesis," *J. Ed. Psych.*, in press.

worked together"; "It also gave me recognition"; "I feel it makes a better man of me." The same students report some other satisfactions *less* frequently than their counterparts in the large school. They report fewer satisfactions referring (*a*) to vicarious enjoyment, (*b*) to affiliation with a large entity, (*c*) to learning about the school's persons and affairs, and (*d*) to gaining "points" via participation. In the students' own words, again, fewer experiences of these kinds come from the small school students: "I enjoyed watching the game"; "I like the companionship of mingling with the rest of the crowd"; "I enjoyed this because I learned who was on the team"; "You get to build up points for honors." Students in the schools with the less consequential behavior settings have more frequent satisfactions relating to themselves as persons of consequence, i.e., as competent, important, valued, and good, than students in the school with more consequential behavior settings.

Evidence from other studies in a variety of institutions has been rereviewed by Willems (1964b). Although not many of the studies are reported in terms of behavior settings, but in terms of work situations and group meetings, they all, in fact, deal with behavior settings as defined here. The evidence of these studies discloses these behavior characteristics of inhabitants of small, frequently undermanned behavior settings, in comparison with inhabitants of large, optimally manned settings:

(4) They are absent less often (Baumgartel and Sobol, 1959; Revans, 1958; Tallachi, 1960; Indik, 1961; Acton, 1953; Hewitt and Parfit, 1953; LeCompte and Barker, 1960).

(5) They quit jobs and positions less often (Cleland, 1955; Tallachi, 1960; Isaacs, 1953).

(6) They are more punctual (Revans, 1958; Acton, 1953).

(7) They participate voluntarily more frequently (Dawe, 1934; Larson, 1949; LeCompte and Barker, 1960; Wright, 1961; Coleman, 1961; Barker and Gump, 1964; Fisher, 1953).

(8) They function in positions of responsibility and importance more frequently, and in a wider range of activities (Barker and Gump, 1964a; Barker and Barker, 1961a, 1961b, 1963a; Wright, 1961).

(9) They are more productive (Revans, 1958; Thomas, 1959; Acton, 1953; Marriot, 1949).

(10) They demonstrate more leadership behavior (Bass and Norton, 1951).

(11) They are more important to settings (Barker and Barker, 1961a; Katz, 1949; Thibaut and Kelley, 1959).

(12) They have broader role conceptions (Thomas, 1959).

(13) They are more frequently involved in roles directly relevant to setting tasks (Dawe, 1934; Bales, 1953; Taylor and Faust, 1952).

(14) They are more interested in the affairs of the setting (Revans, 1958; Acton, 1953).

(15) They exhibit less centralization of communication around one or a few persons and greater social interaction among inhabitants generally (Kelley and Thibaut, 1954; Bales, 1952; Bales and Borgatta, 1955; Taylor and Faust, 1952).

(16) They engage in more greetings and social transactions per person (Wright, 1961).

(17) They exhibit easier communication, both through greater clarity and decreased difficulty (Campbell, 1952; Indik, 1961).

(18) They have greater group cohesiveness and more frequent liking of all fellow members (Katz, 1949; Larson, 1949).

(19) They have greater ability to identify outstanding persons and higher agreement about such persons (Coleman, 1961).

(20) They receive more "satisfaction" (Katz, 1949; Tallachi, 1960; Slater, 1958).

(21) They speak more often of participation as having been valuable and useful (Anderson, Ladd, and Smith, 1954).

(22) They are more familiar with the setting (Wright, 1961).

(23) They report being more satisfied with payment schemes and with the results of group discussions (Campbell, 1952; Hare, 1952).

(24) They find their work more meaningful (Worthy, 1950).

This evidence indicates that behavior settings regulate some aspects of the behavior of their inhabitants, and that most of the attributes of behavior that have been studied in undermanned and optimally manned settings are in accord with the derivations and predictions made on the basis of behavior setting theory. Thirteen of the 24 differences reported are in accord with univocal derivations from behavior setting dynamics (differences 1, 2, 4, 5, 6, 7, 8, 9, 11, 13, 15, 16, 17); nine of the differences are probabilistic predictions on the basis of empirical associations between ecological conditions of behavior settings and psychological states of inhabitants (differences 3, 12, 14, 18, 20, 21, 22, 23, 24). Differences 10 and 19 are of equivocal significance. We have discovered no data that are clearly contrary to the derivations and predictions. In a recent study of churches of different sizes, Wicker (1967) discovered that, in general, the relationships found in large and small schools occur also in large and small churches.

DIFFERENCES IN THE REGULATORY SYSTEMS OF UNDERMANNED AND OPTIMALLY MANNED BEHAVIOR SETTINGS

The school data provide evidence on how regulation of behavior settings is accomplished. In the small schools, with meagerly populated settings, regulation occurs by means of deviation-countering feedback (D-MECH) to all students, i.e., pressures against deviation from the programs of settings. Here, for example, are reports by students of small schools of D-MECH actions toward them: "My teacher talked me into it"; "They needed girls in the cast"; "Everyone was supposed to be there"; "I was assigned to work there." Such deviation-countering inputs occur twice as frequently in the small schools as in the large schools, and all students of the small schools, even marginal ones, receive them. This control system contributes to the harmony between the behavior of individual inhabitants and the programs of the settings by regulating the behavior of all the students.

In the large schools, on the other hand, regulation is in two stages: (*a*) discriminating between students with more and less promising behavior and (*b*) providing deviation-countering feedback to the more promising (regular) students and no feedback at all or vetoing feedback to most of the less promising (marginal) students. In the large school most of the pressures to participate at the performance level of behavior settings are applied to regular students; many marginal students receive no pressures against failure to perform; others are excluded from performing. This control system contributes to the harmony between individual behavior and behavior-setting programs by selecting the students who will require least regulation, and by allowing the others to veto themselves or by actively vetoing them to onlooker or visitor roles.

The behavior settings of the small and large schools do not differ greatly in the number of satisfactions students report, but they differ greatly in the content of the satisfactions. The students of the small schools report more frequently that they achieve satisfactions by being competent, by accepting challenges, by doing important things, by engaging in group activities, and by engaging in valued actions, all of which can be gained only by serious performance in the programs of the settings. The students of the large schools report more frequently that they achieve satisfactions by watching others participate, by mingling with the crowd, by learning about the school, and by gaining points, none of which require serious performance in the schools' settings. Performance satisfactions undoubtedly elicit stronger goal actions than visitor and spectator satisfactions, and the former are available to almost all students of the small schools but only to those students of the large schools who have not been vetoed or allowed to veto themselves from the performance zones of the settings. This is one source of the differential behavior of the inhabitants of the undermanned and optimally manned behavior settings; but it is a psychological resultant of ecological differences that cannot be derived from a theory of behavior settings. Although it is likely that a behavior setting inhabitant who has an important role in a setting will experience gratification, it is not certain.

The different control systems of behavior settings have wide significance for inhabitants. Behavior settings with deviation-countering feedback and central satisfactions to almost all inhabitants for appropriate, responsible performances provide quite a different environment from settings where control is achieved by restricting feedback and central satisfactions to promising inhabitants, and where marginal inhabitants are allowed to, or required to, withdraw from the performance zones.

SOURCES OF BEHAVIOR DIFFERENCES AND BEHAVIOR VARIATION WITHIN BEHAVIOR SETTINGS

According to behavior setting theory, systematic research (Raush *et al.*, 1959 and 1960; Ashton, 1964), and general observation, the behavior of the inhabitants of any behavior setting is less varied than their behavior across all the settings they inhabit. This is true for both individual variation and individual differences. However, restricting behavior to a single setting by no means eliminates either individual variation or individual differences.

Behavior setting programs themselves are sources of individual differences and individual variation within settings; even the most uniform and rigid of behavior setting programs require both. For example, the setting High School Juniors National Merit Scholarship Qualifying Achievement Test has one of the most uniform and rigid programs, but it requires some inhabitants to behave differently from others (the test administrator and the proctors must, according to the program, behave differently from the testees), and the program requires some variation in the behavior of the individual inhabitants (the testees must take their assigned positions, get their writing materials ready, receive the tests, open them on signal, etc.). Within a less uniform setting, for example within the setting Church Wedding, greater individual differences are programmed: the guests, the bride, the bridesmaid, the groom, the best man, the father, the minister, etc. are directed to behave in widely different ways. And the program requires great variation in the behavior of many of the inhabitants; the bride must wait, she must walk slowly, she must repeat after the minister, she must greet the guests, etc.

The internal states of the inhabitants are another source of behavior variety within settings. The varied programs of most behavior settings allow inhabitants to select parts that are to some degree congenial to their needs and abilities (individual differences), and to change these parts in accordance with their changing states (individual variation). In addition, all behavior settings allow some unprogrammed behavior.

Inputs originating outside behavior settings are sources of behavior variety within settings. The inhabitants of behavior settings may receive input via S-MECH from other settings and from the inhabitants of other settings. A message via the telephone in the behavior setting High School Principals Office may bring input from any of innumerable Midwest and out-of-town settings that alters behavior within the setting. The principal may receive information from a parent that causes him to cease the work under way and call a pupil to the office; a message from the state education office may induce further changes in the direction of his actions. Although influences upon behavior setting inhabitants are not limited to those originating within the programs of settings or within the inhabitants, it should be noted that behavior instigated by extra-setting inputs must be harmonious with the standing pattern of the setting if the recipient is to remain an inhabitant.

These sources of behavior variety within behavior settings operate to different degrees in different settings and with respect to different behaviors. There are limiting cases where some sources of behavior variety are not operative. Fawl (1963) and Ashton (1964) found that variation in the frequency of strong negative emotional disturbances in children (tantrums, fits of anger, etc.) was as varied within the average setting as across all settings the children inhabited. In these cases behavior variety was independent of differences in behavior setting programs and ecological conditions. There are unsolved problems concerning the sources and extents of behavior variety within and across behavior settings, including, in the limiting cases, conditions within inhabitants that make some behavior independent of the coercive forces of behavior settings, and conditions within behavior settings that deprive them of coercive power over inhabitants.

CONCLUDING COMMENTS

In the course of our explorations in ecological psychology, we have discovered behavior settings, and we have made systematic descriptions of them. To behavior settings we have brought concepts and theoretical predilections in terms of which we have fashioned an eco-behavioral theory, and on the basis of the theory we have made predictions regarding behavior from nonbehavioral attributes of behavior settings. Finally, we have tested these predictions in limited situations by means of our own and others' data.

The theory and data support the view that the environment in terms of behavior settings is much more than a source of random inputs to its inhabitants, or of inputs arranged in fixed array and flow patterns. They indicate, rather, that the environment provides inputs with controls that regulate the inputs in accordance with the systemic requirements of the environment, on the one hand, and in accordance with the behavior attributes of its human components, on the other. This means that the same environmental unit provides different inputs to different persons, and different inputs to the same person if his behavior changes; and it means, further, that the whole program of the environment's inputs changes if its own ecological properties change; if it becomes more or less populous, for example.

Our present knowledge of behavior settings relates to only a few of their many facets, so the theory we have fashioned on the basis of this knowledge is necessarily incomplete. Hopefully, it is a first approximation to, or a component of, the theory or theories that an eco-behavioral science will finally have.

APPENDIXES

Appendix 1. Occupancy Time Code

See Table 5.3, pp. 110–16.

Interval	Code	Score	Interval	Code	Score
0–1	1	.25	9,456–10,416	31	9,928
2–5	2	2.50	10,417–11,440	32	10,920
6–14	3	8.75	11,441–12,529	33	11,976
15–30	4	21.00	12,530–13,685	34	13,099
31–55	5	41.25	13,686–14,910	35	14,289
56–91	6	71.50	14,911–16,206	36	15,549
92–140	7	113.75	16,207–17,575	37	16,881
141–204	8	170.00	17,576–19,019	38	18,288
205–285	9	242.25	19,020–20,150	39	19,770
286–385	10	332.50	20,151–21,750	40	21,330
386–506	11	442.75	21,751–23,431	41	22,970
507–650	12	575.00	23,432–25,195	42	24,693
651–819	13	731.25	25,196–27,044	43	26,499
820–1,015	14	913.50	27,045–28,980	44	28,391
1,016–1,240	15	1,123.75	28,981–31,005	45	30,371
1,241–1,496	16	1,364.00	31,006–33,121	46	32,441
1,497–1,785	17	1,636.25	33,122–35,330	47	34,604
1,786–2,109	18	1,942.50	35,331–37,154	48	36,860
2,110–2,470	19	2,284.75	37,155–39,555	49	39,212
2,471–2,870	20	2,665.00	39,556–42,055	50	41,662
2,871–3,311	21	3,085	42,056–44,656	51	44,213
3,312–3,795	22	3,548	44,657–47,360	52	46,865
3,796–4,324	23	4,054	47,361–50,169	53	49,621
4,325–4,900	24	4,606	50,170–53,085	54	52,484
4,901–5,525	25	5,206	53,086–56,110	55	55,454
5,526–6,201	26	5,857	56,111–59,246	56	58,534
6,202–6,930	27	6,559	59,247–62,495	57	61,726
6,931–7,714	28	7,315	62,496–65,859	58	65,033
7,715–8,555	29	8,127	65,860–69,340	59	68,455
8,556–9,455	30	8,998	69,341–72,940	60	71,995

Interval	Code	Score	Interval	Code	Score
72,941–76,661	61	75,655	173,011–179,571	81	177,141
76,662–80,505	62	79,438	179,572–186,295	82	183,783
80,506–84,474	63	83,344	186,296–193,184	83	190,589
84,475–88,570	64	87,376	193,185–200,240	84	197,562
88,571–92,795	65	91,537	200,241–207,465	85	204,702
92,796–97,151	66	95,827	207,466–214,861	86	212,012
97,152–101,640	67	100,249	214,862–222,430	87	219,494
101,641–106,264	68	104,806	222,431–230,174	88	227,150
106,265–111,025	69	109,498	230,175–238,095	89	234,983
111,026–115,925	70	114,328	238,096–246,195	90	242,993
115,926–120,966	71	119,298	246,196–254,476	91	251,183
120,967–126,150	72	124,410	254,477–262,940	92	259,556
126,151–131,479	73	129,667	262,941–271,589	93	268,112
131,480–136,955	74	135,069	271,590–280,425	94	276,854
136,956–142,580	75	140,619	280,426–289,450	95	285,784
142,581–148,356	76	146,320	289,451–298,666	96	294,904
148,357–154,285	77	152,172	298,667–308,075	97	304,217
154,286–160,369	78	158,178			
160,370–166,610	79	164,340			
166,611–173,010	80	170,660			

Appendix 2. Programs of the Genotypes of Midwest

EACH GENOTYPE occurring in Midwest is identified by a number and name, and is described by a précis of its program for the inhabitants of its different penetration zones. The format of the genotype survey is as follows: Identification number. Name. Précis of program (with penetration of the different classes of inhabitants).

1. Abstract and Title Company Offices. Abstracter (6) manages office and assistant (4) carries out office routines; both search files and records in County Clerks and Register of Deeds office for information about land titles, prepare summary statement (abstract) of the successive conveyances and other facts upon which a client's title to a piece of land rests, sell title insurance; land buyers and sellers (3) ask for title records, bring land identification, pay for services, discuss issues.

2. Agricultural Advisers Offices. County agent (5) manages office, advises farmers, prepares material and programs, collects, analyzes, and evaluates agricultural data, plans 4-H program; home economics agent (5) manages office, prepares material and lectures on home and family life, distributes literature, advises leaders and homemakers; secretary (4) carries out office routines; interested citizens and members of farm organizations (3) consult, obtain material and literature.

4. Agronomy Classes. County agricultural agent (6) is in charge of arrangements, introduces agronomy specialist; specialist (4) teaches regarding soil fertility, crops, etc.; farmers (3) or 4-H members (3) listen, discuss, ask questions.

5. Animal Feed Mills. Manager (6) manages operation, operates mill, sells fertilizer, etc.; employees (4) fill fuel tank, load trucks, engage in office routines; farmer members (3) bring grain to be ground, weigh in, buy products, pay for service and materials.

6. Animal Feed Stores. Feed store proprietor (5) manages store, buys and sells feed and feed additives, loads feed into trucks and cars; insurance agent (5) sells insurance, arranges for adjustor, engages in office routines; customers (3) buy and pay for feed, buy insurance or make claims.

7. Animal Husbandry Classes. County agricultural agent (6) is in charge of arrangements, introduces livestock specialist; specialist (4) teaches regarding livestock; farmers or 4-H members (3) listen, ask questions, discuss.

8. Athletic Equipment Rooms. Coaches (6 or 5), both local and visiting, prepare for physical education and sports, give out equipment, consult with individuals; athletes (3) get equipment for sports.

9. Attorneys Offices. Lawyers (6 or 5) initiate legal actions, prepare legal defense in civil and criminal cases, give legal advice, draw up contracts, prepare wills, prepare federal and state income tax returns, manage office; secretary (4) carries out office routines; clients (3) seek and pay for advice and service.

10. Auction Sales, Household Furnishings and General Merchandise. Sellers (5) determine what is to be sold, arrange for display articles to be sold; auctioneer (5) determines order of sale, calls for bids, sells to highest bidder; clerks (4) record bidder and accept payment; customers (3) bid, pay clerk, remove purchased articles, converse.

11. Auditing and Investigating Company Offices. Proprietor (6) consults with investigative staff in office and by phone, consults with clients via telephone, manages office; employees (4) get directions; clients (3) seek information.

12. Automobile Washing Services. Teacher and student in charge (5) direct activities and help; other students (4) wash, sweep, polish, get cars from customers, deliver washed cars, accept payment; customers (3) arrange for and pay for having car washed.

13. Award Ceremonies. Master of ceremonies (6) organizes meeting, presents awards to the qualified persons with appropriate remarks; awardees (4) accept awards; audience (2) applaud.

14. Bakery Services, to Order. Baker (6) prepares and bakes food on order, accepts pay; customers (3) order, pick up, and pay for food.

15. Banks. President (6) manages all operations, makes loans, gives financial advice, provides credit information; vice-president (4) makes loans, sells insurance; cashier (4) cashes checks, receives deposits, provides access to safe deposit, keeps records; clerks (4) engage in office routines; bank examiners (4) come at intervals to examine the routines, the assets and liabilities of the bank in relation to legal standards; customers (3) deposit and withdraw money, arrange for or pay back loans, seek advice, use safe deposit boxes, and converse.

16. Barbershops. Barber (6) cuts hair, sells products for grooming, manages shop; customers (3) wait for service, converse, have hair cut, pay barber.

17. Baseball Games. Coach (6) or coaches (5) arrange game or practice and instruct players; players (4) play the game according to rules for baseball or softball; umpire (4) calls "strikes, balls, safe, out"; audience (2) cheer team, comment on play.

18. Basketball Games. Coach (6) or coaches (5) arrange games, instruct players; referees (4) judge plays; players (4) play according to standard basketball rules; cheerleaders (4) lead cheers; salesmen (4) sell popcorn, soft drinks; band (4) plays music in intervals; audience (2) watch, cheer, applaud, eat.

19. Beauty Shops. Operator-manager (6) cuts, washes, sets, styles, colors, combs hair of customer, carries out management routines; assistant (4)

answers phone, assists operator; customers (3) receive operator's services, converse, read, pay for services.

20. Billiard Parlors and Taverns. Proprietor (6) manages business, serves drinks, gives out equipment for billiards, converses; assistant (4) helps manager; customers (3) order and pay for drinks, drink beer, converse, play cards or billiards.

22. Bowling Games. Proprietors (5) manage business, team managers (5) arrange games, keep scores; bowlers (4) bowl according to rules, watch, eat, converse; audience (2) watch, eat, converse.

24. Building, Construction, and Repair Services. Operators (6) manage construction, engage in carpenter work, painting, wallpapering, cement work; helpers (4) do similar work under direction; employers (3) arrange for and pay for work, inspect work; onlookers (1) watch work being done.

25. Bus Stops. Driver (6) sells tickets, loads and unloads luggage; customers (3) get on or off bus.

26. Card Parties. Host (6) greets members, provides place, equipment, refreshments; members (3) or customers (3) play cards, converse, eat.

27. Carnivals. Chairmen (5) of different concessions (games of skill and chance, sales of goods, competitions, exhibits, movie) organize effort, provide objects, act as salesmen, barkers, ticket sellers; helpers (4) assist in all activities; customers (3) buy, watch, eat, play, converse.

28. Cemeteries, including Graveside Services. Minister (5) and mortician (5) arrange and perform burial services according to ritual; casket bearers (4) assist; caretaker (4) mows grass, maintains cemetery; chairman of cemetery board (5) sells lots, oversees caretaker; gravediggers (4) dig graves; mourners (3) attend service; visitors (2) visit cemetery, bring flowers.

29. Charivaris. Ringleaders (5) collect friends of newlyweds, provide wheelbarrow, call on newlyweds; groom (5) wheels bride around Courthouse square; bride and groom (5) act as hosts to friends at their own home; onlookers (2) cheer, laugh, eat, converse.

30. Chiropractors Offices. Chiropractor (6) carries out office routines, consultations, manipulation of patient's vertebral column according to chiropractic theory and practice; patient (3) seeks advice, is treated, pays for services.

32. Civil Engineers Offices. Engineer (6) manages office, consults with county commissioners, county employees, rural residents, and state highway officials regarding roads and bridges and sanitation problems in the county; secretary (4) carries out office routines; county officials (3) and citizens (3) consult, converse, get maps.

33. Classrooms, Free Time. Teacher (6) keeps order; pupils (3) converse, study, play quiet games.

34. Cleaners, Dry Cleaning Plants. Owner-manager (6) manages business, cleans and presses clothes, waits on customers, accepts payment, sells insurance; helpers (4) assist manager in dry cleaning; customers (3) bring clothes to be cleaned, pick up clean clothes, pay for service.

35. Clothiers and Dry Goods Stores. Joint managers (5) manage business,

serve customers, stock shelves; clerks (4) assist managers; customers (3) select, buy, and pay for merchandise.

36. Club Officers Training Classes. Members of agricultural extension advisory council (5) and home economics agent (5) arrange program and teach officers of home economics units their respective responsibilities; officers of home economics units (3) learn, discuss.

37. Commercial Classes. Commerce teacher (6) teaches typing, shorthand, business machine use, bookkeeping, office routines; students (3) learn, practice, and demonstrate office skills and routines.

38. Commercial Company Offices. Proprietors (5) manage office; secretary (4) and bookkeeper (4) engage in office routines; customers (3) come to select and order windows and doors.

39. Cooking Classes. Leader (6) teaches theory and practice of cooking; assistants (4) help leader; members of 4-H club (3) cook under supervision, eat products.

40. Court Sessions, County. Judge (6) opens court, hears charges and witnesses, gives and records judgments in cases involving misdemeanors (including traffic violations), juvenile offenders, matters of probate; sheriff (4) or state traffic officer (4) or individuals (4) bring charges; counsel (4) or accused (4) or witnesses (4) offer evidence; accused may be acquitted, fined, or imprisoned; spectators (2) listen.

41. Court Sessions, District. Judge of the District Court, a professional (6), listens to presentation of case, rules on admissibility of evidence, instructs jury, settles disputes between opposing attorneys, sentences defendant in criminal cases, determines liability in civil cases; Clerk of the Court (4) swears in witnesses; bailiff (4) opens court, keeps order; court reporter (4) records proceedings; attorneys (4) present client's case; witnesses (4) give evidence; defendant (4) gives evidence; plaintiff (4) gives evidence; jury (4) (if present) listens, deliberates, gives verdict; spectators (2) listen.

44. Custodial Work Groups. Person in charge (6 or 5) manages cleaning, gardening, meal or coffee break; volunteer workers (4) scrub, sweep, polish, rake, make minor repairs; others (2) watch, join in recreational eating.

46. Dances. Committee of students and teachers in charge (5) arrange for decorating, music, food, plan program; master of ceremonies (5) carries out program; operator of record player (4) or musicians (4) provide music; refreshment servers (4), decorators (4), ticket-takers (4) carry out specified routines; members and customers (3) dance, play games, converse, eat; audience (2) watch.

47. Day Care Homes and Nurseries. Person in charge (6) cares for young children left in her care, may give them food, put them to bed, entertain, comfort; children (3) are cared for; parents (3) leave and call for children.

48. Delivery and Collection Routes. Deliverers (6) take papers, etc., to homes and leave them, come at regular intervals to collect for goods and service; customers (3) pay for goods and services.

49. Dentists Offices and Services. Dentist (6) examines patients, using

x-rays and mouth mirrors, explores, cleans, fills, extracts, and replaces teeth, using power and hand instruments, manages office; assistant (4) assists dentist, makes appointments, records treatments, accepts payment, develops x-rays, conducts office routines; patients (3) wait, are treated, pay, converse.

50. Dinners and Banquets. Organizers (5) plan, buy, cook, serve meal, and clean up after meal; helpers (4) help with above or in some cases all bring ready-cooked food and place it for diners to serve themselves; members (3) or customers (3) eat and converse.

51. Dinners with Business Meetings. President of organizations (6) arranges for dinner, presides at meeting; cooks (4), waitresses (4) prepare and serve dinner; secretary (4), treasurer (4), committee chairman (4) do prescribed work; invited speakers (4) make speeches; members (3) eat, converse, engage in business meeting activity, listen.

52. Dinners with Dances. Chairmen of committees (5) arrange and manage dinner, program, dance; master of ceremonies (5) introduces speakers (4) and entertainers (4) for program; cooks (4) prepare and waitresses (4) serve food; guests (3) eat, dance, converse, listen.

53. Dinners with Recreational and Cultural Programs. Chairmen (5) arrange for dinner, program, decorations; cooks (4), waitresses (4), decorators (4) prepare and serve dinner, decorate; master of ceremonies (5) presides; speakers (4) and/or entertainers (4) present after-dinner program; members (3) listen, eat, converse, applaud.

54. Drugstores. Pharmacist (5) mixes and dispenses drugs according to prescription issued by physician, manages drug and general variety store; manager (5) manages cosmetic, jewelry departments and fountain; sales persons (4) sell and serve customers at counters or fountain, wash dishes, mix drinks; customers (3) select, buy, pay for merchandise, eat food, converse.

55. Educational Methods Classes. Leaders (6) or co-leaders (5) teach methods and values of teaching to individuals who will teach; members (3) learn, listen, ask questions, discuss.

56. Elections, Polling Places. Election board chairman (5) sees that voting and ballot counting is conducted according to law, makes up final tally for county clerk, seals pouch; bailiff (5) sets up booths, tables, supplies ballots, and canisters; election clerks (4) check off voters, hand out ballots, place ballots in appropriate canisters; counting board (4) counts ballots; watchers (4) watch procedures to detect any deviancy; voters (3) identify themselves, mark ballots, cast ballots.

57. Elections, Public Posting of Returns. County clerk (5) and election board chairmen (5) record votes as they come in; secretaries (4) place results on records and on blackboard for spectators to see; spectators (2) stand before blackboard, read how election is going, converse.

58. Elementary School Basic Classes. Teacher (6) teaches reading, grammar, arithmetic, writing, elementary health, social studies, science, and engages in classroom routines; pupils (3) listen, write, recite, read, figure.

59. English Classes. Teacher (6) teaches English literature, composition,

speech, grammar, and engages in routine classroom management; high school students (3) study, recite, listen.

60. Examinations, Boy Scout. Examining board (5) questions boy scouts regarding requirements for specific badges, makes judgment regarding competence of scout and informs him of decision; scout (4) answers questions, demonstrates knowledge.

61. Examinations, Standardized. School principal (6) gives test according to specific directions accompanying test; students (3) take examination, follow directions.

62. Excavating Contracting Services. Owner-managers (6) direct earth-moving and engage in management routines; employees (4) operate and repair equipment; customers (3) arrange for and pay for earth-moving services; onlookers (1) watch activity.

63. Excursions and Sightseeing Trips. Persons in charge (5) supervise loading and unloading, keep order, keep track of young people; driver (5) drives bus; members (3) gather, wait for bus, enter bus, go on the trip, may sing and converse on the bus, eat, watch, walk.

64. Factory Assembly Shops. Owner-managers (5) manage business, make general plans; foreman (5) directs workers on the floor in assembling aluminum parts; workers (4) assemble glass and aluminum into doors and windows, load and unload trucks.

65. Farm Implement Agencies. Owner-manager (6) manages business, sells parts, sells machinery, attends to office routines, directs repair; repairman (4) works on farm machinery; salesman (4) sells parts, tools; customers (3) buy, bring in machinery for repair, pay; loafers (1) sit around and talk.

67. Fashion Shows. Teachers (5 or 6) in charge help exhibitors dress, arrange order; master of ceremonies (5) announces exhibitors, describes costumes; models (4) walk across stage to exhibit clothing; servers (4) serve refreshments; audience (2) watch, applaud, eat, converse.

68. Fire Alarms and Fire Fighting. Fire chief (6) directs activity, drives truck, helps with chemicals or hose; firemen (4) help extinguish fire; homeowner (3) calls firemen; onlookers (1) watch activity.

69. Fire Drills. Principal (6) rings alarm bell, times and evaluates speed and efficiency of evacuation of building, records result; teachers (4) take charge of evacuating classes; pupils (3) conform to directions of rules and of teachers to leave the building quickly, return in prescribed order.

70. Fire Stations. City engineer (5) and fire chief (5) use building for repair and maintenance of trucks, storage of chemicals; employee (4) and firemen (4) work on trucks under direction; farmers (3) come to purchase water and fill tanks from city hydrant in times of drought.

71. Fireworks Sales Stands. Manager (6) or family members (5) manage the enterprise, sell fireworks; helpers (4) assist in selling; customers (3) buy fireworks; onlookers (1) watch, converse.

72. Floor Laying Services. Co-owners (5) manage business and do work of laying floor covering, building and finishing cabinets and installing

them; helper (4) sometimes assists; customers (3) arrange for work, pay for work.

73. Food and Rummage Sales. Committee members (5) arrange for use of space with building owner, solicit donations, arrange and price goods, sell; helpers (4) assist in all phases; customers (3) buy food or other objects.

74. Football Games, American Football. Coaches (5) in charge instruct players; players (4) play ball according to rules; umpires (4) determine legality of plays, keep time; band (4) plays instruments, marches; concession stand workers (4) prepare and sell food; water boys (4) take water on to field; cheerleaders (4) lead organized cheering; announcer (4) tells audience of players involved in game, introduces band for its performance; Boy Scouts (4) have flag ceremony before band plays the national anthem; audience (2) watch, cheer, eat, applaud, converse.

75. Funeral Directors Services, including Funerals. Mortician-owner (6) embalms body, arranges for and directs all preparations for funeral and burial, takes care of management routines; assistants (4) help mortician, usher at service, arrange flowers; minister or priest (4) conducts service; pianist (4) plays; singers (4) sing; pallbearers (4) carry casket; customer (3) selects casket, makes plans with mortician; mourners (2) come to view body, attend funeral service.

76. Funeral Services, Church. Minister in charge at the church (6) conducts service according to ritual, accompanies casket out of the church; mortician and assistants (4) arrange and remove flowers, place casket, move casket from front to back of church, usher mourners, hand out order-of-service folders; singers (4) sing; organist (4) plays; pallbearers (4) carry casket out; mourners (3) sit, listen, sign order-of-service folders, view the deceased as they leave, wait outside until hearse drives away.

77. Furniture Stores. Owner-manager (6) manages business, waits on customers, gives information regarding products; employees (4) keep books, wait on customers, service appliances; customers (3) look at merchandise, select, buy, pay for merchandise.

78. Garages. Owner-manager (6) manages garage, repairs cars, services cars; mechanic (4) repairs cars; attendant (4) puts in gas, oil, washes windshields; assistant (4) carries out office routines; customers (3) have cars serviced or repaired, pay.

79. Gift Showers. Hostesses (5) provide decorations and refreshments, invite guests, plan and introduce games; honoree (4) opens gifts, expresses thanks; assistants (4) record gifts, serve refreshments; guests (3) bring gifts, converse, play games, eat.

80. Golf Games. Executive committee (5) arranges tournament play, plans for upkeep of course; workmen (4) mow the course; volunteers (4) mow or do other upkeep work; members (3) and guests (3) play on the course; audience (2) watch play, converse.

81. Government Offices: Business and Records. Elected or appointed gov-

ernment official (6) manages office, is responsible for records and accounts, answers questions, confers with county commissioners or other boards, works as required by law; clerks (4) carry out office routines; customers (3) pay fees, obtain information.

82. Graduation and Promotion Ceremonies. Master of ceremonies (6) arranges program to honor and compliment graduates, speaks, introduces other speakers; speakers (4) speak; official (4) gives out diplomas; musicians (4) play or sing; graduates (4) receive diplomas; audience (2) listen, applaud, congratulate.

83. Grocery Stores. Manager (6) manages business, prices goods, prepares advertising, takes inventories; cashier (4) totals charges, takes money; butcher (4) cuts meat, serves customers, stocks meat case, weighs meat; stock clerk and carry-out boy (4) stock shelves, mark price on merchandise, carry out sacks to customer's car; salesmen, wholesale (4), interview manager; customers (3) select goods from shelves and cases, pay for merchandise.

84. Hallways. Principal or teacher (5) keeps order; janitor (4) keeps halls clean; employees (3), students (3), visitors (2) walk, converse.

85. Hardware Stores. Owner-manager (6) manages business, sells merchandise, repairs appliances; assistants (4) work with manager; customers (3) inspect and buy goods, pay for service; onlookers (1) watch TV, converse.

86. Hayrack Rides. Host-driver (6) drives tractor, host at farm visited; committee members (4) arrange picnic, provide food; members (3) and guests (2) ride, sing, eat.

87. Hikes and Camps. Scout leader (6) directs total camp activities; patrol leaders (4) direct small group activities; scouts (3) make camp, hike, cook, engage in programmed scout activities.

88. Home Economics Classes. Home economist (6) in charge teaches skills and theory of homemaking, including cooking, sewing, family life; specialist (4) in one field may lecture; high school students (3), or 4-H members (3), or home economics units lesson leaders (3) learn, listen, practice.

89. Home Economics Competitions. 4-H advisers (5) set up program and act as masters of ceremonies; judges (4) evaluate entries; contestants (4) exhibit clothing or other 4-H project work; 4-H leaders (4) help set up club members' exhibit; committee (4) sells sandwiches and beverages; members (3) see exhibits, learn points important for judging, eat.

90. Horseshoe Pitching Contests. Game organizers and referees (5) set up order of play, provide horseshoes, keep score, award prize; players (4) play regulation horseshoe pitching game; spectators (2) watch.

92. Hotels. Proprietor (6) or proprietors (5) manage business, greet, register, and conduct guests to rooms, clean rooms; employees (4) help with work; guests (3) stay in rooms, pay bills.

93. Ice Cream Socials. President or hostess (6) in charge of arrangements greets members; helpers (4) serve, clean up; members (3) eat, converse.

96. Installation and Induction Ceremonies. President of organization and installing officer (5) arrange program, preside over ritual; persons installed (4) participate in ritual; other performers (4) take prescribed parts in ritual; refreshment committee (4) serves refreshments; members (3) watch, applaud.
97. Insurance Offices and Sales Routes. Insurance agent (6) manages office, sells insurance, records claims, arranges for claim adjuster; secretary (4) engages in office routines; adjuster (4) gets and gives information; customers (3) buy insurance, make claims.
98. Ironing Services. Ironer (6) prepares clothes for ironing, irons, folds, charges for service; customers (3) bring and call for clothes, pay for service.
99. Jails. Sheriff (6) has responsibility for security and management of jail, places offenders in jail, releases offenders, admits visitors; sheriff's wife (4) prepares meals, sees to laundry, takes charge of jail during sheriff's or deputy's absence; deputy sheriff (4) may act as sheriff; offenders (3) are confined to cells.
100. Jewelry Stores. Owner-operator (6) manages business, waits on customers, examines and repairs watches and clocks; clerk (4) waits on customers, wraps packages; customers (3) examine and purchase merchandise, bring in watches for repair, pay for service and goods.
101. Judges Chambers. Judge (6) directs work of court reporter, clerk of the court, bailiff or deputy; confers with attorneys and their clients, often seeking out-of-court settlement, advising, admonishing; court reporter (4), clerk of the court (4), bailiff (4) carry out the judge's directives; attorneys (3) and their clients (3) consult with judge.
102. Kennels. Owner-managers (5) feed, breed, care for, show, and sell dogs; assistants (4) help care for dogs; customers (3) look at, buy, and pay for dogs.
103. Kindergarten Classes. Teacher (6) engages in classroom routines, teaches, supervises activities; pupils (3) play, draw, construct, sing individually and in groups.
104. Knitting Classes and Services. Teacher-knitter (6) teaches knitting, knits herself, sells knitted garments; customer-pupils (3) learn knitting, pay for lessons or garments.
105. Land Condemnation Hearings. Commission members (5) hear complaints regarding fair pay for condemned land; complainants (4) make complaints orally to commission meeting for judgment.
106. Landscaping and Floriculture Classes. County agents (5) in charge of arrangements introduce specialists; specialists (4) teach landscaping and floriculture; interested persons (3) attend as class members.
107. Latin Classes. Latin teacher (6) teaches Latin language and literature, engages in classroom routines; high school students (3) study, recite.
108. Laundries, Self-Service. Owner (6) services machines, collects money from machines weekly; cleaner (4) cleans premises daily; customers (3) wash and dry own clothes; sit in chairs and converse while waiting for machines to complete cycles.
109. Laundry Services. Owner-operator (6) manages laundry, washes, irons,

receives payment; assistant (4) irons; both converse with customers; customers (3) bring clothing to be washed and ironed, pick up clean clothes, rent machines to wash own clothes, pay operator, converse.

110. Libraries. Librarian (6) checks out, checks in, orders, catalogues books, assists in finding information for patron, engages in managerial functions; assistants (4) act as librarian, reshelve books, clean, beautify surroundings; patrons (3) read, study, select, and check out books, return books.

111. Locker and Shower Rooms. Physical education teachers in charge (6) set and enforce standards of conduct; students (3) dress for athletic events and physical education, take showers, put on school clothes, converse.

112. Lodge Meetings. Chief officer (6) conducts meeting; secretary (4), treasurer (4), lodge officers (4), committee chairmen (4) take their assigned responsibilities, engage in ritual activities and business meetings; members (3) attend, listen, vote, participate in ritual, eat, socialize.

114. Lumberyards. Owner-manager (6) manages business, attends customers, loads truck; assistant (4) helps manager; customer (3) looks at merchandise, selects, buys.

115. Machinery Repair Shops. Foreman (6) manages shop, may or may not engage in actual repair work; mechanics (4) repair and maintain machines, weld, grease, oil, adjust, service the buses, trucks, road equipment belonging to the county, state, or school district; bus drivers and road crews (3) store equipment, converse while waiting for workday to begin.

116. Mathematics Classes. Teacher (6) teaches mathematical subjects of algebra, geometry, calculus, etc., engages in classroom routines; high school students (3) study, recite, converse.

117. Meetings, Business. President or chairman (6) presides at meeting and conducts it in general accordance with Roberts' Rules of Order; secretary (4), treasurer (4), committee chairmen (4) engage in prescribed work; members (3) participate in meeting according to prescribed rules.

118. Meetings, Cultural. President (5) conducts business meeting; secretary (4), treasurer (4), committee chairmen (4) participate appropriately in business meeting; program chairman (5) arranges program, introduces program; hostess (5) has charge of social hour and refreshments; performers (4) present program; members (3) participate in business meeting, listen, applaud, eat, socialize.

119. Meetings, Discussion. Chairman (6) presides, may introduce speaker (4); hostess or servers (4) serve refreshments; members (3) discuss topic under consideration, eat, converse.

120. Meetings, Social. President or chairman (5) presides; treasurer (4), secretary (4), other officers (4) take prescribed responsibilities; recreational chairman (5) organizes card and other games, provides food; others assist (5) in amusing program or games; members (3) engage in meeting behavior, play games, eat, converse.

121. Memorial Services. Commander (6) of American Legion directs march

of squad (4) to center of cemetery; gun bearers (4) fire salute; chaplain (4) offers a prayer; flag bearer (4) carries flag; bugler (4) plays taps; audience (2) watch quietly.

122. Motor Vehicle Operators Classes and Examinations. Driver Education teacher (6) teaches technique and theory of safe driving, drives with students in practice, engages in classroom routines, examines students; state traffic officer (6) administers driving test to applicants for license; clerk (4) administers eye test and written examination; students (3) study, drive dual-control car, take examination on theory and practice; applicants for license (3) take written examination and driving test with oral questions.

123. Moving Picture Shows. Projectionist-owner (6) projects film; ticket seller (4) sells tickets; usher (4) takes tickets, pops and sells popcorn, soft drinks; customers (3) watch picture, eat popcorn, drink pop.

124. Music Classes, Instrumental. Music teacher (6) teaches skills and theory of instrumental music, engages in classroom routines; students (3) study and practice.

125. Music Classes, Vocal. Teacher (6) or choir master (6) teaches technique and theory of singing, may engage in classroom routines; accompanist (4) plays organ or piano; pupils (3) or choir members (3) learn about singing, practice.

126. Music Competitions. Master of ceremonies (6) arranges order of appearance of music groups; judges (4) evaluate quality of playing, offer critique; director (4), performers (4) play instruments or sing singly or as a group; audience (2) listen.

127. Newspaper Reporters Beats. Reporter (6) seeks news; interviewees (4) answer questions, volunteer information.

128. Newspaper and Printing Plants. Proprietor (6) manages business, runs printing presses, writes and corrects copy, plans layout; employees (4) run job press and linotype, address and mail papers, get news; customers (3) subscribe to paper, arrange for printing and advertising, bring in news and announcements.

129. Nursing Homes. Owner-operator (6) manages enterprise, cares for patients, gives medication, baths, etc.; employees (4) cook, serve meals, care for patients; patients (3) receive care, live housebound lives.

130. Optometrists Services. Professional optometrists (5) test eyesight of all pupils; older students (4) assist in making records, bring children for testing; pupils (3) obey directions, respond to tests of visual acuity.

131. Painting Classes. Teacher (6) teaches theory and technique of oil painting, accepts pay; students (3) listen, learn, paint, pay.

132. Parades. Band leader (6) or a committee (5) plans route and leads parade over designated route; judges (4) evaluate costumes and decorations, give prizes; paraders (4) play instruments, walk or ride in parade, behaving appropriately to costume; spectators (2) watch, applaud, converse.

133. Parking Lots. School principal (4), teachers (4), custodians (4) correct deviations from rules governing parking positions and individual behavior in lot; users (2) park cars.

134. Parks and Playgrounds. Principal (6), principal and teachers, or committee members (5) are responsible for proper behavior of users and for upkeep of property; school custodians or city employees (4) keep areas tidy; schoolchildren, citizens, and lake club members (3) use facilities and equipment for games, picnics, fishing (in case of lake); visitors (2) also use playgrounds and parks.

135. Parties. Committee members (5) or host and hostess (5) plan and decorate, supervise games and entertainment, provide refreshments; servers (4) may assist; members (3) play games, eat food, converse.

136. Parties, Stag. American Legion officers (5) plan party, cook dinner, set up tables, make guests welcome; members (3) eat, play games, converse.

137. Pastors Studies. Pastor (6) consults with individuals and groups, studies, takes care of correspondence; secretary (4) carries out office routines; church members (3) consult minister.

138. Photographic Studios. Photographer (5) takes pictures; school official or proprietor of business (5) arranges for photographer, makes appointments, takes the pay; customers (3) have pictures taken, bring children for pictures.

139. Physical and Biological Science Classes. Science teacher (6) teaches and directs laboratory work in biology, chemistry, physics, engages in classroom routines; students (3) study, recite, take examinations, do laboratory work.

140. Physical Education Classes. Physical education teacher (6) directs calisthenics and games, engages in classroom routines; pupils (3) exercise, play games.

142. Piano Recital. Teacher (6) acts as master of ceremonies; pupils (4) play the piano; audience (2) listen, applaud.

143. Picnics. Organizer (6) or organizers (5) make arrangements, bring food, direct cooking, plan transportation; helpers (4) assist organizers; members (3) eat, play, converse.

144. Plays and Programs. Director (6) or directors (5) plan, direct rehearsals, produce plays or programs including skits, speeches, vocal or instrumental numbers; performers (4) act, sing, dance, speak, play instruments; stage crew (4) arranges stage, shifts scenery; audience (2) watch, listen, applaud.

145. Plumbing, Heating, and Electrical Service and Appliance Companies. Plumber-electrician (6) or partners (5) make installations in new and old houses, sell and repair appliances, manage business; assistants (4) help plumber-electrician; customers (3) arrange for work, examine appliances, pay for service and materials.

146. Post Offices. Postmistress (6) manages post office according to regulations; postal clerks (4) sell stamps and money orders, sort in-mail, place in boxes, sort and cancel out-mail, place in sacks; rural mail carriers (4) sort route mail, get stamps; contract carrier (4) brings and takes mail bags; custodian (4) cleans premises; customers (3) buy stamps and money orders, mail packages, get mail from boxes and packages from employees.

147. Programs of Band Music. Director-teacher (6) conducts band, determines program; players (4) play instruments, march; audience (2) listen, applaud.

148. Programs of Choral Music. Director-teacher (6) or teachers (5) plan, rehearse, and conduct program; members (4) sing, play instruments; audience (2) listen, applaud.

149. Psychological Research Offices. Directors (5) manage office, plan work; secretaries (4) engage in office routines; research associates, students (4) code, write, compute; visitors (2) seek information, attend conferences.

150. Psychological Service Offices. School psychologist (5) manages office, interviews clients, tests children; speech therapist (5) writes reports, prepares for teaching; secretary (4) types reports, engages in office routines; clients (3) talk, take tests.

151. Public Speaking and Drama Competitions. Play director (6) or 4-H leaders (5) organize contestants, direct activity; judge (4) evaluates performance, gives criticism and rating; contestants (4) perform in play or make speech; audience (2) listen, applaud.

153. Real Estate Agents Offices. Licensed real estate broker (6) lists farms and homes for sale, shows property to customers, closes sale; customers (3) consult with broker, sign papers, pay.

154. Receptions. Hostesses (5) make arrangements, greet guests; honorees (4) receive congratulations, converse with friends; assistants (4) register guests, serve refreshments; guests (3) bring gifts, converse, eat.

155. Refreshment Stands. Scout leaders (5) take charge of arrangement; scouts (4) sell pop, retrieve bottles, accept pay; customers (3) buy and drink pop, converse, pay.

156. Refuse Hauling Services. Truck owner (6) collects trash from homes and businesses, collects pay for service; customers (3) arrange and pay for service.

157. Religion Classes. Teacher (6) or teachers (5) conduct short worship service, teach about church history, doctrine, the Bible, lead discussion; class members (3) listen, study, discuss, pray, contribute money.

158. Religion Study Groups. Chairman (5) conducts business meeting; program leader (5) presents lesson, leads discussion; assistants (4) may present parts of lesson, play the piano, or serve refreshments; members (3) listen, discuss, eat.

159. Religious Fellowship Meetings. Adult sponsor (5) and youth leader (5) or president (5) and program chairman (5) arrange meeting, preside; program participants (4) speak, pray, lead discussion; accompanist (4) plays piano; refreshment committee (4) provides and serves refreshments; members (3) discuss, sing, pray, eat.

160. Religious Prayer and Meditation Services. Minister (6) or co-leaders (5) plan meeting, preside, speak, read, pray; assistants (4) play piano, take assigned parts; members (3) listen, sing, pray.

161. Religious Worship Services. Minister (6) or Sunday school superintendent (6) prays, speaks, reads scripture; minister (6) performs rituals, e.g., baptism; organist (4) or pianist (4) plays instrument; choir direc-

tor (4) directs choir; choir members (4) sing; ushers (4) seat congregation, take up collection; candlelighters (4) light and extinguish candles; members (3) and visitors (2) listen, sing, pray.

162. Restaurants and Organization Dinners for the Public. Cafe proprietor (6) or proprietors (5), school lunchroom manager (5) and principal (5), organization chairman (5) plan, order food, establish prices, may aid in cooking and serving food; assistants (4) cook and serve food, clean up; customers (3) eat, pay for food, converse.

163. Retarded Childrens Classes. Director (6) organizes program of activities for retarded children, secures volunteer teachers, teaches; assistants (4) teach and care for children, prepare and serve snacks; members (3) learn, play, eat.

164. Roller Skating Parties. Adults (6) or (5) plan and conduct excursion to rink; may have assistants (4) drive cars or buses; members (3) skate, eat, converse.

166. Sales Promotion and Patron Attracting Openings. Proprietor (6) or proprietors (5) invite the public to inspect new or remodeled premises, greet guests, show guests around premises, offer refreshments, give souvenirs; assistants (4) assist proprietors; guests (2) inspect premises, eat, accept gift.

167. Sales Promotion Parties. Hostess (5) invites guests, prepares and serves refreshments; saleswoman (5) shows wares, directs games, takes orders; helpers (4) assist in serving guests; customers (3) inspect and order wares, eat, play games, converse.

168. Sales Routes: Cosmetics, Household Supplies, Magazines. Salesman-agents (5) plan route, sell, take orders, deliver goods; or sales organizers (5) plan sales route and campaign, give out order blanks, etc.; salesmen (4) sell, take orders, deliver goods, report to organizer; customers (3) inspect, order, pay.

169. Savings Stamp Sales Stands. Teacher (6) organizes and directs; pupil-salesmen (4) sell U.S. savings stamps; teacher and pupil customers (3) buy U.S. savings stamps.

170. School Administrators Offices. Principal (6) manages office routines, confers with school board members, faculty, students, parents, sales people, administers and deals with curricular, disciplinary, business problems of school; secretary (4) attends to office routines; board members (3), faculty (3), students (3), sales people (3), parents (2) talk with, are admonished by, or sell supplies to principal.

172. School Enrollment Periods. Principal (5) and teacher (5) interview pupils and parents, enroll pupils in appropriate classes; clerks (4) issue books, accept book rental fee; pupils (3), parents (3) fill out information forms, pay book rental fee, discuss program.

173. School Offices. Principals (5) manage offices; secretaries (4) carry out office routines; student assistants (4) assist secretary; teachers (3) may use equipment; pupils (3) run errands, get supplies.

174. School Rallies. Principal or teacher (5) on hand if control is necessary; head cheerleader (5) acts as master of ceremonies, calls for cheers, directs cheerleaders; cheerleaders (4) yell, do acrobatics, lead cheering;

athletic team members (4) introduced; students (3) cheer in concert, applaud.

175. Scout Meetings. Scout leaders (5) or den mothers (6) plan and direct activities, demonstrate skills; patrol or den leaders (4) assist leaders, take roll, raise flag; members (3) engage in games, handicraft, study, discussion, ceremony.

177. Service Stations. Manager (6) manages business, fills tanks of cars and trucks with gasoline, checks oil, water, and tires, washes windshields, changes oil, greases cars, sells accessories; assistants (4) service cars as prescribed; customers (3) buy gasoline, oil, accessories, pay for servicing.

178. Sewing and Dressmaking Classes. Teacher-leader (6) teaches theory and skills of sewing, demonstrates sewing techniques; members (3) sew by hand and machine, learn principles of sewing.

179. Sewing Club Meetings. Chairman (6) plans activities, distributes work (piecing quilts, sewing rags for rugs, mending); committee (4) prepares and serves refreshments; members (3) sew, converse, eat.

180. Sewing Services. Seamstress (6) manages work, takes orders, fits garments, sews, charges for service; customers (3) arrange for work, are fitted, pay for service.

181. Sheriffs Offices. Sheriff (6) manages office, keeps in radio contact with sheriff's cars, state police, and other law enforcement agencies, keeps records, directs deputy, responds to calls for assistance; deputy (4) takes duty when sheriff is out; visitors (2) come for information, to give information.

183. Sign Painting Services. Sign painter (6) designs and paints signs.

184. Social Science Classes. Social science teacher (6) teaches history and government of United States and other countries, engages in classroom routines; students (3) study, write, discuss.

185. Soil Conservation Service Offices. Soil conservationist (6) manages office, directs assistants (4) in conducting surveys of soil erosion and water conservation projects, plans management practices such as contour plowing, reforestation, prepares plans in cooperation with farmers for soil and water conservation on individual farms; secretary (4) engages in office routines; farmers (3) come in for consultation on problems relating to soil and water conservation, give necessary information for planning.

186. Solicitation of Funds. Organizers (6) or (5) plan campaign, direct solicitors to designated areas of town, distribute information leaflets and receipt forms to solicitors; solicitors (4) solicit donations from individuals, accept money, give receipt; donors (3) give or refuse to give money.

187. Solicitation of Goods. Drivers (5) distribute solicitation leaflets over town, return to pick up goods in Salvation Army truck; donors (3) leave donated goods in accessible place with Salvation Army sign.

188. Speech Therapy Services. Speech therapist (6) teaches children correct enunciation of words, demonstrates placement of tongue and lips, uses taped speech to assist teaching; pupil (3) practices correct speech, demonstrates progress.

189. Spelling Bees. County superintendent (6) arranges contest, appoints judge; judge (4) pronounces words, indicates success or failure in correct spelling; contestants (4) representing county schools spell words; audience (2) listen.

190. Staff Lounges. Janitors (4) keep room clean; teachers (3) use room for coffee break, smoking, correcting papers, conversing.

191. Street Fairs. Chamber of Commerce committee (5) arranges for carnival, provides facilities; carnival manager (5) directs placement of concessions, deals with committee; concessionaires (4) set up own concession or ride, take tickets, act as barkers, give prizes; ticket sellers (4) sell tickets usable at any concession; food sellers (4) sell popcorn, cotton candy, hot dogs; customers (3) ride on equipment, try games of skill, buy and eat food, stroll about, converse.

192. Swimming Excursions and Classes. Leaders (6) or (5) organize swimming group, arrange transportation, are responsible for group until return to point of departure; bus drivers (5) drive school bus; members (3) ride in bus, converse, go swimming for enjoyment and instruction.

193. Tank Truck Lines. Driver-agent (6) takes orders for bulk fuel oil and gasoline, fills tank at depot, delivers fuel oil to town customers, charges for oil and delivery; customers (3) order and pay for gasoline and oil.

194. Taverns. Owner-manager (6) manages business, serves beer, accepts pay, converses; assistant (4) helps in serving customers; customers (3) drink, converse, play pinball machine, play juke box, pay.

195. Teacher Conferences with Parents. Teacher (6) confers with parent or parents of each elementary school child at an appointed time, gives parent child's report card; parents (3) listen, ask questions, confer with teacher, receive child's report card.

196. Telephone Automatic Exchange Buildings. Telephone service man (6) uses building as headquarters, services automatic equipment; customers (3) may leave payment for telephone service at the building.

197. Telephone Booths. Telephone service man (6) services phone, takes money from box at regular intervals; customers (3) put coins in phone, dial, talk.

199. Timber Sales and Tree Removal Services. Tree faller (6) fells large trees, determines desired direction for tree to fall, saws undercut in bole of tree, saws backcut, using wedges to tip tree, cuts felled tree into lengths, removes on truck; assistant (4) helps, drives and loads truck, using winch; customers (3) arrange for and pay for service. (The Dutch elm disease made felling of large trees an important service in Midwest in 1963–64.)

200. Tool Sharpening Services. Owner-operator (6) sharpens saws and other tools, receives pay, keeps books; customers (3) bring tools to be sharpened, pay for service.

201. Track and Field Meets. Track coaches (5) are in charge of arrangements, schedule, and organization; officials (4) at each event judge and record winners and their records; starters (4) start races; competitors (4) run, jump, throw; public address announcer (4) announces contests, winners; audience (2) watch, cheer, applaud.

202. **Tractor Pulling Contests.** Organizers (5) take entries, explain rules, announce winners, start contests, give awards; contestants (4) drive tractors; designated spectators (4) jump on sled to add weight; judges (4) on flatbed truck record number of men on sled when tractor can no longer move sled, measure number of feet pulled, judge winner in each class; audience (2) watch, applaud.

203. **Trafficways.** City employees (4) repair streets; city marshall (4), county sheriff (4), and state traffic officers (4) enforce traffic regulations; pedestrians (2) walk on streets and sidewalks; automobile drivers (2) drive on streets; children (2) play in streets.

204. **Trips by Organizations to Visit the Sick.** President (6) organizes trip; members (4) gather at one member's home and drive to nearby nursing home, where they visit all able to receive visitors, sew, or write letters for them, converse.

205. **TV and Radio Repair Shop.** Owner-operator (6) repairs TV sets and radios, charges for service and parts, manages business; helper (4) assists; customers (3) bring in sets or phone for service, pay for service.

208. **Variety Stores.** Owner-operators (5) manage store, sell merchandise, interview wholesale salesmen, stock shelves; clerk (4) sells merchandise; customers (3) look, select, buy, converse.

210. **Vocational Counseling Services.** High school principal (6) organizes trip for seniors to Career Day in another high school; members (3) gather at high school bus stop, ride to neighboring town, learn about possible careers, ask questions, discuss.

211. **Volleyball Games.** Coaches (5) arrange game and umpire; players (4) play volleyball according to rules; audience (2) watch, applaud.

212. **Wallpapering and Painting Services.** Operator (6) papers and paints as arranged, charges for service; customer (3) arranges for and pays for service.

213. **Water Supply Plants.** City engineer (5) and assistant (5) check plant daily, add chemicals, take samples of water, make minor repairs.

214. **Weed Inspectors Offices.** Weed supervisor (6) arranges with farmers to inspect for noxious weeds or to spray along county roads; assistant (4) helps supervisor; farmers (3) come for advice and to make request for spraying and chemicals.

215. **Weddings, Church.** Minister (5) is in charge of marriage service; bride's parents (5) are in charge of reception; bride (4), groom (4), attendants (4), ushers (4), musicians (4), helpers at reception (4) fill designated roles in marriage ceremony; guests (2) watch, congratulate, eat refreshments, may bring gift.

216. **Weddings, Civil.** Probate judge (6) performs marriage; bride (4), groom (4), witnesses (4) carry out prescribed roles; guests (2) watch, offer good wishes.

217. **Welfare Offices.** Welfare director (6) manages office, interviews clients, works with county commissioners and state welfare officers, makes reports, presides at staff conferences; welfare workers (4) interview clients, implement law; secretaries (4) engage in office routines; clients (3) come to see welfare workers, get information, assistance.

218. Welfare Workers Classes. Welfare director (5) organizes class, arranges for place, etc.; teacher (5) teaches class, engages in classroom routines; students listen, take notes, discuss.
219. Woodworking and Machine Shop Classes. Teacher (6) teaches skills and theory of working with wood, demonstrates proper use of tools, teaches reading and drawing of plans, engages in classroom routines; students (3) work with wood, engage in mechanical drawing, study.
220. X-Ray Laboratories. X-ray specialist (5) is in charge of taking x-rays; local chairman (5) organizes volunteer help; clerical workers (4) get information from clients, type cards, give directions; clients (3) have chest x-ray taken, respond to directions, give information.

References

Items with asterisks are Midwest Psychological Field Station Publications.

Acton Society Trust. 1953. *Size and morale.* London.

Allport, F. H. 1955. *Theories of perception and the concept of structure.* New York: Wiley.

Anderson, K. E., G. E. Ladd, and H. A. Smith. 1954. A study of 2,500 Kansas high school graduates. *Kansas Studies in Education* (Univ. of Kansas), *4.*

Ashby, W. R. 1956. *An introduction to cybernetics.* New York: Wiley.

*Ashton, Margaret. 1964. An ecological study of the stream of behavior. Master's thesis, Univ. of Kansas.

Bales, R. F. 1952. Some uniformities of behavior in small social systems. In G. Swanson, T. Newcomb, and E. Hartley, eds., *Readings in social psychology* (New York: Holt), pp. 149–59.

————— 1953. The equilibrium problem in small groups. In T. Parsons, R. Bales, and E. Shils, eds., *Working papers in the theory of action* (Glencoe, Ill.: Free Press), pp. 111–61.

Bales, R. F., and E. F. Borgatta. 1955. Size of group as a factor in the interaction profile. In A. Hare, E. Borgatta, and R. Bales, eds., *Small groups: studies in social interaction* (New York: Knopf), pp. 396–413.

*Barker, Louise S., Maxine Schoggen, P. Schoggen, and R. G. Barker. 1952. The frequency of physical disability in children: a comparison of three sources of information. *Child Developm., 23,* 215–26.

*Barker, R. G. 1957. Structure of the stream of behavior. In Proceedings of the 15th international congress of psychology, pp. 155–56.

*————— 1960a. Ecology and motivation. In M. R. Jones, ed., *Nebraska symposium on motivation* (Lincoln: Univ. of Nebraska Press), pp. 1–49.

*————— 1960b. Small high schools (letter). *Science, 131,* 1560–61.

*————— 1963a. On the nature of the environment. *J. Soc. Issues, 19* (4), 17–38.

*—————, ed. 1963b. *The stream of behavior.* New York: Appleton-Century-Crofts.

　　Barker, R. G. The stream of behavior as an empirical problem, pp. 1–22.

　　Barker, R. G., and Louise S. Barker. Social actions in the behavior streams of American and English children, pp. 127–59.

　　Dickman, H. R. The perception of behavioral units, pp. 23–41.

Dyck, A. J. The social contacts of some Midwest children with their parents and teachers, pp. 78–98.

Fawl, C. L. Disturbances experienced by children in their natural habitats, pp. 99–126.

Schoggen, Maxine, Louise S. Barker, and R. G. Barker. Structure of the behavior of American and English children, pp. 160–68.

Schoggen, P. Environmental forces in the everyday lives of children, pp. 42–69.

Simmons, Helen, and P. Schoggen. Mothers and fathers as sources of environmental pressure on children, pp. 70–77.

Simpson, J. E. A method of measuring the social weather of children, pp. 219–27.

*——— 1964. Observation of behavior: ecological approaches. *J. Mt. Sinai Hospital, 31,* No. 4, 268–84.

*——— 1965. Explorations in ecological psychology. *Amer. Psychologist, 20,* No. 1, 1–14.

*——— 1967. Naturalistic methods in psychological research: some comments on the symposium papers. *Human Developm., 10,* 223–29.

*Barker, R. G., and Louise S. Barker. 1961a. Behavior units for the comparative study of culture. In B. Kaplan, ed., *Studying personality cross-culturally* (New York: Harper & Row), pp. 457–76.

*——— 1961b. The psychological ecology of old people in Midwest, Kansas and Yoredale, Yorkshire. *J. Geront., 16,* 144–49.

*——— 1963a. Sixty-five and over. In R. H. Williams, C. Tibbitts, and Wilma Donahue, eds., *Processes of aging* (New York: Prentice-Hall), pp. 246–71.

——— 1963b. See Barker, R. G. 1963b.

*Barker, R. G., and P. V. Gump. 1964. *Big school, small school.* Stanford, Calif.: Stanford Univ. Press.

Barker, R. G.(a). Community size and activities of students, pp. 154–71.

Barker, R. G.(b). Ecological units, pp. 11–28.

Barker, R. G.(c). The ecological environment, pp. 3–10.

Barker, R. G., and Louise S. Barker. Structural characteristics, pp. 41–63.

Barker, R. G., and Eleanor Hall. Participation in interschool events and extracurricular activities, pp. 64–74.

Barker, R. G., and W. F. LeCompte. Adolescents in the towns of Midwest County, pp. 172–92.

Campbell, W. J. Some effects of high school consolidation, pp. 139–53.

Gump, P. V., and R. G. Barker. Overview and prospects, pp. 195–202.

Gump, P. V., and W. V. Friesen(a). Participation in nonclass settings, pp. 75–93.

Gump, P. V., and W. V. Friesen(b). Satisfactions derived from nonclass settings, pp. 94–114.

Willems, E. P.(a). Forces toward participation in behavior settings, pp. 115–35.

Willems, E. P.(b). Review of research, pp. 29–37.

Barker, R. G., and Eleanor Hall. 1964. See Barker, R. G., and P. V. Gump, 1964.

Barker, R. G., and W. F. LeCompte. 1964. See Barker, R. G., and P. V. Gump, 1964.

*Barker, R. G., and H. F. Wright. 1949. Psychological ecology and the problem of psychosocial development. *Child Developm.*, 20, 131–43.

*———— 1951a. Maud Pintner: a full day study. Unpublished manuscript, Univ. of Kansas, Midwest Psychological Field Station.

*———— 1951b. *One boy's day.* New York: Harper & Row.

*———— 1951c. The psychological habitat of Raymond Birch. In J. H. Rohrer and M. Sherif, eds., *Social psychology at the crossroads* (New York: Harper & Row), pp. 196–212.

*———— 1953. Mary Chaco: a full day study. Unpublished manuscript, Univ. of Kansas, Midwest Psychological Field Station.

*———— 1955. *Midwest and its children.* New York: Harper & Row.

Barker *et al.* 1941. (Coauthors Tamara Dembo and K. Lewin.) Frustration and regression: a study of young children. *University of Iowa Studies in Child Welfare,* 18, No. 1.

*———— 1950. (Coauthors H. F. Wright, J. Nall, and P. Schoggen.) There is no class bias in our school. *Progressive Educ.,* 27, 106–10.

*———— 1951. (Coauthors H. F. Wright and W. A. Koppe.) The psychological ecology of a small town. In W. Dennis, ed., *Readings in Child psychology* (New York: Prentice-Hall), pp. 552–66.

*———— 1955. (Coauthors Maxine Schoggen and Louise S. Barker.) Hemerography of Mary Ennis. In A. Burton and R. E. Harris, eds., *Clinical studies of personality* (New York: Harper & Row), pp. 768–808.

*———— 1961. (Coauthors H. F. Wright, Louise S. Barker, and Maxine Schoggen.) *Specimen records of American and English children.* Univ. of Kansas Press.

*———— 1967. (Coauthors Louise S. Barker and D. D. M. Ragle.) The churches of Midwest, Kansas and Yoredale, Yorkshire: their contributions to the environments of the towns. In W. Gore and L. Hodapp, eds., *Change in the small community* (New York: Friendship Press), pp. 155–89.

Bass, B. M., and Fay-Tyler M. Norton. 1951. Group size and leaderless discussion. *J. Appl. Psychol.,* 35, 397–400.

Baumgartel, H., and R. Sobol. 1959. Background and organizational factors in absenteeism. *Personnel Psychol.,* 12, 431–43.

Brunswik, E. 1955. The conceptual framework of psychology. *International encyclopedia of unified science.* Vol. 1, Part 2. Chicago: Univ. of Chicago Press, pp. 656–750.

———— 1957. Scope and aspects of the cognitive problem. In H. Gruber, R. Jessor, and K. Hammond, eds., *Cognition: the Colorado symposium* (Cambridge: Harvard Univ. Press), pp. 5–31.

Campbell, H. 1952. Group incentive pay schemes. *Occup. Psychol.,* 26, 15–21.

Cleland, S. 1955. *Influence of plant size on industrial relations.* Princeton: Princeton Univ. Press.

Coleman, J. S. 1961. *The adolescent society.* Glencoe, Ill.: Free Press.

Dawe, Helen C. 1934. The influence of size of kindergarten group upon performance. *Child Developm., 5,* 295–303.

Dickman, H. R. 1963. See Barker, R. G., 1963b.

Dollard, J., L. W. Doob, N. E. Miller, O. H. Mowrer, and R. R. Sears. 1939. *Frustration and aggression.* New Haven: Yale Univ. Press.

*Dyck, A. J. 1958. A study in psychological ecology: a description of social contacts of twelve Midwest children with their parents. Master's thesis, Univ. of Kansas.

*——— 1963. See Barker, R. G., 1963b.

*Fawl, C. L. 1959. Disturbances experienced by children in their natural habitat: a study in psychological ecology. Doctoral dissertation, Univ. of Kansas.

*——— 1963. See Barker, R. G., 1963b.

Fisher, P. H. 1953. An analysis of the primary group. *Sociometry, 16,* 272–76.

*Gump, P. V. 1964. Environmental guidance of the classroom behavioral system. In B. J. Biddle and W. J. Ellena, eds., *Contemporary research on teacher effectiveness* (New York: Holt, Rinehart & Winston), pp. 165–95.

*——— 1967a. Persons, settings, and larger contexts. In B. Indik and K. Berrien, eds., *People, groups and organizations: an effective integration* (New York: Teachers College, Columbia Univ. Press).

*——— 1967b. *The classroom behavior setting: its nature and relation to student behavior.* Final report to U.S. Office of Education, Project No. 2453, Contract No. OE-4-10-107.

Gump, P. V., and W. V. Freisen. 1964. See Barker, R. G., and P. V. Gump, 1964.

Gump, P., P. Schoggen, and F. Redl. 1957. The camp milieu and its immediate effects. *J. Soc. Issues, 13,* No. 1, 40–46.

——— 1963. The behavior of the same child in different milieus. In R. G. Barker, ed., *The stream of behavior* (New York: Appleton-Century-Crofts), pp. 169–202.

Gump, P., and B. Sutton-Smith. 1955. Activity-setting and social interaction. *Amer. J. Orthopsychiat., 25,* 755–60.

*Hall, Eleanor R. 1965. An ecological study of parent-child influencing behavior. Master's thesis, Univ. of Kansas.

Halverson, H. M. 1943. The development of prehension in infants. In R. G. Barker, J. S. Kounin, and H. F. Wright, eds., *Child behavior and development* (New York: McGraw-Hill), pp. 49–65.

Hare, A. P. 1952. A study of interaction and consensus in different sized groups. *Amer. Sociol. Rev., 17,* 261–67.

Heider, F. 1959. On perception, event structure and the psychological environment, selected papers. *Psychological Issues, 1,* No. 3 (entire issue).

Hewitt, D., and J. Parfit. 1953. A note on working morale and size of group. *Occup. Psychol., 27,* 38–42.

Indik, B. P. 1961. Organization size and member participation. Paper read at Amer. Psychol. Assoc., New York, September.

Isaacs, D. A. 1953. A study of predicting Topeka high school drop-outs one year in advance by means of three predictors. Doctoral dissertation, Univ. of Kansas.

Isaacs, Susan. 1950. *Intellectual growth in young children.* London: Routledge & Kegan Paul.

James, W. 1950. *Psychology.* New York: Dover Publications.

Jordan, N. 1963. Some formal characteristics of the behavior of two disturbed boys. In R. G. Barker, ed., *The stream of behavior* (New York: Appleton-Century-Crofts), pp. 203–18.

Katz, D. 1949. Morale and motivation in industry. In W. Dennis, ed., *Current trends in industrial psychology* (Pittsburgh: Univ. of Pittsburgh Press), pp. 145–71.

Kelley, H. H., and J. W. Thibaut. 1954. Experimental studies of group problem-solving and process. In G. Lindzey, ed., *Handbook of social psychology* (Cambridge, Mass.: Addison-Wesley), pp. 735–85.

Kendall, M. 1948. *Rank correlation methods.* London: Charles Griffin.

*Koppe, W. A. 1954. A study in psychological ecology: a survey of the behavior settings of Midwest. Doctoral dissertation, Univ. of Kansas.

Larson, Carol M. 1949. School-size as a factor in the adjustment of high school seniors. *Bull. No. 511, Youth Series No. 6,* State College of Washington.

Lawrence, D. H. 1963. The nature of a stimulus: some relationships between learning and perception. In S. Koch., ed., *Psychology: a study of a science* (New York: McGraw-Hill), Vol. 5, pp. 179–212.

*LeCompte, W. F., and R. G. Barker. 1960. The ecological framework of cooperative behavior. Paper read at Amer. Psychol. Assoc., Chicago, September.

Leeper, R. W. 1963. Learning and the fields of perception, motivation, and personality. In S. Koch, ed., *Psychology: a study of a science* (New York: McGraw-Hill), Vol. 5, pp. 365–487.

Lewin, K. 1951. *Field theory in social science.* New York: Harper & Row.

Marriot, R. 1949. Size of working group and output. *Occup. Psychol., 23,* 47–57.

Miller, G. A., E. Galanter, and K. H. Pribram. 1960. *Plans and the structure of behavior.* New York: Holt, Rinehart & Winston.

Murray, H. A. 1959. Preparations for the scaffold of a comprehensive system. In S. Koch, ed., *Psychology: a study of a science* (New York: McGraw-Hill), Vol. 3, pp. 7–54.

*Newton, M. R. 1953. A study in psychological ecology: the behavior settings in an institution for handicapped children. Master's thesis, Univ. of Kansas.

*Ragle, D. D. M., A. Johnson, and R. G. Barker. 1967. Measuring extension's impact. *J. Cooperative Extension,* Vol. 5, No. 3, 178–86.

Ratliff, F. 1962. Some interrelations among physics, physiology, and psychology. In S. Koch, ed., *Psychology: a study of a science* (New York: McGraw-Hill), Vol. 4, pp. 417–82.

Raush, H. L., A. T. Dittmann, and T. J. Taylor. 1959. Person, setting, and change in social interaction. *Human Relat., 12,* No. 4, 361–78.

———— 1960. Person, setting, and change in social interaction: II. A normal control study. *Human Relat.*, *13*, No. 4, 305–32.

Revans, R. W. 1958. Human relations, management, and size. In E. Hugh-Jones, ed., *Human relations and modern management* (Amsterdam: North Holland Pub. Co.), pp. 177–220.

Schoenfeld, W. N., and W. W. Cumming. 1963. Behavior and perception. In S. Koch, ed., *Psychology: a study of a science* (New York: McGraw-Hill), Vol. 5, pp. 213–52.

Schoggen, Maxine, Louise S. Barker, and R. G. Barker. 1963. See Barker, R. G., 1963b.

*Schoggen, P. 1951. A study in psychological ecology: a description of the behavior objects which entered the psychological habitat of an eight-year-old girl during the course of one day. Master's thesis, Univ. of Kansas.

*———— 1954. A study in psychological ecology: structural properties of children's behavior based on sixteen day-long specimen records. Doctoral dissertation, Univ. of Kansas.

———— 1963. See Barker, R. G., 1963b.

Simmons, Helen, and P. Schoggen. 1963. See Barker, R. G., 1963b.

*Simpson, J. E. 1956. A study in psychological ecology: social weather of children in the behavior settings of Midwest. Doctoral dissertation, Univ. of Kansas.

*———— 1963. See Barker, R. G., 1963b.

Slater, P. E. 1958. Contrasting correlates of group size. *Sociometry*, *21*, 129–39.

Soskin, W. F., and Vera P. John. 1963. The study of spontaneous talk. In R. G. Barker, ed., *The stream of behavior* (New York: Appleton-Century-Crofts), pp. 228–81.

Tallachi, S. 1960. Organization size, individual attitudes and behavior: an empirical study. *Administrative Sci. Quart.*, *5*, 398–420.

Taylor, D. W., and W. L. Faust. 1952. Twenty questions: efficiency in problem-solving as a function of group size. *J. Exp. Psychol.*, *44*, 360–68.

Terman, L. M., and Maud A. Merrill. 1937. *Measuring intelligence.* Boston: Houghton Mifflin

Thibaut, J. W., and H. H. Kelley. 1959. *The social psychology of groups.* New York: Wiley.

Thomas, E. J. 1959. Role conceptions and organizational size. *Amer. Sociol. Rev.*, *24*, 30–37.

Warner, W. L., Marchia Meeker, and K. Eells. 1949. *Social class in America.* Chicago: Science Research Associates.

Warriner, C. K., and Jane Emery Prather. 1965. Four types of voluntary associations. *Sociological Inquiry*, *35*, 138–48.

*Wicker, A. W. 1967. Students' experiences in behavior settings of large and small high schools: an examination of behavior setting theory. Doctoral dissertation, Univ. of Kansas.

Wiener, N. 1963. The mathematics of self-organizing systems. In R. E. Machol and P. Gray, eds., *Recent developments in information and decision processes* (New York: Macmillan), pp. 1–21.

*Willems, E. P. 1963. Forces toward participation in behavior settings of large and small institutions. Master's thesis, Univ. of Kansas.

*——— 1964. See Barker, R. G., and P. V. Gump, 1964.

*——— 1965a. An ecological orientation in psychology. *Merrill-Palmer Quarterly, 11,* No. 4, 317–43.

*——— 1965b. Participation in behavior settings in relation to three variables: size of behavior settings, marginality of persons, and sensitivity to audiences. Doctoral dissertation, Univ. of Kansas.

*Willems, E. P., and Gwendolyn J. Willems. 1965. Comparative validity of data yielded by three methods. *Merrill-Palmer Quarterly, 11,* 65–71.

Worthy, J. C. 1950. Organizational structure and employee morale. *Amer. Sociol. Rev., 15,* 169–79.

*Wright, H. F. 1961. The city-town project: a study of children in communities differing in size. Interim research report. Univ. of Kansas.

——— 1967. *Recording and analyzing child behavior.* New York: Harper & Row.

*Wright, H. F., and R. G. Barker. 1950a. *Methods in psychological ecology.* Lawrence: Dept. of Psychology, Univ. of Kansas. (Out of print.)

*——— 1950b. The elementary school does not stand alone. *Progressive Educ., 27,* 133–37.

*Wright, H. F., R. G. Barker, W. A. Koppe, Beverly Meyerson, and J. Nall. 1951. Children at home in Midwest. *Progressive Educ., 28,* 215–26.

*Wright, H. F., R. G. Barker, J. Nall, and P. Schoggen. 1955. Toward a psychological ecology of the classroom. In A. P. Coladarci, ed., *Readings in educational psychology* (New York: Holt, Rinehart & Winston), pp. 254–68.

Zener, K., and Mercedes Gaffron. 1962. Perceptual experiences: an analysis of its relation to the external world through internal processings. In S. Koch, ed., *Psychology: a study of a science* (New York: McGraw-Hall), Vol. 4, pp. 516–618.

Index

Midwest, 126; behavior mechanisms Midwest, 123; genotypes Midwest, 110–16; total Midwest, 104–7

Nutrition action pattern, 27; definition, 60; ERI, 119–21, 130–32; occupancy time Midwest, 130–32; present Midwest, 119–21, 132; prominent Midwest, 119–21, 132; rating example, 99, 101; rating guide, 60–61

Occupancy time (OT), 27; action patterns Midwest, 130–32; authority systems Midwest, 135–36; autonomy Midwest, 133–35; availability of data, 49; behavior mechanisms Midwest, 132–34; definition, 48–49; ERI Midwest, 130–36; genotypes Midwest, 110–16; Midwest residents, 110–16; out-of-town residents, 110–16; total Midwest, 129

Occupancy time code, 209–10

Occurrence (O), 26; action patterns Midwest, 120; authority systems Midwest, 129; autonomy Midwest, 126; behavior mechanisms Midwest, 123; definition, 47; genotypes Midwest, 110–16; total Midwest, 106

O data, *see* Operator data

O-Mech, 170–74

Operator data, 141–45

Parfit, J., 200, 232

Penetration, 27; data example, 98, 99, 101, 103; definition, 49–52; Midwest genotypes, 211–28; Midwest settings, 127–28; source of data, 52

Performer: autonomy rating, 76–80; data example, 99, 101; definition, 27, 52. *See also* Penetration

Personal appearance action pattern, 27; definition, 61; ERI, 119–21, 130–32; occupancy time Midwest, 130–32; present Midwest, 119–21,

132; prominent Midwest, 119–21, 132; rating example, 99, 101; rating guide, 61–62

Physical health action pattern, 27; definition, 62; ERI, 119–21, 130–32; occupancy time Midwest, 130–32; present Midwest, 119–21, 132; prominent Midwest, 119–21, 132; rating example, 99, 101; rating guide, 62–63

P-Mech, 170–74

Population (P), 26–27, 47–48; data example, 50, 99, 101; nonresident, 110–16; town resident, 110–16

Prather, Jane Emery, 90, 234

Predictions from theory, 189–98

Preperceptual environment, *see* Ecological environment

Pressure, 27; adolescent, 123–24; children, 123–24; definition, 70–71; Midwest, 123–24; rating example, 99, 101; rating scale, 71–75

Pribram, K. H., 138, 171, 233

Professionalism action pattern, 27; definition, 63; ERI, 119–21, 130–32; occupancy time Midwest, 130–32; present Midwest, 119–21; prominent Midwest, 119–21; rating example, 99, 101; rating guide, 63–64

Program circuits, 168–69, 178–79

Psychological environment, *see* Life space

Psychologists: operators, 141–45; transducers, 140–45

Ragle, D. D. M., 233

Ratliff, F., 150, 233

Raush, H. L., 4, 17, 203, 233, 234

Recreation action pattern, 27; definition, 64; occupancy time Midwest, 131–32; present Midwest, 119–21; prominent Midwest, 120–21; rating example, 55, 99, 101; rating guide, 64–65

Redl, F., 17, 232

Religion action pattern, 27; definition, 65; occupancy time Midwest,